How to Ice Climb!

T0346527

Help Us Keep This Guide Up to Date

Every effort has been made by the authors and editors to make this guide as accurate and useful as possible. However, many things can change after a guide is published—trails are rerouted, regulations change, techniques evolve, facilities come under new management, etc.

We appreciate hearing from you concerning your experiences with this guide and how you feel it could be improved and kept up to date. While we may not be able to respond to all comments and suggestions, we'll take them to heart and we'll also make certain to share them with the authors. Please send your comments and suggestions to the following address:

FalconGuides
Reader Response/Editorial Department
246 Goose Lane, Suite 200
Guilford, CT 06437

Thanks for your input!

How to Ice Climb!

Second Edition

Sean Isaac and Tim Banfield

FALCON GUIDES

UT

FALCONGUIDES®

An imprint of Globe Pequot, the trade division of
The Rowman & Littlefield Publishing Group, Inc.
4501 Forbes Blvd., Ste. 200
Lanham, MD 20706
www.rowman.com

Falcon and FalconGuides are registered trademarks and Make Adventure Your Story is a
trademark of The Rowman & Littlefield Publishing Group, Inc.

Distributed by NATIONAL BOOK NETWORK

British Library Cataloguing in Publication Information available

Library of Congress Cataloging-in-Publication Data

Names: Banfield, Tim, 1977– author. | Isaac, Sean, 1972– author.
Title: How to ice climb! / Sean Isaac and Tim Banfield.
Description: Second edition. | Guilford, Connecticut FalconGuides, 2021. | Includes
   bibliographical references and index. | Summary: "How to Ice Climb! covers the
   equipment and techniques that will allow beginners to safely enjoy this sport. It also
   provides experienced climbers with advanced skills that will make them more
   efficient"—Provided by publisher.
Identifiers: LCCN 2021017421 (print) | LCCN 2021017422 (ebook) | ISBN
   9780762782772 (trade paperback) | ISBN 9781493031351 (epub)
Subjects: LCSH: Snow and ice climbing.
Classification: LCC GV200.3 .L84 2021 (print) | LCC GV200.3 (ebook) | DDC
   796.9—dc23
LC record available at https://lccn.loc.gov/2021017421
LC ebook record available at https://lccn.loc.gov/2021017422

♾™ The paper used in this publication meets the minimum requirements of American
National Standard for Information Sciences—Permanence of Paper for Printed Library
Materials, ANSI/NISO Z39.48-1992.

Contents

Stas Beskin climbing French Reality (WI6+ 5.8) at the Stanley Headwall in Kootenay National Park, British Columbia, Canada.

Acknowledgments

Writing a book is a major project and is in no way just the sole labor of the authors. There were many people involved in this process that we would like to acknowledge and thank. All of these people have helped make *How to Ice Climb!* the best it can be. We (Tim and Sean) thank you for your words, edits, photos, advice, knowledge, skills, belays, and much more.

Writing contributions: Conrad Anker (foreword), Grant Staham (avalanche), Steve House (training), Nikki Smith (Utah), Brandon Pullan (northern Ontario), Jas Fauteux (Quebec)

Technical advisors: Marc Piche (ACMG), Dale Remsberg (AMGA), Marc Beverly (Beverly Mountain Guides), Kolin Powick (Black Diamond), Grant Statham (Parks Canada)

Extra photos: Jon Glassberg, Austin Schmitz, Sebastian Taborszky, Alex Popov, Alex Ratson, Aaron Beardmore, Tim Emmett, Dane Christensen, Jim Elzinga, Chic Scott

Climbing models: Larry Shui, Tiff Carleton, Jeff Mercier, Maarten van Haeren, Patrick Lindsay, Chris Wright, Aaron Mulkey, Jon Walsh, Alex Pedneault

Proofing: Ian Welsted, Maarten van Haeren, Chris Wright, Raf Andronowski, Jon Jugenheimer, Aaron Mulkey

FalconGuides staff: David Legere, Ellen Urban, Mason Gadd

Equipment: Adam Peters of Petzl, Kolin Powick and Adam Riser of Black Diamond Equipment, Glen Griscom of CAMP, Jeff Perron and Dale Robotham of Edelrid/Sasso

Images: Avalanche Canada, Parks Canada

Studio space: Jeremy Regoto

And many more: Ian McCammon, Quentin Roberts, Paul McSorley, Shaun King, Jordy Shepherd, Zac Bolan, Kat Wood, Zhou Peng, Brent Peters, Manoah Ainuu, Nathalie Fortin, Stas Beskin, Etienne Rancourt, Doug Shepherd, Ryan Vachon, Takeshi Tani, Lindsay Fixmer, Samira Samimi, Erik Wellbourn, John Frieh, Nate Goodwin, Daniel Harro, Pierre Raymond, Barry Blanchard, Jack Tackle, Mark Howell, Marco Delesalle, Steven Campbell, Kris Irwin, Marianne van der Steen, Gord McArthur, Brette Harrington, Pack L'Hirokoi, and Trango (Tim's canine companion)

Jon Walsh climbing Superlite, (WI5+ 5.10, 230 m), in Protection Valley, Banff National Park, Alberta, Canada.

Foreword

Ice climbing, the pursuit of frozen waterfalls, as a subset of mountaineering is relatively new. As mountain adventure in the Alps and Rockies progressed from attaining a summit to seeking out aesthetic and challenging lines, alpinists found themselves on steep terrain. The alpine ice that welcomed them was a good stepping-stone to seek out frozen waterfalls. Water ice was a good training ground for the greater ranges. Eventually it became its own discipline in the many-faceted sport of climbing.

Water ice forms seasonally when cascades and seeps are suspended in place with the lock of winter. Climbs, ephemeral in nature, vary according to temperature, precipitation, and the position of the sun. Whereas a rock climb will have the same features, a frozen waterfall can and will change on a daily basis. There is no prescribed route to follow. This seasonality is akin to surfing or powder skiing—when the conditions are "in," there is a palpable level of excitement that runs through the respective sport communities. Word spreads, plans are made, and adventures are shared.

Water, be it liquid, solid, or vapor, is tricky and demanding. Not enough liquid and we become parched; too much we drown; and vapor as clouds can obscure the horizon and visibility. In its solid state, water can be lethal. Unconsolidated snow becomes an avalanche. Falling water ice can take our lives. This understanding of the material and its changing nature is part of what draws us to climb frozen cascades. Knowing the characteristics of ice and how it changes is integral to the art of ice climbing. This awareness makes the experience that much more real.

Humans are tool makers and users—it's only logical that we would apply this ability to the mountains. Excepting climbing shoes and a bit of chalk, rock climbing is a direct interface with the cliff. It's pretty elemental. Ancient societies around the world climbed rock for safety, storage, and divine purposes. Ötzi, the hunter-gatherer entombed in an Austrian glacier, had specific tools that allowed him to traverse the ice. Five thousand years forward, ice climbing still has a mechanical interface with the mountain. Part of the fun we find in ice climbing is our gear—understanding limitations, maintaining functionality, and allowing our tools to take us to places unknown.

—Conrad Anker

Nathalie Fortin lost in a sea of ice on Rio del Lobo (WI5, 40 m) in Rivière-du-Loup, Quebec, Canada.

The Ice Climbing Game

Ice climbing was once upon a time a fringe of a fringe sport. In recent years, its continual gain in popularity has pushed it to the threshold of almost mainstream. There are many reasons why someone would ice climb. It is beautiful. It is fleeting. It is physical. It is cerebral. It is social. It is adventurous. And, it is simply a fun way to enjoy winter.

This book is aimed at every level of ice climber, from the never-ever novice all the way up to the seasoned veteran looking to catch up on modern advancements. It is the long-awaited follow-up to Craig Luebben's *How to Ice Climb!* (FalconGuides, 1999). Unfortunately, Craig was tragically killed in a mountaineering accident in 2009, so we are honored to take up the torch and continue where he left off. The idea is that all climbers can hopefully glean something from these pages. Ice climbing is indeed a risky activity, but if armed with knowledge and training and experience, it can provide an incredible opportunity to explore winter in a wild way.

The three main fundamentals that must be mastered to be a skilled ice climber are hazard management, movement technique, and technical systems. All three of these skill sets are equally important to develop in order to decrease risk. This trilogy of ice education is meticulously described throughout the book. But . . . it is very important to note that a book is in no way a replacement for proper hands-on training. It doesn't matter if you are a first-time neophyte or have been leading ice for many years—continued skill acquisition and mentorship from trained professionals is an investment in your longevity as an ice climber. Hire a guide, join a climbing club, or attend an ice festival. Ice climbing is a lifelong activity with many lessons to learn.

The transient nature of ice is intriguing. You can climb the same route several times and every time have a different adventure. Climbing a route at the start of the season when days are short, the ice is thin, and temperatures are low can be a much different experience than climbing that same route in March when days are longer, the sun is out, and the ice is thick.

As children, many of us found pleasure in swinging at things with a stick or dreamed of cracking open a piñata on our birthday. Ice climbing is the adult manifestation of smashing things with a bat; there is something eerily enjoyable about swinging sharp, spiky objects into frozen water.

On top of being fun, some people seek out ice climbing for the additional challenge that the mountain environment provides. Not only do you need the skills to climb ice, but you also need to know how to stay warm in frigid temperatures, often in compromising locations. There is an art to staying warm when you are out ice climbing that isn't usually required on sunny summer days. Winter nurtures mental and physical robustness, which is extremely empowering.

Zhou Peng heads up the crux pillar on Ice Nine (WI6, 95 m) located along the Icefields Parkway in Banff National Park, Alberta, Canada.

Mountaineers generations before us laid the foundation of ice climbing, wanting to expand their abilities to push their limits and open new possibilities on high peaks. Over time, in particular, starting in the 1980s and 1990s, ice climbing became a sport in its own right. Not only were practitioners learning to ice climb to apply those skills to larger mountains, but some individuals began to ice climb strictly for the enjoyment and pursuit of the sport. The concept of climbing a frozen waterfall is unique and better appreciated in the moment.

Differences Between Rock and Ice Climbing

Ice climbing has a degree of unpredictability that is not found in rock climbing. Typically, rock climbs don't change in difficulty unless a hold breaks, but in ice climbing, the complexity of a climb can vary throughout the season and sometimes day to day. Many factors come into play with ice variability. If someone has climbed the route previously, it alters the ice, making the climb less difficult. If temperatures are frigid, it becomes harder to climb. If the sun is out and blasting on a warm day, it might all fall down around you. These are factors that, for the most part, rock climbers don't have to consider. If temperatures dip while rock climbing, your fingers can get cold, but if it's cold while ice climbing, then the density of the ice can change, and large portions can begin to fracture off.

Ice climbs form differently every year: Sometimes they can be steeper, other years they can be more straightforward, some seasons they can develop technical features like petals and mushrooms whipped up by the wind, and other years they might not form at all. Ice routes are ephemeral in our world. They appear for several months a year and then disappear. They are continually changing. It is not always a given that an ice route will form; some form once every several years, and others might only develop once every couple of decades. Usually, an ice climber's tick-list will have several routes that they would like to climb but that have not formed in recent years; then, when the climbs form, they become the center of attention for that season.

The systems used in ice climbing and rock climbing do not greatly differ, but the technique required to climb is entirely different. With both, you read the features: In rock climbing, you are seeking out the next handhold, a crimp or a side-pull, while with ice climbing you are looking for the next place to swing your tool. Reading features on both mediums is equally as crucial, except ice climbing tends to be repetitious while the movement in rock climbing is usually more varied. While climbing ice, you swing your tool, get a solid stick, step up with your feet, kick in your crampons, stand up, and repeat the process for the length of the route. It is often considered less technical than rock climbing but can seem more physical and mentally taxing.

Leading a steep ice route, you can pretty much guarantee you will feel more runout than on most rock climbs. The difference is that you always have a big jug to hold on to—the handle of an ice tool. Placing protection for ice climbing is typically easier than learning all the subtle nuances of traditional rock gear. However, while falling off is often acceptable on rock routes, it is a big no-no on ice routes. In fact, movement skills on ice should be so dialed in that falling is never an option.

Adding ice climbing to your quiver of climbing skills will take a bit more than just learning the climbing technique. You must also learn about reading the ice, how it changes in different weather, the gear required, and the technical know-how of using that gear. If you have rock climbed before taking up ice climbing, it will accelerate the learning curve dramatically. Within a few dedicated weeks, it's possible to transition comfortably to leading ice, given the right instruction and mentorship.

Tim Auger on the first ascent of Bourgeau Righthand in 1973, Banff National Park, Alberta, Canada.
ROB WOOD

A Short History of Ice Climbing

The advent of ice climbing has its roots in Europe. During the early 1900s in Scotland, climbers started exploring peaks such as Ben Nevis, while at the same time climbing technique and climbing gear were evolving in the Alps. Guides and adventurers climbing snow and ice to the summits of mountains made the first advancements in ice climbing. Guides leading people up snowy and icy slopes completed many first ascents while chopping steps with their ice axe to create what amounted to a staircase up the mountains.

Then, 10-point crampons were invented, and the flatfoot technique was adopted. Walking uphill using this style reduced the need for chopping steps. The first crampons made it easier to ascend slippery slopes and saved the energy it took to cut steps up the side of a mountain. Those climbing the icy north faces of mountains incorporated a new climbing style, developed shortly after the advent of crampons, using both a longer axe and a shorter axe to climb harder lines.

Ice climbing was born, and starting around the 1930s, many of the large European north faces began to be climbed. The Eiger, Matterhorn, and Triolet all saw ascents, while at the same time, more changes were occurring to the equipment being used. Twelve-point crampons were adopted, and the transition from flatfoot technique to front pointing began. Until about the mid-1950s, the technical difficulty of climbing in the mountains would have been equal to around AI3 and M4 in the modern grading system.

Early in the 1960s, after helping retrieve the bodies of three climbers, Hamish MacInnes created an ice axe made entirely of metal. In the accident he responded to, all three climbers' wooden ice axes broke, failing the group, and they fell to their death in Scotland. The new metal shaft gave climbers more confidence in their equipment.

In the mid-1960s, photos started to emerge of climbers using an ice axe with a downturned pick. The pick angle change allowed for advancement in climbing abilities, as it became easier to get a secure ice axe placement, providing additional security on icy slopes. Changing the pick angle along with shortening the length of ice axes allowed for the pursuit of more technical ice routes. Around the same time, the advent of tube ice screws for protection also began to make ice climbing less dangerous.

By the early 1970s, shorter, all-metal ice axes with downturned and drooped picks were in full production, the most popular built by MacInnes and Yvon Chouinard. At this time, the upper limit of ice climbing grades was approximately AI4 and AI5. Most ice climbing was in the alpine, but waterfall ice climbing was fast approaching.

Technical advancements in ice axes and screws allowed climbers to begin to ascend vertical ice and push grades. The beginning of the sport of ice climbing as we know it today started. These changes, especially the introduction of MacInnes's Terrordactyle ice tool, allowed for advancement in grades in both Scotland and the Canadian Rockies.

In the 1970s in North America, the first waterfall ice routes were climbed, with first ascents of the Black Dike (WI4/5 M3) and Repentance (WI5 M4/5) taking place in New Hampshire. Initially, in the Canadian Rockies, some of the longer ice routes were climbed using fixed ropes and aid technique because of their length, but that didn't last long; in a few years routes such as Polar Circus (WI5), Weeping Pillar (WI6), and Nemesis (WI6) were all climbed free.

Throughout the 1970s, harder ice grades were climbed, and by 1977 testpieces were being climbed around the world. In 1979 a route that is on most ice climbers' tick-list as their dream route, Slipstream (WI4+) in the Canadian Rockies, was climbed by Jim Elzinga and John Lauchlan. In the following few years, both the Pomme d'Or (WI5+) in Quebec and Gimme Shelter (WI7) in the Canadian Rockies were also climbed.

As skills on ice were advancing, so were the tools themselves. In 1980 curved tools came into fashion, and the ice tool as we know it today was born. These curved tools allowed for added security on steeper ice but had reduced capabilities on more general terrain. The specificity of tools for steep ice further evolved with the advent of hammers and modular picks.

In the 1980s, the actual sport of ice climbing began. The change was starting to happen, and climbers were no longer pursuing ice climbing to merely push grades in the mountains—they began to seek out ice climbing as a sport unto itself.

The 1990s marked further improvements in tools and also in leashes. Leashes help a climber hold on longer when ice climbing, but present

Jim Elzinga on Weeping Wall in 1974, Banff National Park, Alberta, Canada.
JOHN LAUCHLAN

The spray ice routes of Helmcken Falls in central British Columbia are the future of steep ice climbing. Tim Emmett on Mission to Mars at Helmcken Falls.
JON GLASSBERG OF LOUDER THAN ELEVEN (WWW.LT11.COM)

The Ice Climbing Game   **5**

issues when trying to disconnect from the ice tool. Tools were still reasonably straight compared to technical tools today, or had a slight curve without the large grip rests of modern tools. Eventually, quick-release leashes became popular. These leashes allowed climbers to disconnect from their ice tools relatively quickly without removing their wrist strap, allowing them to shake out or place an ice screw faster and with fewer complications.

Leashless tools became popular in the early 2000s. Initially, just a larger trigger grip at the base of the tool was added, but within several years, larger Z-grip handles became popular. These steep ice and mixed climbing tools became easier to hang on to and increased the freedom of movement in climbing. The new wave of ice climbing tools was very sport-specific. Larger curve angles in the shafts of ice tools also made climbing harder ice features easier, giving more clearance over mushrooms, pet-als, and other awkward ice features.

Screws were also updated, and now climbing ice was becoming a little less scary. With solid pick placements becoming easier to make and protection that was more than just cerebral, more people began to engage in the sport.

The changes in climbing gear allowed for more people to push harder on ice, and ascents of WI6 testpieces started to happen more regularly. Around this time, the harder grades became accessible to the weekend warrior as well.

Since the start of the twenty-first century, there hasn't been much change in the difficulty of ice climbing. Some think it has become easier to climb ice because of technological advances in gear and increased traffic on climbing routes. Still, with one exception, there has not been a notable advance-ment in pure difficulty. In 2010 at Helmcken Falls in Wells Gray Provincial Park in British Colum-bia, Spray On was climbed by Will Gadd and Tim Emmett and given the grade WI10. Before this climb, the hardest ice climbing difficulty grade was WI7. In the following years, several other climbs have taken place at the extremely overhanging Helmcken Falls, with additional routes being graded as high as WI13.

Ice Climbing Then and Now

Ice climbing is thriving, and is not just a medium for older alpinists looking to hone their skills for the bigger mountains anymore. The advances in ice tools, crampons, protection, and clothing have made the sport more enjoyable than ever. Reading the stories of the first generation of ice climbers in Europe and North America, it is hard to imagine the willpower it took to climb ice with hobnail boots, ice pitons, and chopped steps. The advances in gear and access to information on where to climb have helped the sport skyrocket in popularity.

It wasn't long ago that ice climbers were using straight-shaft tools and leashes, swinging at the ice with straight picks that fractured the ice into siz-able and dangerous dinner plates. Now ice tools are made ergo-dynamically, so that with as little effort and ice displacement as possible, a secure stick is easy to make. Advances in protection are as notable as those of the axes. There was a time when placing an ice screw took a long time; the screw was placed by sticking the end of your tool into the screw and twisting it around in a circle to get it deeper into the ice. Now climbers grab the screw off their har-ness and get it to bite into the ice without much effort, then spin away single-handed until it's all the way in after a couple of quick turns. It is advances like these that have helped the ice climbing com-munity grow and brought ice climbing into the forefront of winter sports.

Participation in ice climbing is proliferating; the increase in the number of new climbers has become much more substantial in just the last few years alone. It's not surprising that advances in hard-ware and winter clothing, along with the advent of social media, helped increase the attractiveness of the sport. Swinging axes into frozen waterfalls is rewarding, but in addition to the regular challenges

Ice Climbing by the Book

How to Ice Climb! is but one in a long and distinguished line of ice climbing how-to books. It stands on the shoulders of past tomes written by top ice climbers of the time. The past five decades have witnessed vast changes in equipment and technique, which is reflected in the pages of these now-historical books. In fact, the sport of ice climbing seems to progress so quickly that most instructional books become outdated within a few years. However, knowing where you came from helps set the trajectory of where you are going. All the books listed below are still great references and entertaining reads that should adorn the shelf of all ice aficionados.

1978: *Climbing Ice* by Yvon Chouinard (Sierra Club Books)

1995: *Ice: Tools and Technique* by Duane Raleigh (Elk Mountain Press)

1996: *Ice World: Techniques and Experiences of Modern Ice Climbing* by Jeff Lowe (Mountaineers Books)

1999: *How to Ice Climb!* by Craig Luebben (Falcon Publishing /Globe Pequot Press)

2003: *Ice and Mixed Climbing: Modern Technique* by Will Gadd (Mountaineers Books)

2005: *Mixed Climbing* by Sean Isaac (Globe Pequot Press)

2012: *The Art of Ice Climbing* by Jerome Blanc-Gras and Manu Ibarra (Blue Ice Press)

2019: *Climbing: From Rock to Ice* by Ron Funderburke (FalconGuides)

2021: *How to Ice Climb!* by Sean Isaac and Tim Banfield (FalconGuides)

of climbing, ice climbing has the added trials of cold temperatures and the ever-changing consistency of ice. Both bring an added difficulty to the sport that must be learned over time, in addition to the systems of climbing.

It is the goal of this book to provide you with the knowledge and skills to enjoy the winter medium of ice and start your ice climbing journey with the skills and expertise to make it as efficient as possible.

Ice Grades

Understanding the grading system for ice climbing is important so that you know which routes to choose and how to progress without getting yourself into trouble. The number one rule about ice climbing is no lead falls. Understanding the difficulty of a climb and your abilities is crucial when selecting what route to climb. Every ice climb,

from the easiest flow to the hardest testpiece, has a given grade for a reason, and it is your responsibility to understand what that grade means. Unlike rock climbs, waterfall ice climbs can fluctuate in difficulty throughout the season. Another factor that is specific to ice climbing grades is how many people have climbed a route before you. Most grades that you find in guidebooks are based on one or two things: a consensus grade after many repeat ascents or the grade given during the first ascent.

Waterfall ice climbing gets more difficult when the ice hasn't been climbed previously, has regrown overnight, the ice is thin, or the quality of protection is poor. If someone has climbed the route before you, then the swings and sticks of your ice tools are much easier to make than if you are confronted with a vertical sheet of untouched ice. A grade can also depend on the season and time of year; in the early season, often a route is more challenging, with thinner ice requiring more technique and affording fewer options for protection. If an area is having a banner ice season, ice climbs can be a grade easier than their established guidebook ratings. The reverse is also true if an area is having a bad season; the grades can be more challenging than indicated. In general, a waterfall ice difficulty grade gives you a good idea of what you might encounter when you head out to go climbing, but the difficulty of the ice can change on any given day for numerous reasons.

There are a few different aspects of a grade that are important to understand: The technical grade of the ice is indicated with WI (which stands for water ice), the serious grade is indicated by an R or X, and the commitment grade is indicated by a Roman numeral.

Technical Waterfall Ice Grades

WI1—Often referred to as a frozen lake or a streambed; only crampons are required; some low-angled gullies and approaches.

WI2—Generally around 60 degrees with perhaps a short section reaching 80 degrees but not vertical. Ordinarily there are good possibilities for protection and anchors.

WI3—70-degree ice with short sections of 80 to 90 degrees on a pitch, Normally good ice, with good stances and anchors. The ice is more sustained and requires skills like placing protection and making belays.

WI4—80-degree ice with few options for rest, or 90-degree ice with good possibilities to rest. Sometimes really wild formations like the first pitch of Whiteman Falls or La Meduse are graded WI4 and feature crazy mushrooms and petals to climb but have perfect rests between features. Getting excellent protection is usually not a problem.

WI5—85- to 90-degree ice that is often a long and sustained pitch. If the pitch is shorter, then there can often be poor and featureless ice. There can be short sections of lousy protection due to thin or rotten ice. Protection is harder to place, and sometimes pillars, daggers, and thin ice are encountered.

WI6—90-degree vertical or overhanging ice for a full pitch. If a route is shorter, the ice is usually more challenging than a longer pitch. Typically, there are limited options to rest, and protection is placed while standing on front points or while in challenging positions. Features such as mushrooms, cauliflowers, petals, and chandelier ice can be encountered. Options for protection are limited, and technical climbing is required.

WI7—A rare grade that doesn't get climbed often. The climbing is similar to WI6, but the ice is thinner and usually poorly attached. The climbing requires creativity by the leader. Technical climbing with equally as technical protection skills are required; often protection is nonexistent, difficult to place, or psychological in nature only and wouldn't hold a fall. A physically and mentally challenging pitch.

WI7+—Only a handful of climbs worldwide exist at this grade, which psychologically is like soloing. A fall would have grave consequences.

WI10 to 12—These grades came from the spray ice at Helmcken Falls in British Columbia, Canada. Close in climbing style to mixed climbing, with ultra-steep terrain using crampons and boots. Described by Will Gadd as "Like M10 but you have to swing for placements not hook."

If you see a + when looking at an ice grade, it indicates that the route is a little bit harder than the given grade, but not quite hard enough to necessitate a change in grades. WI4+ indicates that the route is more challenging than WI4 but not quite hard enough to be considered a WI5; it is typically an amalgamation of the two grades.

Waterfall ice grades can range in difficulty from season to season and can sometimes be almost a grade difference in difficulty. The guidebook grade is a good indicator of what to expect, but a consistent grade is not guaranteed.

Seriousness Grades

Ice climbing difficulty grades can also feature the letters R and X, which have a similar meaning as in rock climbing. R is an indicator of a runout pitch. In ice climbing, this typically means that the ice is thin. Unlike rock climbing, an ice climb gets thicker as the season goes on. In the early season, when ice is still forming, many routes can be in R condition, but the guidebook grade may not indicate that. If you see an R in a guidebook, it typically means that it is a thin route throughout the season. If climbing earlier in the season or if you see the R grading, consider taking some additional stubbies and rock protection with you on the climb. Often, protection is tricky, nonexistent, or takes creativity to place. X means protection is limited and practically nonexistent. If you fall, you may die. These can be fragile free-standing pillars that may collapse if you decide to climb them.

Picked-Out Ice

The increase in popularity of ice climbing has led to increased traffic on climbs, which is further changing the grades of ice climbing. If the ice on a climb is virgin and it hasn't had traffic for a significant period or if it is the first ascent of the season, it is often much harder to lead than for subsequent parties. Seconding a route is significantly easier on ice, as the tension is released and the ice is cleaned by the leader, making it easier to get good sticks with your tools. After a couple of parties have climbed an ice route, this becomes increasingly more noticeable, and the route is described as being "picked out." There was a running joke in the Canadian ice climbing scene about suggesting picked-out grades along with difficulty grades to represent how the ice was manufactured before your climb.

In many ice climbing forums across North America, there are posts about virgin ice being more challenging to find, but for the creative few who are willing to venture on longer approaches, there are always options; it just takes more work to get to the ice.

Commitment Grade

Commitment grades in ice climbing differ from those used in grading rock climbs and alpine routes. A system was designed specifically for ice climbs, and the two rating systems are not the same. The commitment grade for ice climbs takes these considerations into account:

- Length of the approach and descent
- Length of the climb
- Objective hazards

I—A friendly route, close to the car and short in length, that is not in avalanche terrain, with either a straightforward rappel or a quick walk-off.

II—A short climb, one or two pitches, that is close to the car; the route may have avalanche danger and a rappel or a walk-off.

III—The climb can take a few hours to most of a day to complete, including the approach. Often used for multi-pitch climbs; or if the climb is short, there may be no trail for the approach, and the approach will likely be longer than an hour. The approach and the climb may have avalanche danger.

IV—A multi-pitch route that may take multiple hours to approach. The climb is often in serious alpine terrain with significant elevation gain on the approach. The climb and approach are likely subject to avalanche danger.

V—A full-day climb in alpine terrain, often with a long approach and a long descent requiring multiple rappels. The climb, approach, and descent are typically in serious alpine terrain and continuously threatened by objective hazards.

VI—Some of the longest ice climbs in the world with all the objective hazards that accompany a serious winter alpine route. Some parties will be out longer than a day, and faster parties will still have a full day in the mountains threatened by avalanches and weather changes.

VII—Reserved for routes like Reality Bath—long, technical routes. Longer and harder than grade VI climbs, continually threatened by overhanging seracs or large avalanche bowls.

Mixed Grades

Mixed grades are easier to define because, like in rock climbing, the holds are somewhat permanent so the difficulty should be the same from ascent to ascent. Having said that, though, ice tools can either destroy or enhance holds, potentially altering the grade. The crowbar leverage applied by ice tools can pry off even seemingly solid holds, thus making a route harder. Conversely, the chisel effect of steel picks on soft stone can make originally small holds deeper, thus making a route easier. Also, the ice on a mixed route obviously can change, either from the progression of the season (bulking out or sublimating) or from climbers' actions (breaking ice or adding hooks). Pure drytool routes are more akin to rock grades since they are not affected by ice conditions changing, but the grade can still (and most likely will) change due to rock holds either breaking or improving over time. Mixed grades use the M-system while pure drytool routes use the D-system, which is essentially the same except a D-grade denotes the routes are "dry" (therefore no ice) and can be climbed outside of the winter season. Like rock climbing grades (Yosemite Decimal System), both M-grades and D-grades are opened-ended scales.

M3 = 5.5

M4 = 5.7

M5 = 5.8

M6 = 5.9

M7 = 5.10

M8 = 5.11-

M9 = 5.11+

M10 = 5.12-

M11 = 5.12+

M12 = 5.13-

M13 = 5.13

M14 = 5.13+

Scottish Grades

Scotland, the birthplace of mixed climbing, uses two numbers to define the difficulty of a pitch. The first number is an overall grade represented by Roman numerals. It describes the whole experience, taking into account seriousness, difficulty, and how sustained the difficulties are. The second number is the technical grade of the hardest single move on the pitch, which is indicated by an Arabic number. Generally, Scottish technical grades are slightly easier than an M-grade of the same number. V 5 is an example of a benchmark Scottish mixed climb and would be similar to M4 with good protection for the crux. VII 6 would feel like M5 but with a more serious crux, and VIII 7 like a dangerously runout M6. If the commitment grade is lower than the technical grade, you can be assured that the pitch is very well protected with gear pretty much wherever you want it.

Environmental Considerations

Minimizing our impact when we travel in both the frontcountry and backcountry is essential, not only for the ecological impact but also the aesthetic impact. Tracks on the snowy white canvas tell others where you have been—that is, until it snows again. For that reason, visible signs of travel and impact in the winter environment can be short-lived (seasonal); however, when ice climbing, you should think and visualize what effects might extend beyond and into the summer season.

Winter Travel

Snow is a moldable and low-impact surface. Unlike the effects climbers can have on a fragile alpine environment in the summertime, the winter provides a durable and protective surface. When traveling in areas with low snow, remember what the surface may look like in other seasons. Stick to trails and more durable surfaces, avoiding, for example, impacting alpine meadows. Traveling in a smaller group and being aware of noise, especially in popular areas, help mitigate the social impact for other user groups and potentially reduces crowding in high use areas.

Crowding

With the popularity of ice climbing on a steady rise, crowding at routes and crags is becoming an obvious issue. Weekends are often very busy and can lead to frustration, while weekdays still can offer a bit of solitude. At crags, be courteous and willing to share topropes with your fellow climbers so as not to dominate classic routes all day. Portable speakers have no place in the wilderness, especially if other users are present. Music at the crag not only is annoying but can also be distracting to the point of being a hazard.

On multi-pitch routes, be sure to write your intended objective in the dirt on the back window of your vehicle (and maybe even your departure time). This helps other parties arriving after you to decide if they should go somewhere else. There should never be a race for a route. Communicate with other parties and come up with a plan. The first group to the base of the route has the right of way. Passing parties is bad form due to the ice fall hazard, but it is also very poor practice to climb under other parties.

Access to our public lands as climbers should be thought of as a privilege and not a right. Be aware

Ice climbing is popular, and crags and routes are becoming very busy.
SEAN ISAAC

of any access issues and heed any closures. You do not want to be the person responsible for having an area shut down to climbing.

Human Waste

Poor disposal of human waste has the potential to affect the cleanliness of not only our ice climbing crags and routes but ultimately also our waterways. Check for best practices in your area and requirements from land managers. Disposal of urine and feces can be addressed differently in a winter environment. Aesthetically, it is best to concentrate urine in one area, such as a designated pee-tree. Do not urinate near the base of routes or belay stances. Also, avoid urinating beneath rock overhangs. These might seem like a suitable and private bathroom spot, but snowfall will not cover the stain, and the rock will start to hold the odor.

During times of snow drought, urine stains may not be covered by new snowfall for a long time, so make sure to move far away from the routes to urinate. Pack out all toilet paper and feminine hygiene products. While burning toilet paper is an option with a hot fire, burning it with a lighter is often incomplete, leaving remnants of toilet paper bits. Disposing of feces with little environmental impact is more challenging in the winter. This is due to the spring water running through the snowpack, eventually joining streams and waterways. Depending on the land manager and best practices for the area, options may include:

- Packing it out in a disposable bag for solid waste. Both individual and group systems are manufactured commercially with chemicals that work to solidify, decrease odor, and eliminate the waste as a biohazard. Packing out solid waste is becoming more common and sometimes required in high use and winter areas.

- Digging to the soil, then disposing of waste as per other seasons—100 meters (328 feet) away from any water source or existing trails, dug 15 to 20 centimeters (6 to 8 inches) deep in organic soil and covered up. Of course, this may be impossible if the ground is frozen.

- Digging a group trench or pit system in the snow with the thought that eventually the sun will melt it out and UV radiation will sterilize it. This is only appropriate where there will not be a great aesthetic impact.

- With small user numbers, dispersal rather than concentration of feces may be more appropriate. Digging individual pit systems could then be considered. Think about what the environment looks like in the summertime, and ask yourself what this environment can handle, and is this a good place to urinate or defecate?

Human's Best Friend

Taking your dog ice climbing is not like taking your dog to the rock crag. For the majority of people and locations, bringing a dog to the crag is not the best idea, especially a busy crag with lots of ice falling and people walking around with crampons on their feet. With that said, if you are contemplating taking your dog to the crag, here are some things to consider:

- Clean up after your dog, no exceptions. No one wants to see dog poop at the crag. Also, have your dog pee away from the climbing area. Yellow snow is not aesthetic.

- Keep your dog on a leash and away from falling ice. Tie up your dog away from where it can

Human's best friend: Ice crags can be hazardous for dogs with the cold, falling ice, and crampon points.

be hit by ice and rocks or be in the way of people. Dogs have also been known to find their way around a pitch and make it to the top or halfway up a climb. Claws are not crampons, so a scrambling dog could easily slip off a climb.

- If your dog barks and cries a lot, leave and go home. Dogs barking and crying at the crag can be very annoying and distracting to others.

- Prepare for the cold. Although Fido has some extra fur, it's likely not enough to sit out in the cold without moving for several hours. Consider packing an insulated bed and a synthetic puffy that you can wrap around your dog to keep it warm.

- People have crampons on. Ensure your dog is not around people's feet. Seeing a dog have its paw stepped on by crampons is not enjoyable.

- Taking your dog into avalanche terrain is risky and not recommended.

Ice Climbing Responsibility Code

Be Respectful—Everyone deserves a safe and enjoyable experience. Educate others with respect and be educated with grace. Engage in online forums as you would when face to face. Pack out trash, cigarette butts, and excrement (bring a wag bag to popular venues). Urinate away from the base.

Leave a Note—on your dashboard or in the dirt on your rear window, with route name, party size, and time, to aid others in their decision making at busy venues. Have a backup plan for when others are on your intended route, if it will not accommodate multiple parties.

Parties Ahead Have Right of Way—It is your responsibility to steer clear of them. Do not climb beneath or pass others without clear communication and a plan to which all parties agree. Multi-pitch climbers have right of way over those only climbing the first pitch of established multi-pitch climbs.

Expect Falling Ice from Other Climbers—Falling ice is inevitable. Climbing beneath others is dangerous to you and compromises their security. Plan your movements and belay stances to maximize shelter from ice fall, which can bounce far, and in unexpected ways.

Avalanche Rescue Equipment—A transceiver, shovel, and probe should be carried by all party members in avalanche terrain when sufficient snow exists for an avalanche hazard to be present. This may be on the approach, the climb, or the descent.

Jeff Mercier gets ready at the base of the mixed climb Big Brother (M4 WI5, 200 m) on the Little Sister in Canmore, Alberta, Canada.

CHAPTER 2

Equipment

I ce climbing is, by its very nature, fully dependent on gear since ice cannot be climbed without crampons and ice tools. Modern waterfall ice climbing gear is necessary to successfully scale frozen waterfalls. This chapter will focus on the equipment required for ice climbing as well as strengths and limitations of equipment. It is poor form to use outdated or worn-out equipment, since old equipment is a hazard in itself. The chapter will also discuss clothing systems for winter ice climbing.

Ice Tools

Ice tools have come a very long way from the classic alpenstock of yore. In fact, the ice axe's early ancestor is the shepherd's cane used by herders since the Middle Ages to cross glaciers in order to reach high alpine pastures for their flocks of sheep. Over the centuries, the shaft shrank and curved while the crook of the cane evolved into a pick. Modern ice tools are high-tech engineered implements that have made climbing frozen waterfalls easier and safer.

Ice tools basically break down into three categories: general all-mountain tools, waterfall ice tools, and drytooling/mixed tools. All-mountain tools excel in the alpine but still hold their own on vertical waterfall ice climbing. They tend to have straighter shafts than the more specialized ice tools, which allow them to plunge into snow more efficiently, but they still have enough of a curve to allow for technical ice ascents. Modern waterfall ice tools have a curved shaft and a handle that offers two grip positions: lower and upper. They also usually have modular heads that accept different picks.

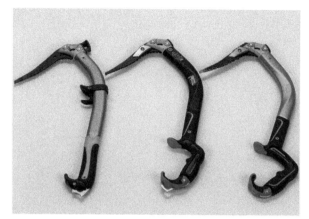

Ice tools: All-mountain, waterfall ice, and drytooling (left to right).

These types of tools are suitable for every genre of waterfall ice and mixed climbing. Specific mixed and drytooling tools have an even more aggressively curved shaft with a steeper pick angle for very featured ice and stable hooking on rock but are more awkward to use on lower-angled ice.

In addition to these three types of tools, there are also competition tools that are just designed to hook, so they are not appropriate for real ice climbing. There are also speed tools, which are manufactured to hook your way up ice as fast as possible in speed climbing competitions. Again, they are not suitable for real ice climbing either.

For climbers who are undecided about what style of climbing they enjoy, or for someone looking for a single set of ice tools for both intermediate ice and advanced mixed climbing, there are modular tools on the market that allow you to change components of the ice tool. You can customize your tool by adjusting the handle angle, pick, pommel, and other attachments to your preferred setup.

Ice tools are made from a variety of materials. Luckily, wooden-shaft ice axes are considered antiques, while modern tools are made from various metals and even carbon fiber. Most ice tools are of metal construction, either aluminum or steel components. Carbon shaft tools have the advantage of being lighter and stiffer, thus reducing the vibration of the tool when impacting the ice. They do not conduct heat from your hand as well as metal tools. In theory this should keep your hands warmer.

Lighter tools are great for long approaches and drytooling, but the savings in weight may end up costing more energy while swinging into ice. What is most important is a well-balanced tool with a weighted head or pick. Some tools have steel heads for weight, while others have aluminum heads with pick weights for more forward weight. For pure drytooling, pick weights can be removed to provide a lighter tool for rock moves.

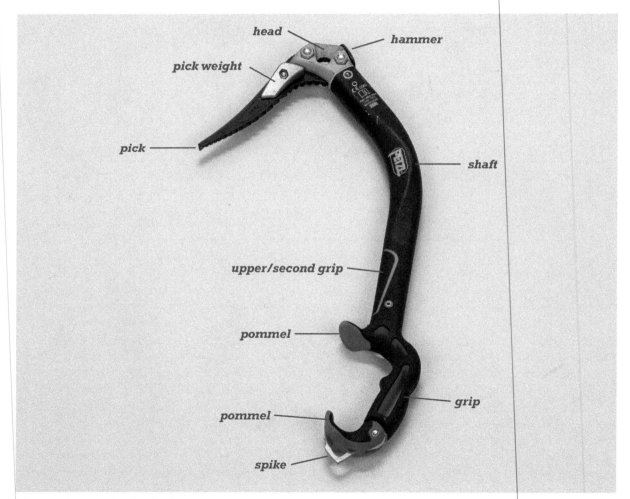

The anatomy of an ice tool.

Picks

Ice picks have changed over time. They used to be straight with no teeth, until the reversed-curved design was born in the 1960s. Now, ice tools and picks are modular, thus offering different options for different terrain.

Pure ice picks tend to be the narrowest of all the picks, which helps get a solid tool placement in ice faster and easier. The narrower the pick, the less ice that is displaced when ice climbing, which means a reduced number of swings and more efficient climbing. The upper edge of ice picks is usually beveled and does not have teeth that would impede cleaning a placement. Pure ice picks are often the lightest of picks and generally measure around 3 mm at the tip. Ice picks can be B or T rated (see sidebar), depending on the manufacturer.

Pick weights greatly improve the swinging performance of an ice tool by adding some heft to the swing and dampening vibration. If an ice tool is too light in the head, the pick simply bounces off cold, hard ice.

Dry picks are designed specifically for dry-tooling. They are wider picks compared to ice picks, which adds rigidity to the pick for when it is torqued and cammed in rock. They also have a more aggressive front tooth for better hooking and

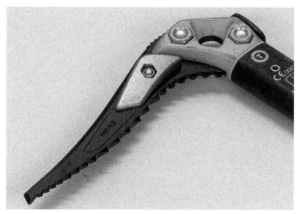

Pick weights help picks penetrate better in hard ice.

B versus T Rating

The B (basic) and T (technical) ratings are based on tests to the shaft and pick. Technical ice tool shafts should be rated T. Picks are rated Type 1 (B) or Type 2 (T). Type 1 picks are not as strong or durable as Type 2 picks but perform better on pure ice because they are often thinner.

teeth on the top side of the pick for added purchase when camming the head against rock. Most dry picks measure approximately 4 mm along the entire length of the pick. The wider pick means they are heavier and often T rated.

Mixed picks try to merge the stability of a dry pick on rock with the performance of an ice pick. The front tooth isn't as aggressive as on a dry pick, which is better for ice, while the pick is often wider and T-rated. The teeth on the top side of the pick are also not as aggressive, so that a placement made in ice can be cleaned a little easier. Often, they vary in size from 3.3 to 4 mm depending on the manufacturer.

Some things to consider with ice and mixed picks:

- What style of climbing will you be doing? If you are simply climbing ice, there isn't often a need to have a mixed pick.

- Occasionally picks break in the field. Some people carry an extra one and the tools to change it in case this happens on a route.

- If you will be mixed climbing as well as ice climbing, take two picks that you can change the night before for each style of climbing that interests you.

- Picks will touch rock and start to dull. Sharpening picks is a bit of an art, and some climbers have specific ways they like to sharpen them.

- In the early season, when ice is thin, the possibility of hitting rock with your tools is higher. Consider using last year's picks or mixed picks until the ice fattens up. The skinnier ice picks dull faster when they hit rock compared to the wider mixed-specific picks.

Hammers

Ice tools can be purchased with no hammer, a mini hammer, or a proper hammer depending on the make and manufacturer. Hammers are useful for placing and testing pitons and tapping an ice tool deeper into a moss- or ice-choked crack. Most technical ice tools have gotten away from coming stocked with an adze as the default setup, since an adze is a snow-digging implement more useful for mountaineering than ice climbing. In fact, an adze is dangerous if a tool pops while drytooling and hits you in the face. A hammer can also add much-needed weight to the head of the tool if pick weights are not available.

Grip

The grip is located at the bottom of the shaft. Ideally it is ergonomically shaped and adjustable to fit different hand sizes and should have a rubber

Modern waterfall ice tools have two grips.

surface for good contact. Most grips have a pommel under the pinky finger to assist in supporting the hand. Modern ice tools should have two grips: an upper and a lower. Some handles have a trigger hook for the index finger. In theory this might seem like a good idea; the reality is that it chokes the wrist-flicking action of a swing. Traditionally, a spike protrudes from the bottom of the grip. This metal spike offers traction when holding the ice tool by the head to use it as a walking cane, but also could be a stabbing hazard on difficult drytool routes. Some ice tools have removable spikes for this reason. The spike also often has a hole for attaching umbilical leashes to prevent dropped tools.

Leashes

In the early to mid-2000s, the transition away from leashes began. A leash attaches to an ice tool and to the wrist of a climber, allowing the climber to let the leash take some of their weight while climbing. Using one reduces the freedom of a leashless tool and makes it more difficult to shake out and place ice screws.

Now, almost unanimously, climbers favor the increased freedom that leashless tools offer, and seeing someone climbing with a leash has become a rarity. Not being attached to the tool with a leash allows the climber to shake out and de-pump significantly easier than when they are attached to an ice tool.

Most tools now offer a clip-in point for an elasticized bungee umbilical leash that attaches and rotates on a swivel from the belay loop of a harness. This helps maintain the freedom of leashless tools while at the same time prevents dropping a tool. Umbilical leashes, however, have their own drawbacks, as they can get twisted around themselves.

Crampons

Like ice tools, crampons come in a variety of styles depending on the intended purpose. For winter waterfall ice climbing, full step-in crampons with a

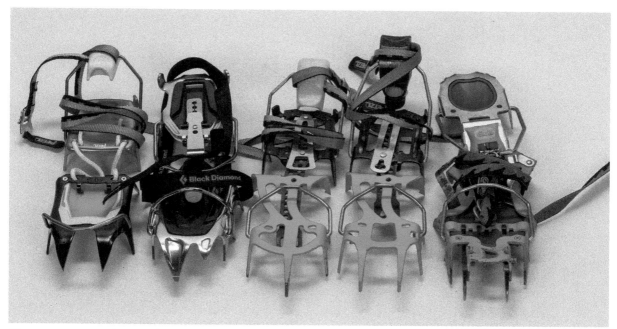

Crampons come in a variety of styles.

metal toe bail and a heel lever are the best. Strap-on or semi-strap-on (with a toe strap instead of toe bail in the front) are not appropriate for ice climbing due to the fact that a solid boot-to-crampon interface is difficult to achieve. Crampons can have either dual or mono front points. Novice ice climbers are encouraged to begin with dual front points since they offer more purchase in the ice and more stability; however, they also displace more ice. Mono-point crampons are for more experienced ice climbers with refined movement skills and for mixed climbing. Having a single point allows for better precision and displaces less ice but requires more body tension to maintain stability.

Crampons come in three materials: steel, stainless steel, and aluminum. Steel is durable but is heavy and will rust. Stainless steel offers the same benefits in durability as steel crampons plus some additional protection against rust and corrosion.

Aluminum crampons are light but only appropriate for snow walking. A recent advent is hybrid crampons with a steel front piece and an aluminum back piece, so durability and performance is up front where it's needed, while the back is lightweight.

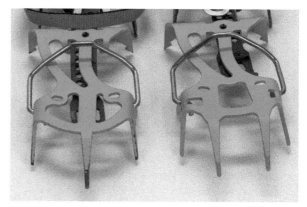

Mono and dual front points.

CRAMPON ADJUSTMENT

A well-fitted crampon should be very tightly attached to the boot. There should be absolutely no play between the crampon and the sole of the boot. This is important to ensure that crampons do not unexpectedly fall off. Crampons are asymmetrical, so there is a right and left (often signified with lettering or symbols). Adjust the length of the crampon first with the center bar and then fine-tune with the heel lever dial. Unfortunately, crampons are designed for men's size 9 boots, so they do not fit super well on very small or very large boots.

Make sure the the bottom of the boot as well as the toe and heel welts are free of snow and ice when putting crampons on.

Longer center bars can be bought for big shoe sizes, and smaller toe bails can be bought for small shoe sizes. A tight crampon fit should require a forceful snap of the heel lever. It is recommended to spend some time toproping before leading when using a new crampon/boot combination, to prevent any nasty surprises.

Front points also need to be adjusted. Points should protrude beyond the toe of the boot by approximately 3.5 to 4 centimeters (about 1.5 inches). If they are too short, there is not enough purchase in the ice; if they are too long, there is too much leverage. The length of the front points is most commonly adjusted by moving the toe bail forward or backward. Some front points can be adjusted by moving the actual point.

Be sure to knock off all snow and ice from the tread of your boots before putting on crampons. Also, scrape out the boot's toe and heel with an ice tool pick so they are completely clear. It is important to do a full visual inspection of the toe bail and heel lever to make sure they are properly in place. It is actually quite easy to miss the heel welt of the boot with the crampon's heel lever, so brush all snow away in order to check the attachment carefully.

The ankle strap is necessary not only to keep the heel lever from accidentally prying off but also to prevent losing a crampon if one unexpectedly parts ways from the boot. The excess strap is usually a nuisance. Various ways to deal with it include:

- Tie it off to itself with half hitches
- Tuck it into the Velcro of gaiters
- Trim it permanently
- Wrap it once more around the ankle

Comp Boots

Comp boots are lightweight boots with a stripped-down crampon bolted directly to the sole. Originally designed for competition climbing, they are also used for very steep, difficult drytool and mixed

Comp boots.

Picks and crampon points need to be sharpened regularly to maintain performance.

lines at crags. This combo hybrid allows for more precision while forgoing the weight of a traditional boot and crampon setup. They are not as warm as regular ice boots and are not practical for approaches or multi-pitch routes.

Heel spurs had their heyday for a few years in the early 2000s. They are points that stick out the back of a comp boot and are used to heel hook rock and ice. They were deemed to make steep mixed routes too easy, so went the way of the dodo bird.

Ice Tool and Crampon Maintenance

Inspecting your ice tools and crampons for damage needs to occur every climbing day. As ice climbers, our gear is our safety net, so it must always be in top-notch condition. It is not uncommon to hear about a fall while ice climbing from a crampon or ice tool breaking. Always check that parts are tight, picks and points are sharp, and everything is dry.

- Inspect your ice tools and crampons before and after every use. Over time metal fatigues, bolts loosen, straps wear out, and plastics crack.

- Sharpen your ice tool picks and crampon points as needed. Try to maintain the original angles and bevels.

- Make sure all bolts and screws are tight.

Gear breaks so always be prepared with a repair kit that includes all the specific wrenches and Allen keys for your crampons and ice tools as well as tie wire for crampon field repairs.
SEAN ISAAC

- Dry out ice tools and crampons after each climbing day to prevent rust, corrosion, and/or plating issues.

- Check boot laces for frays or broken eyelets.

- Carry a field repair kit that includes a file, multi-tool, tie wire (for lashing broken crampon to boot), spare boot lace, duct tape, and the specific Allen keys and wrenches that come with your ice tools and crampons.

Climbing Boots

The advancement in boots over the last several years has improved fit and functionality tenfold. Winter boots are one of the most essential pieces of kit that you will use ice climbing. Keeping your feet warm and having comfortable boots can make or break a day out. Boots have become warmer, lighter, and less cumbersome for technical climbing. Ice climbing boots tend to fit into three categories:

- Lightweight warm-weather climbing boots
- Heavier cold-weather climbing boots
- Double boots with a removable insulated liner

Ice climbing boots are made of a combination of leather and synthetic materials and can be either single or double (a shell and an insulated liner) boots. Specific ice climbing boots should have both a toe and heel welt (deep grooves for crampon bails and levers) and a stiff sole with little to no flex. Hiking boots or general mountaineering boots are not appropriate for ice climbing for many reasons: They are not rigid enough, not warm enough, and may not have a toe welt for step-in crampons. Some ice climbing boots have a built-in gaiter system

Ice climbing boots with full built-in gaiter.

Ice climbing boots with built-in mini gaiter.

Double boots with removable liner.

to keep snow out and to protect the laces from becoming iced up.

Boot Fit

Fitting ice climbing boots correctly is more important than in any other genre of mountain sports. Ice climbing boots have different fit considerations than even mountaineering boots. A properly fitted ice boot should be snug in the heel so your foot doesn't lift off the bottom, but also have enough room in the front so your toes do not bang into the end. When kicking the ice repeatedly, if the boot fit is not right it can lead to jamming your toes against the end of your boot all day, which usually leads to bruised toes and even lost toenails. Boots also have to be warm and comfortable for long approaches over snow, dirt, and rock. A lot of fit can be accomplished by adjusting/tightening the laces. Have the laces a bit looser for approaching, then tighten them at the base of the climb for more of a performance fit.

Choosing the right boots mostly depends on the fit. What boots fit your feet the best? Your climbing objectives and cold tolerance should also be considered. When in the store, make sure to try on both right and left boots, then try kicking the boots into the wall at the store and see if your toes hit the end of the boot. If they do, maybe try a size bigger. If possible, stand on an edge with your feet in a horizontal position to simulate your foot position when front pointing on ice, and you should get a better sense of whether or not you will get heel lift in the boots. Ideally, the heel will stay glued to the bottom of a well-fitted boot.

Harness

Even though a rock–climbing harness will work for ice climbing, there are a few features to look for when purchasing a harness for ice climbing. First, you'll want to make sure that the harness has slots in the waist belt to attach racking clips. Racking

Ice climbing harnesses.

clips are large, plastic, carabiner-like devices for clipping ice screws and ice tools to. Some racking clips are designed to attach around the waist belt and do not need specific slots. The second thing to look for is adjustable leg loops. Not everyone uses harnesses with adjustable leg loops, and they do add a little bit more weight to the harness, but they make it a lot easier to put your harness on over big boots. Hanging belays on ice routes are not comfortable but fortunately usually a rare occurrence, which reduces the need for lots of extra padding, which is commonly found on rock climbing harnesses.

Helmet

A climbing helmet is designed to protect your head from falling ice and rock as well as the impact from a fall. There are specific ice climbing helmets available with eye protection visors, but despite seeming like a good idea, they have not become popular. There are two styles of climbing helmets: hard shell and soft shell. Hard shell helmets have a hard plastic shell and tend to be more durable. Soft shell helmets are made from a foam material and are very lightweight but potentially not as durable, so care

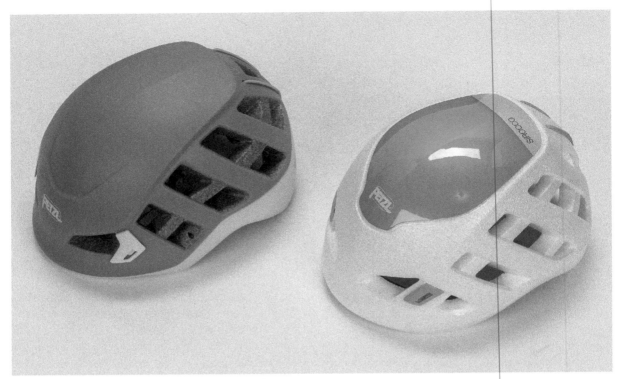

Climbing helmets can be used for rock or ice.

Proper helmet fit covering forehead.

Improper helmet fit leaving forehead exposed.

must be taken when packing them. Most modern helmet designs use a combination of soft shell and hard-shell materials for a hybrid construction. Most helmets come in at least a couple of different sizes and should be fitted with a hat or balaclava. A properly fitting helmet should cover the entire forehead down to the eyebrows. If the helmet is too small and sits too high or too far back on the head, the forehead will be exposed to being hit by ice.

Ice Screws

Gone are the days of pounding in ice pitons and hoping for the best. Ice screws have been the main form of ice protection for several decades now. Ice screws have evolved over the last decade to bite easier, screw in faster, and weigh less. All ice screws consist of a tube, threads, teeth, a hanger with clip-in hole(s), and, in recent times, a crank knob or lever. The tube of modern ice screws is manufactured from plated stainless steel or aluminum. The hanger is also made from stainless steel or aluminum, and previously from chromoly steel. Chromoly is becoming less common in ice screw designs since it is heavy and rusts. Most hangers either have two clip-in holes or one large hole that will accept two carabiners.

In the quest for lighter ice screws, aluminum is currently being used in lightweight versions for the tube of the screw, with the teeth of the screw being made of steel. This has helped reduce the weight of an ice rack by 30 percent but has made ice screws less durable as well. It can also be harder to place aluminum screws in wet ice conditions.

Ice screws come in approximately five different lengths:

- 10 cm (red)—used for thin ice and not as strong as other screw sizes because of fewer threads on the tube.
- 13 cm (yellow)—stronger than a 10 cm screw due to more threads; used for lead protection.

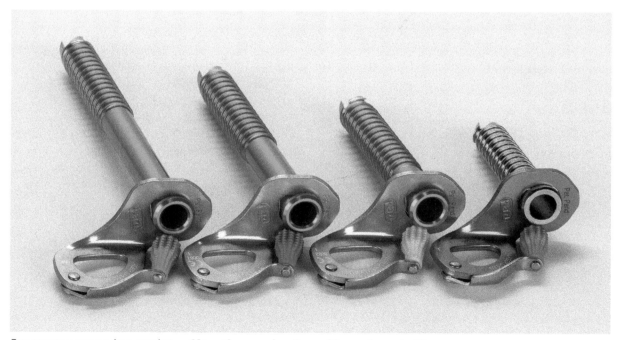

Ice screws come in a variety of lengths ranging from 22 cm down to 10 cm.

- 16/17 cm (blue)—the most popular length and bulk of an ice screw rack; used for lead protection and anchors.
- 19 cm (gray)—an in-between length for lead protection in poor ice quality and for anchors.
- 21/22 cm (green/purple)—the longest length ice screw; used for constructing V-threads and anchors.

Ice Screw Maintenance and Repair

Ice screws should be packed in a commercially bought sleeve to protect the threads and teeth from getting damaged. Dull teeth and burred threads prevent ice screws from going in as smooth and fast as when they are new, so every measure should be taken to preserving their sharpness. Once they do become dull, a trained amateur machinist might be able to sharpen them, but this takes much skill. Some companies sell sharpening devices that do a satisfactory job of re-sharpening. Another option is sending them off to someone who specializes in sharpening ice screws. Even though modern screws are stainless steel plated and should not rust, there can be issues with the plating if they are not dried out after being used.

Slings

Slings are commercially sewn closed loops of nylon or high-modulus polyethylene (HMPE), more commonly known as Dyneema. Nylon is bulkier and heavier but is cheaper and holds knots better. Dyneema is incredibly strong for its weight and is more cut-resistant than nylon.

Dyneema can't be dyed, so slings are white with colored nylon thread running through them. Both nylon and Dyneema are considered static, but nylon offers a bit of stretch while Dyneema is essentially as static as steel chain. The repeated flexing of Dyneema degrades the fibers much quicker than nylon, especially when knots are tied; therefore,

Dyneema slings need to be replaced more frequently than the nylon equivalent.

Sewn slings come in a variety of lengths. They are commonly used to connect carabiners to create a protection runner (alpine draw), to construct anchors, or as a tether to secure to an anchor when rappelling. Commercially sewn slings come in standard lengths of 60 cm (shoulder length), 120 cm (double-shoulder length), 180 cm (triple length), and 240 cm (quads).

All slings are constructed to meet the industry's full-strength standard of 22 kN. Nylon slings are reduced in strength by roughly 30 percent when a knot is tied in them (more or less depending on the type of knot), while Dyneema experiences a reduction of 50 percent strength when a knot is introduced due to its low melting point.

Cord

Cord, commonly referred to as accessory cord, is essentially smaller-diameter static rope. At roughly 10 kN strength, 7 mm cord should be the minimum diameter used since it is already well below full strength. Due to its smaller diameter, it is important that the ice climbing leader understand the strength limitations of cord and ensure that in any full load-bearing application the cord is doubled. Two 5-meter (16-foot) lengths (cordelettes) and one 1.5-meter (5-foot) section of cord (personal prusik) should be carried for anchor construction and rescue applications. Once a knot is added to cord, its strength is reduced by roughly 30 percent.

Belay and Rappel Devices

Belay devices create friction by forcing the rope through a series of bends where it rubs against the device or itself, or some form of cam is engaged. Some belay devices are designed for skinnier ropes, so be sure to have the correct device paired up with the diameter of the ropes being used. All devices, including auto braking, require constant

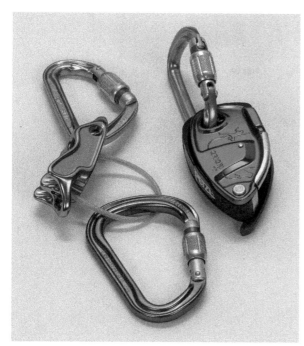

Auto-braking (left) and assisted-braking (right) belay devices.

on the rope when an abrupt force is applied. Braking engagement is assisted and automatically maintained (examples include Petzl Grigri, Mammut Smart, Trango Cinch, Edelrid Mega Jul). Assisted-braking devices place 30 percent more force on the top piece of protection in a lead fall compared to a manual-braking device because there is no rope slippage through the device. With this in mind, they are best used for top rope belays or for lead belays on sport mixed and drytooling routes where a dynamic belay can be added by the belayer jumping up with the fall. When the ground is snow covered, Grigri use should be avoided because they can clog up with snow. Some newer belay devices, like the Edelrid Giga Jul, have a feature to switch modes from manual braking to assisted braking, making it more versatile for various situations.

Auto-Braking Device

Auto-braking devices only allow rope to go in one direction. The rope can be pulled in but the device automatically locks when force is applied to the active strand. A number of manual-braking devices also have an auto-brake mode, and some even have an assisted-braking mode possibility. Examples of a manual-braking device with an auto-locking option are the Petzl Reverso, DMM Pivot, and Black Diamond ATC Guide. Plate device examples with an auto-locking mode are the Camp Oyo and Kong Gigi. Plate devices provide an extra benefit of reduced friction versus a manual-braking device set up in auto-braking mode when belaying from the top, saving your elbows extra stress while belaying. Auto-braking does not mean hands free. A hand must be kept on the brake strand while belaying, or a backup blocking knot needs to be tied before taking your hand off the rope.

Carabiners

Carabiners can be either locking or non-locking and constructed of either aluminum or steel. The

management. Most belay devices can also be used for rappelling. They can be divided into three categories: manual braking, assisted braking, and auto braking.

Manual-Braking Device

Manual-braking devices are two-way devices that allow rope to be pulled in or paid out. They are typically tube-style devices that require braking to be done manually to engage them and manually maintained. Manual-braking devices are also used for rappelling.

Assisted-Braking Device

Assisted braking devices are two-way devices that allow rope to be pulled in or paid out but assist with braking force. Devices like the Petzl Grigri use a camming function to create friction. Assisted implies that the device is designed to clamp down majority of carabiners used in modern climbing activities are aluminum due to its lightweight properties in comparison to steel. Non-locking carabiners may be used at noncritical connection points. These are the connection points in a technical system that would not have catastrophic consequences if they were to fail. All critical connection points in a technical system should employ locking carabiners. In situations where movement of the critical connection point is anticipated and monitoring of that point will be limited, such as the master point of a toprope anchor, two locking carabiners in opposition should be used. Locking carabiners can either be large HMS style or small offset-D style. A few of both types are recommended—the HMS lockers for anchor clove hitches, rescue Munter hitches, and the main carabiner for your belay device, and the offset-D lockers for personal tethers and prusiks and the eye of an auto-braking device in auto-brake mode. A triple-action, captive-eye locking carabiner is useful for fixed-point lead belays with a Munter hitch.

Carabiners are commonly rated (stamped on the spine) between 20 and 24 kN when loaded along their long axis. Their strength decreases drastically (roughly by a third) when loaded across their short axis (cross-loading) or with the gate open. Carabiners can also be much weaker when levered over an edge or torqued in a crack.

Larger carabiners with larger gate openings are typically easier to clip, especially in winter with gloves on. Wire-gate carabiners do not freeze as easily as normal gate carabiners when they get wet.

Runners

A runner is a length of sling with two carabiners used to connect the rope to protection points like ice screws, bolts, and traditional rock gear.

Runners: load-limiter draws, quickdraws, and alpine draws.

Quickdraw

A quickdraw is a short (10 to 18 cm) length of sling (nylon or high-strength material) that is sewn through the middle creating a loop at either end for non-locking carabiners. The bottom end of the quickdraw should have a rubber restraint to hold the carabiner in place so it can't flip upside down when trying to clip the rope in and feature a bent-gate carabiner to also make clipping easier. The gate of the other end is typically a straight-gate carabiner used to clip into the piece of protection. Both the upper and lower carabiner need to be facing the same direction. Like most things in climbing, there are several quickdraw options depending on your budget, with the lightest ones being the most expensive. For pure ice climbing ten to twelve quickdraws and a couple of alpine draws should be adequate for most climbs.

Alpine Draw

An extendable form of the quickdraw made out of a 60 cm sewn sling (shoulder-length sling) with two non-locking carabiners. These are also called triple or extendable draws because the sling is tripled to make it short like a quickdraw, to hang from a harness gear loop, and then it can be extended. It is usually beneficial to have at a minimum a couple of alpine draws on your rack so that you can extend protection and reduce rope drag.

Locker Draw

A locker draw is the same as a quickdraw except that it has locking carabiners at either end. Only one should be carried for use on critical protection points like high first bolts on sport mixed routes or backup V-thread rappel anchors.

Load-Limiter Draw

Load-limiter draws (aka Screamers) are force-absorbing runners that can decrease peak force on protection by roughly 15 percent (about 2 kN). They are designed in such a manner that when activated, the stitching rips to decrease the shock on the protection. Despite their weight, bulk, and expense, it is wise to carry a couple. They are used for clipping to an ice screw instead of a quickdraw and are useful on questionable protection placements in thin or unconsolidated ice and for protecting the anchor on multi-pitch routes.

Accessories

Various other accessories that should be carried on an ice climber's harness include a V-thread hooker, a knife, quick links, and a personal prusik.

V-thread Hooker

There are numerous V-thread hookers available on the market. Some feature a built-in cutting tool, while others have the ability to tighten a nut on a bolt. Some are flexible wire and others are rigid plastic, which is useful for poking stuck ice cores out of ice screws. It's best to experiment to see which ones work best for you. Be careful with them in your pack and ensure the sharp hook is covered well; if not, it can easily rip soft goods inside your backpack. It is not uncommon for someone to pull out their down jacket from the top of their pack only to have it followed by a cloud of feathers as the hook slices through the shell fabric.

Knife

A knife is an essential piece of personal kit when ice climbing, especially for making V-threads and cutting cord. A small knife with a locking blade that can be clipped to your harness is best.

Quick Links

Quick links, also known as maillons, are small stainless-steel links that, instead of having a hinged gate like a carabiner, have a threaded sleeve that can be tightened, making them strong for their size and weight. They are often used when rappelling,

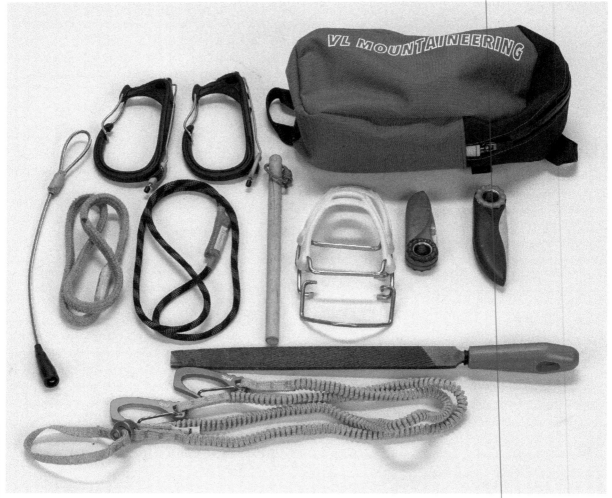

Accessories: V-thread hooker, Hollowblock, racking clips, umbilicals, knife, spare parts.

lowering, retreating, or in rescue applications. They can be found in varying sizes, but typically the climbing-specific links are ⅜ inch and stamped with a CE strength rating.

Personal Prusik

A personal prusik made out of 1.5 meters (5 feet) of 7 mm cord is carried for backing up rappels and non-standard lowers. Sewn loops of cord like Hollowblocks (13.5-inch) have become popular

because they are quicker and easier to set up.

Climbing Ropes

One of the most important pieces of kit in climbing is the rope—your lifeline. Climbing ropes need to be dynamic (i.e., stretch) in order to absorb force and dissipate it through elongation. For ice climbing, you always want a dry-treated rope, since it will invariably get wet. Most ropes used in ice climbing

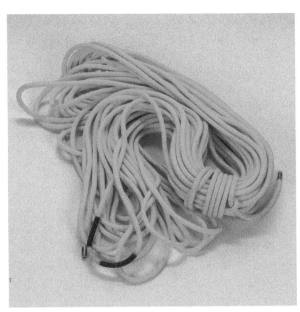

Dry treated 70 m single-rated rope with middle marker.

are either 60 or 70 meters long and range in diameter from 10 mm down to 7.5 mm depending on their rating: single, half, or twin. There now are also triple-rated ropes that are suitable to be used on their own as a single rope, a half rope clipped separately in a double-rope system, or even as a twin rope clipped together.

When looking at ropes, you will notice UIAA safety ratings. These indicate the number of falls that the rope held during the certification tests. Usually the fall forces created in the testing environment are higher than when actually climbing. It doesn't necessarily mean that once you have fallen on a rope that number of times that it is time to retire the rope.

When a rope is stretched under load when toproping, it is called static elongation. This number can vary anywhere from 6 percent stretch to 11.5 percent stretch depending on the ropes and setup you are using. Typically, single ropes stretch less than double ropes. The numbers are tested with

an 80-kilogram (176-pound) load. When climbing, static elongation is something to consider. If you have climbed a 60-meter pitch and the rope you are using has a 7.5 percent elongation and the follower falls, the stretch in the rope could still lead to a 4.5-meter fall!

Buy ropes with middle markers—usually a wide black band at the halfway mark. Bi-colored or bi-patterned ropes have a distinct change at the middle of the rope. If your rope does not have a halfway indicator, a specialized rope pen can be bought to mark the middle.

Rope Care

Ice climbing ropes tend to stay fairly clean due to their constant exposure to water (and not much dirt). However, mixed climbing and drytooling may expose ropes to dirt and mud. Rope bags and tarps are not required for ice climbing and should be left at home or in the car since they just collect snow and get punctured with crampons. However, rope bags can be of use at mixed and drytool crags if the ground is dirt instead of snow. This will help extend the life span of a rope. If a rope becomes extremely dirty, it can be hand-washed in lukewarm water with very mild detergent.

Always be aware of crampons and ice tools around ropes since they can easily nick or cut ropes. If white core filaments are visible through the sheath, that section should be considered suspect and be cut off. Cut ropes with an electrical hot knife, found at most climbing equipment stores. A sharp knife heated over a flame will also work. Either way, be sure that the end of the rope is well sealed by melting the nylon.

Retire a climbing rope immediately if it has arrested a large fall with extreme loads or if it shows damage, such as cuts, flat spots, stiffness, or excessive fuzziness. Even a rope that shows no visible signs of damage eventually needs to be retired after a few years with regular use.

Climbing Packs

Many manufacturers make climbing-specific backpacks. Most packs will work for ice climbing as long as they are large enough to carry winter climbing gear and warm clothes, and you can find a way to attach your ice tools to the backpack. If you are just trying out the sport, there is no need to buy an ice-specific pack, but if you plan on ice climbing a lot, here are some features you might want to consider:

- Ice tool/axe attachments: Climbing-specific packs should have a way to attach ice tools to the backpack. With the advent of new ergonomic tools, the older method of attaching ice tools to a pack was changed, as the older loop-style attachment no longer works easily. Depending on the tools you use, make sure the pack has an attachment system that works with your tools.

- Crampon pouch: Depending on how you like to carry your crampons, this could be a key

Ice climbing packs have specific features for attaching ice tools and crampons.

feature to look for. Some people like to carry their crampons on the outside of their pack to avoid having sharp crampon teeth in their pack next to their delicate winter parka. If a pack has a crampon pouch, it is easy to stash your crampons and keep them separate from the rest of your gear. Instead of a pouch some packs have a bungee system that serves a similar purpose.

- Top loading: A top-loading pack is better for ice climbing than a zipper-panel style for many reasons. It can be overstuffed, a rope can be lashed under the lid, and the lid can be tucked inside the pack to make it smaller when climbing. A top-loading pack also allows access when it is clipped into a belay.

- Size: A 40- to 60-liter pack is large enough to carry everything that is required for a day of ice climbing. It is suitable as a crag pack or to be left at the base of a multi-pitch route. A 30- to 40-liter pack is more suitable for the actual climbing, but packing will be tight. Small, lightweight "summit packs" ranging from 15 to 20 liters are sometimes a good idea for multi-pitch climbs as a second pack carried to the base in your larger pack.

Clothing Systems

With ice climbing, clothing is more important than in other styles of climbing. While rock climbing, you can get away with a T-shirt and a pair of jeans, but a little more thought needs to be put into what you will wear when ice climbing. Your clothes are what will keep you dry and warm, and choosing correctly will make ice climbing more enjoyable, not to mention the safety factor of having the right gear to avoid hyperthermia or cold injuries like frostbite.

When you are just starting out at the crag, you can get away with borrowed clothing or your ski/snowboard gear for the first few days; just be careful not to snag or put a hole in your expensive pants with your crampons. Wearing gaiters will help protect those loose-fitting ankles. After you decide that you like ice climbing (and you will), then start thinking about what clothing you'll need.

Do some weather research before heading out for a day of climbing, then dress for the conditions but be ready for it to be wetter and colder too. Some questions to ask yourself when planning your clothing choices:

- What is the temperature going to be?
- Is it going to rain or snow?
- Is the climb in the sun?
- Is the temperature at the base the same as higher up?
- Is the day warming up?
- How long is the approach?
- Will the climbing take longer than normal because it is technical, and will you be standing still for long periods of time?
- Are there recent trip reports that suggest the climb might be wet?

Layering ensures comfort throughout the day in a multitude of conditions. Appropriate layering will enable you to stay warm when belaying and avoid overheating when approaching and climbing. Layers for ice climbing are commonly separated into four categories: a base layer that sits next to the skin; a mid-layer that traps in heat; an outer layer

Layers: base, mid, outer, and insulating.
ALEX POPOV

that protects from the elements such as wind, rain, snow, and dripping ice; and an insulating outer layer for times of non-activity, often referred to as a belay jacket and belay pants.

Base Layer

There are lots of base layer options on the market. The key is to not choose cotton, because in ice climbing there is a lot of stop-and-go movement. Cotton is a poor insulator when wet; fabrics such as merino wool and synthetic materials work best. Base layers need to wick moisture away from the skin, be close fitting, dry quickly, and be breathable. Features to look for in your base layers are a hood for cold days and a long waist so it stays tucked in. The bottom layer should have a crotch zip for going to the bathroom.

Mid-Layer

Mid-layers provide insulation and warmth. They should be air permeable and breathable and fit comfortably over a base layer but still fit close to the body. Like base layers, tops should be long enough to stay tucked into your pants and harness. Common mid-layer materials include synthetics like fleece and sometimes down. A chest pocket is a handy feature on mid-layer tops to stash your phone in a warm spot, helping save its battery life. Often you only need a base or mid-layer for legs, but not both unless it is very cold.

Outer Layer

Your outer layer is what protects you from the elements when the conditions turn bad. It should block wind and precipitation while still being breathable. Jackets should stay tucked into the harness even when arms are in an overhead climbing position. The front needs to be streamlined so it does not become baggy and bulgy. Hoods need to be large enough to fit over helmets.

Pants should have tapered legs so there is not a lot of excess material around the ankles to snag with crampon points. This will increase the life span of your pants by reducing the number of holes in them, and in certain terrain increase the safety factor by preventing stumbles. Two other features that can be beneficial are reinforced scuff guards around the ankles, which will protect the area of the pant leg that comes into contact with crampons the most, and zips along the legs that open to vent off extra heat on the approach.

Outer layers fall into two categories: hard shell and soft shell. Hard shells are waterproof, while soft shells are traditionally only water resistant but much more breathable and often better fitting due to stretchy materials. Over the past decade, the difference in performance between hard-shell and soft-shell clothing has diminished and typically a good soft-shell jacket or pants can be effective most of the time unless the climate is very wet. At the same time manufacturers are adding stretch fabrics to hard shells, blurring the line between these two categories.

Insulating Layer

There tends to be a lot of standing around with ice climbing. Belay time can be a fight to stay warm, so insulating layers are crucial to maintaining comfort but also function as an emergency layer if something goes wrong. A belay jacket is a large, hooded parka that can be put on over all your other clothing when not climbing. Belay jackets are insulated with either down or synthetic fibers.

Down jackets are often warmer for the same size, lighter, take up less volume, and last longer but are more expensive. One downside to down insulation is that if it gets wet it loses its insulating abilities. There have been recent improvements in the water resistance of down. Hydrophobic down is becoming popular and loses less of its insulating properties when wet. Normal down insulation likely loses 90 percent of its insulating properties when wet; hydrophobic down loses much less, closer to a 25 percent loss in insulating capabilities.

A big, puffy belay jacket that fits over everything is the key to staying warm.

Many down parkas now offer a highly water-resistant membrane for the outer layer.

Although synthetic parkas are often a bit heavier, they usually keep more of their insulating properties when wet. If for any reason you think you will have to move in your parka or that the climb will be wet, then synthetic insulation is typically a better option than down. On the plus side, a synthetic belay parka is often cheaper than a down parka.

Features to look for in a climbing-specific belay parka include:

- Interior mesh pockets that allow you to stash gloves inside it to keep them warm while you belay

- An option to squish the parka inside a stuff sack to clip to your harness for when you are climbing

- A front zipper that zips both ways so you can use your belay device with the bottom of the zipper opened slightly

Belay pants are nice for cold days but not as critical as a belay jacket. Belay pants should have full side zips so they can be donned over crampons, and also have a fly zipper to access the harness belay loop for belaying.

Gloves

Gloves are your interface between hands and ice tools. They should keep your hands warm while not being too bulky. Maintaining warm hands while ice climbing can be one of the more challenging aspects of the sport. No one wants the screaming barfies! Barring poor circulation, glove choice can play a large role in keeping your hands warm while they are above your head holding onto ice tools. Multiple pairs of gloves are the key to comfort and performance—a pair for the approach, a pair or two for climbing, a pair for belaying, and maybe even an older pair for rappelling.

Ice climbing requires multiple pairs of handwear ranging from thin to thick.

Climbing gloves need to be warm, water resistant (waterproof gloves are a myth), and dexterous. Snug fitting and ergonomically shaped means better contact with the grip. A tacky palm material is obviously better than something slick and slippery. Thinner gloves mean more dexterity, which in turn makes most tasks, such as tying knots and placing ice screws, easier.

It is a fine line between too little and too much insulation. Too little and hands will get cold pressed up against the ice or plunging into powder snow. Too much, though, and you'll need to squeeze through all that bulk. The more you squeeze the more you get pumped, and the more you get pumped the more you get cold hands. More insulation doesn't necessarily always mean warmer hands when climbing.

Belay gloves can be thicker as long as they are not too bulky to properly grip the brake strand of the rope while belaying. Rappelling and belaying reduces the life span of gloves, so it is wiser to carry a pair of cheaper work gloves or an older pair of climbing gloves so that you do not wear out new gloves too quickly.

Another glove feature to look for is a loop on one of the fingers that you can clip a carabiner through. This allows for clipping the gloves to the back of your harness with the opening facing down so they do not fill with snow.

For mixed climbing and drytooling, very thin gloves with a tacky palm can make a difference. Insulation is less important since the hand is not constantly in contact with ice and snow.

The Electric Age

A modern advancement in cold comfort is electric heated gloves and socks. Despite being expensive, they work very well to keep hands and toes warm. They operate on rechargeable batteries and have controls to manage the output of heat and monitor battery life. Some of the sock brands even have an app to control the temperature settings via your smartphone. If you have previously suffered from frostnip or frostbite or struggle with Raynaud's syndrome, an investment in heated technology might be worth the money, or it might simply be worth it just to be warm and comfortable on cold days.

Maarten van Haeren leads pitch three of Big Brother (M4 WI5, 200 m) on the Little Sister in Canmore, Alberta, Canada.

Planning and Preparing

Proper planning is stacking the cards in your favor. Going through the steps of preparing before any mountain pursuit is fundamental to not only a successful climb but also risk management. Preparation not only means packing the necessary equipment for the day but also researching and gathering information on current route conditions, approach beta, weather, and avalanche hazard. In addition, proper preparation includes understanding risk management principles to mitigate the various and numerous hazards that can potentially be encountered and determining what third-party rescue resources are available if an accident were to occur.

Guidebooks are an important resource for planning your ice climbing outing. They should have

Ice climbing guidebooks are a key tool in the planning process.
SEAN ISAAC

specific route beta for the approach, pitches, and the descent, as well as more general information about the area, including local ethics, access issues, and avalanche risk. There should be route photos that show what normal ice conditions look like and give visual clues to associated hazards. The front matter in guidebooks will often also provide details for traveling climbers like dining and accommodations, supplies, and gear stores, in addition to rescue options and how to contact them in case of an emergency. If a guidebook is not available for an area or is out of date or out of print, then an internet search most likely will provide what you are looking for.

Conditions

Conditions are probably the single most important factor affecting a day of ice climbing. Collect information pertaining to the route that you want to climb by researching what state the ice is in, what the road and highway travel conditions are like, the forecasted weather for the day, and, if the approach, route, or descent is in avalanche terrain, what the avalanche forecast is rating the danger.

Ice Conditions

Ice conditions can vary from month to month, week to week, and even day to day, so it is important to get up-to-date information on the state of your proposed route. There are many online resources for gathering information on general ice conditions or specific route conditions. Online forums, Facebook pages and groups, and social media posts can all offer insight into current or recent ice conditions. Information might also be gleaned from park rangers, local guiding companies, and equipment retail staff.

In general, ice conditions tend to be more challenging at the beginning of the season when routes are first forming and often in lean shape. As the season progresses, the ice usually fattens up and fills out, taking away some of the initial sting of thin ice. By mid-season, popular routes might have seen significant traffic, leaving a wake of steps and holes to hook. This picked-out or pegboard ice is much easier to climb than fresh, brittle ice. As days become longer and spring approaches, the ice softens, becoming plastic in texture. Solar-aspect routes will become sun baked, making the ice surface almost snow-like. At some point near the end of winter, the inevitable happens—the route either fully melts out or, more dramatically, collapses. A more in-depth treatment on the various types of ice is discussed in Chapter 7: Leading Ice.

Road Conditions

Driving is a major winter hazard and in some cases might be the most dangerous part of an ice climbing day depending on road conditions and weather. Snow- and ice-covered roads can greatly slow a day down or, worst-case scenario, cause an accident. Monitor road conditions and possible closures through one of the many online resources like www.safetravelusa.com or www.theweathernetwork .com or specific state, provincial, or park reports. In addition, the 511 (toll free) traffic system program is becoming widely adopted through the United States and Canada, with up-to-the-minute travel and traffic information.

Weather Conditions

Current, short-range, and long-range weather forecasts can be quickly accessed online through a variety of sources. There are many spot weather forecasting tools (like https://spotwx.com) that offer specific location forecasts. During periods of stable and predictable weather, these forecasts tend to be quite accurate and highly reliable. However, during periods of instability or changing weather, the forecasts and modeling on which they are based become less reliable, and the ice climbing leader may need to complete further research to obtain an accurate depiction of the weather systems that will affect the outing. A professional weather forecast will also provide a confidence rating of low, moderate, or high, depending on the quality of the information they are basing the forecast on. Finally, take all forecasts with a grain of salt. The best forecasting is ongoing (nowcasting), so step outside and pay attention to what is actually happening.

The key weather factors to note are:

- Temperature (current and if increasing or decreasing)
- Cloud cover (clear, few, scattered, broken, overcast)
- Precipitation and intensity (nil, snow, rain, graupel, hail)
- New snow (amount/depth overnight, past 24 hours, or total storm)
- Wind (speed and direction)
- Barometric pressure (more the trend than the actual value)

A critical mountain weather phenomenon to be aware of is a temperature inversion, which is a reversal of normal temperature behavior in the troposphere (the region of the atmosphere nearest the earth's surface), in which a layer of cool air at the surface is overlaid by a layer of warmer air. Under normal conditions air temperature usually decreases with elevation. With an inversion, valley bottom temperatures may present fairly cold, but temperatures on ridgetops and at avalanche start zones above ice routes will be much warmer. Valley fog is often present during an inversion. An inversion can be confirmed by checking both valley bottom and ridgetop temperatures to ascertain which one is higher. Most ski areas have weather stations at the top and will post temperatures for the base area as well as the upper elevations. This is a good resource to confirm if an inversion is suspected.

Chinook or foehn winds are common to the eastern slope of continental ranges. They can raise winter temperatures up to 30 to 40 degrees Celsius and are almost always accompanied by strong, gusting winds up to 100 kilometers (62 miles) per hour on ridgetops. The winds originate from the Pacific Ocean and blow eastward over the Rocky Mountains of North America, warming significantly as they descend to the flatlands of the American Midwest and Canadian Prairies. In addition to significant warming and strong winds, Chinooks are often accompanied by a Chinook arch—a long line of cloud spanning parallel to the mountains with a definitively clear sky to the west and clouds to the east. Chinook literally means "snow eater" and can make 30 cm of snow disappear in one day. It can also make ice disappear through a combination of melting and sublimating.

Weather factors also obviously affect ice conditions, namely temperature and precipitation. Temperature could be said to be the main overall factor affecting ice conditions, since without cold weather there would be no ice. However, during the season, temperature fluctuations can make the ice brittle, hard, soft, or wet. Snowfall can cover low-angle ice, making tool and crampon placements hard to see and assess. Rain, while less common in the colder continental climates, is very possible in maritime climates on either coast. Light, short rainfalls can soften the ice surface, making the actual climbing easier, but extended rainfall events in winter will deteriorate the ice to the point that a route's structural integrity should be considered dubious.

Avalanche Conditions

Avalanche forecasting has come a long way in the past couple of decades. Agencies like the National Avalanche Center, Avalanche Canada, and Parks Canada post daily avalanche bulletins for various areas throughout the winter season. These

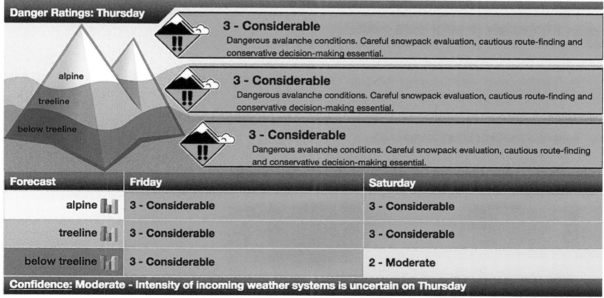

An avalanche bulletin forecasts a danger rating for the alpine, treeline, and below treeline.
PARKS CANADA

North American Public Avalanche Danger Scale

Avalanche danger is determined by the likelihood, size and distribution of avalanches.

Danger Level		Travel Advice	Likelihood of Avalanches	Avalanche Size and Distribution
5 Extreme		Avoid all avalanche terrain.	Natural and human-triggered avalanches certain.	Large to very large avalanches in many areas.
4 High		Very dangerous avalanche conditions. Travel in avalanche terrain not recommended.	Natural avalanches likely; human-triggered avalanches very likely.	Large avalanches in many areas; or very large avalanches in specific areas.
3 Considerable		Dangerous avalanche conditions. Careful snowpack evaluation, cautious route-finding and conservative decision-making essential.	Natural avalanches possible; human-triggered avalanches likely.	Small avalanches in many areas; or large avalanches in specific areas; or very large avalanches in isolated areas.
2 Moderate		Heightened avalanche conditions on specific terrain features. Evaluate snow and terrain carefully; identify features of concern.	Natural avalanches unlikely; human-triggered avalanches possible.	Small avalanches in specific areas; or large avalanches in isolated areas.
1 Low		Generally safe avalanche conditions. Watch for unstable snow on isolated terrain features.	Natural and human-triggered avalanches unlikely.	Small avalanches in isolated areas or extreme terrain.

Safe backcountry travel requires training and experience. You control your own risk by choosing where, when and how you travel.

The North American Public Avalanche Danger Scale.

AVALANCHE CANADA

incorporate the North American Avalanche Danger Scale, in which there are five ratings, ranging from Low (1) to Extreme (5). The avalanche danger is based on the likelihood, size, and distribution of avalanches. While Low and Extreme appear relatively straightforward and intuitive, ice climbers need to pay particular attention to Considerable (3). It is this rating that is often the most uncertain,

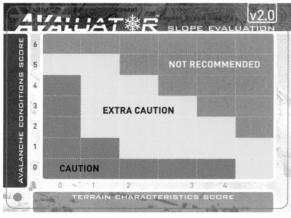

The Avaluator Trip Planner.

AVALANCHE CANADA

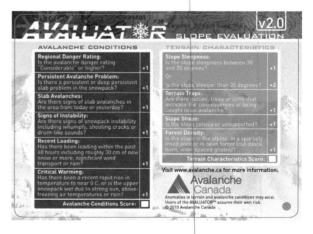

and careful terrain selection needs to be exercised as the Considerable description suggests. The danger scale also incorporates travel advice for each rating.

One tool that ice climbers may find useful for planning an outing in avalanche terrain is the Avaluator 2.0TM Trip Planner from Avalanche Canada. This tool plots avalanche conditions against terrain to determine one of the following three actions: normal caution, extra caution, or not recommended. Constant monitoring of the avalanche forecast, current weather, and avalanche clues (whumpfing, shooting cracks, recent avalanche observations) may see a change in the danger rating and hence may change the caution level suggested by the trip planner.

Avalanche Safety for Waterfall Ice Climbing

by Grant Statham, IFMGA Mountain Guide, Parks Canada Visitor Safety Specialist,
Canadian Avalanche Association Professional Member

Avalanches are a very significant threat to waterfall ice climbers. After deciding which route you'd like to climb and seeing if it's formed, your next move should be figuring out whether it's threatened by avalanches or not. This is a crucial bit of early research. Some areas have no avalanche hazard, but in other locations, such as Colorado's Rocky Mountains, Utah's Wasatch Range, the Canadian Rockies, or Alaska, avalanches are the most significant hazard ice climbers need to deal with.

If the route is threatened by avalanches, the game just changed and you need to know a lot more. Is the climb located in a big gully with avalanche start zones overhead, or will you be climbing through steep snow slopes that hang over cliffs? How about the approach, will you be walking under avalanche paths or climbing up a long 40-degree slope to reach the base of the route? How hard is the route; can you climb fast or will you be exposed to avalanche terrain for hours?

These are just some of the considerations you need to be aware of for climbing in avalanche terrain. This section describes the basics for dealing with avalanche risk when ice climbing but is no substitute for training and experience. Everyone who climbs in avalanche terrain should take an avalanche course, develop their avalanche skill set, and carry avalanche rescue gear.

Avalanche Risk

Avalanche risk in ice climbing requires three main ingredients: 1) enough snow to produce an avalanche, 2) avalanche-prone terrain, and 3) climbers exposed to this hazard. If you remove any one of these three elements, there is no avalanche risk.

For example, if you show up for your climbing trip and happen to arrive in the middle of an avalanche cycle, you still have options for going climbing and being safe—but you need to do some homework. Find a route with no avalanche terrain, drive somewhere where there is no snow, or do something else like go skiing. All three of these options will eliminate the avalanche risk to you.

But while eliminating avalanche risk ensures safety, it might not get you up many of the routes on your hit list. In this case, you need to dive into that same avalanche risk triangle in much finer detail and figure out how to understand and carefully manage all three ingredients.

Avalanche Risk Triangle.
GRANT STATHAM

Snow

Until there is enough snow on the ground to smooth over the irregularities of the ground cover, the avalanche hazard is said to be "below threshold." This is an important early season distinction and not always easy to know. Keep in mind that snow depth increases with elevation, so just because there is only 20 centimeters (8 inches) of snow in the valley does not mean there isn't 100 centimeters (39 inches) in the start zone, 600 meters (1,970 feet) above your route.

The best source of information regarding the snowpack, weather, and avalanche conditions is the local avalanche forecast (www.avalanche.org in the United States and www.avalanche.ca in Canada). Information is provided regarding the current and future avalanche conditions as well as danger ratings for alpine, tree line, and below tree line zones. In some regions you can also access real-time weather data from remote weather stations. Keep in mind that these reports are often for large regions and describe the general conditions. Local variation is common, and climbers need to remain vigilant in their assessment of the immediate conditions while climbing.

The weather forecast is also a critical resource for predicting what will happen with the snow. Learn the basics of how to understand a good weather forecast for different elevation zones and use any available real-time weather station data to help you understand the current weather conditions, and thus the snow conditions.

The best indicator of unstable snow is avalanche activity. Both slab avalanches and sluffs are a threat to ice climbers, as it doesn't take much to knock you off your front points. If avalanches are occurring near your route, it's safe to assume the snow on your route is also unstable. Evaluating the stability of the snowpack is complex and takes a lifetime to try and understand, but here are three of the big factors to watch for:

1. **Precipitation:** New snow can overload the snowpack, and rain will immediately destabilize it. Don't climb in the rain and be wary of increasing avalanche danger after any new snowfall. New snow needs a period of time to settle and stabilize. Be wary of cracking in the snowpack or whumpfing sounds as you walk through it—these are prime indicators of unstable snow.

2. **Wind:** Wind moves significant amounts of snow (ten times the snowfall rate) from windward slopes and deposits it onto leeward slopes, causing locally deep windslabs. This is very common on slopes in and around ice climbs as the wind can swirl in there. Wind alone can cause an immediate rise in the avalanche danger and build large cornices that often overhang ice climbs.

3. **Temperature:** Warm temperatures and direct sun exposure can dramatically reduce the stability of the snowpack and cause cornices to collapse. When the snowpack reaches 0°C (32°F) it loses all strength. Rain, warm air, and solar radiation will all contribute to this; if you are climbing in the sun and feeling hot—just imagine how the snowpack feels!

Terrain

Understanding avalanche terrain is your best strategy to reduce avalanche risk because, unlike snow, you can see the terrain and therefore make conscious and informed decisions about how and when to move through it. Terrain is the gas pedal of risk: When the avalanche danger is high you ease off on the pedal (choose mellow terrain), and when the avalanche danger is low you can push down on the pedal (choose bigger terrain). It's these terrain choices that give you the ability to control your own risk.

ATES Chart

Description	Class	Terrain Criteria
Simple	1	Routes surrounded by low-angle or primarily forested terrain; possible brief exposure time to infrequent avalanches.
Challenging	2	Routes with brief exposure to start zones or terrain traps, or long exposure time in the runout zones of infrequent avalanches.
Complex	3	Routes with frequent exposure to multiple overlapping avalanche paths or large expanses of steep, open terrain; multiple avalanche start zones and terrain traps or cliffs below.

Great ice routes form in the middle of avalanche paths; that's just the plain and simple truth. Certainly not all routes, but many of them. It's not uncommon to spend your entire day exposed to avalanche slopes overhead, or to walk up a steep avalanche-prone slope to reach the base of the route. The Avalanche Terrain Exposure Scale (ATES) rates terrain as simple, challenging, or complex based on unchanging physical characteristics.

Here are a few avalanche terrain basics:

- **Slope angle**—The prime slope angle for slab avalanches is 30 to 45 degrees. Below 25 to 30 degrees, the snow normally settles into the ground, and on terrain steeper than 45 degrees, the snow usually sluffs regularly—which is a big concern for climbers in precarious spots in gullies.

- **Aspect**—The way in which a route faces the sun and the wind makes a huge difference. In the northern hemisphere, north-facing routes are shady and cold while south-facing routes can be sunny and warm. You might need to wait for a cloudy day to climb under south- or west-facing slopes, or you might need to seek out north-facing terrain during a spell of warm and sunny weather.

- **Elevation**—In general the snowpack is deeper, the temperature is colder, and the wind is stronger at higher elevations. Recognizing the avalanche conditions at different elevations is important because you may be climbing well below the avalanche start zones, yet still trying to figure out what is going on above you. Be wary of temperature inversions—you can be freezing down in the valley while the slopes 1,000 meters (3,280 feet) above you are much warmer.

- **Terrain traps**—These are terrain features that increase the consequences of being caught in an avalanche. Obvious examples on waterfall ice routes are deep gully features or slopes over cliffs. In these locations even small avalanches can bury you or knock you off your feet and cause you to fall.

Becoming skilled at how to move safely and efficiently through complex alpine terrain is the very essence of alpine and waterfall ice climbing. Minimizing your exposure to avalanches by positioning the belays, moving together when you can, moving one at a time when necessary, belaying across exposed slopes, and in general spending no unnecessary time exposed to avalanches are the strategies that keep experienced climbers alive.

Avalanche is a major hazard on ice routes in avalanche terrain.

People

For risk to exist, something must be "at risk," and in the case of waterfall ice climbing it is people exposing themselves to the threat of avalanches. While we like to think we can be logical people, human beings are well known for their fallible, impulsive, subjective, and emotional traits. "Human factors" are well-recognized as one of the major contributors to avalanche accidents. Here are some considerations to help mitigate the unavoidable bias that we all bring to our decision making:

- **Partners**—Climb with people you trust and who share your values around avalanche risk. It's no fun to be worried about avalanches while your partner plows on ahead and ignores you. You want a partner who sees what you see and who thinks like you do about how to manage risk. You need to know that you can rely on your partner when the decision making gets difficult or, worse, when you get buried. The very best partnerships are with people with whom the decision making is not stressful and you are on the same page.

- **Decision making**—In the mountains decision making can be difficult at the best of times, but is made worse when human dynamics create undue stress and pressure to do things you otherwise would not. Climbing is a fine balance between pushing yourself beyond what is comfortable and knowing when to pull back because the risk is too high. When push comes to shove, make the conservative choice and live to climb another day. Human factors can exert extreme stress on the situation; try to distance yourself from the emotion and consider all the evidence available. In the end, trust your instincts—if it just doesn't feel right, then bail.

- **Trophy hunting**—All climbers have a hit list, including old climbers whose hit list contains routes they have stared at for years while they wait for the right combination of conditions, weather, and partners. Sometimes that never comes. Flexibility is the key to safety and success in the mountains, so recognize when your timing just didn't work out for the weather or avalanche conditions. Swallow your disappointment, climb something else, and try again next time.

- **Group size and speed**—The number of people in your group makes a big difference to your safety. Large groups that spend a lot of time in the same place are more exposed than smaller groups that can move faster. The typical two-person partnership can weave in and out of risk much more efficiently and safely than a group of six standing in place and toproping. Ice routes with avalanche risk require being lightweight and moving skillfully through the terrain. If your plan is to take your time, then reduce your stress and don't expose yourself to avalanche hazard.

Research shows that while terrain, weather, and snowpack are important contributors to avalanche accidents, human factors are the primary contributor. Humans are inherently biased and seeing clearly while under the influence of such powerful factors as desire, ego, overconfidence, and assumption can be extremely difficult. The antidote is recognizing that none of us are immune to these influences. Accept that you are too, have those difficult conversations with your partner, and trust your instincts when things just don't feel right.

Avalanche Equipment for Ice Climbing

If you're exposed to avalanche risk when climbing, you must carry and know how to use avalanche rescue gear. If someone gets buried, you have about 10 minutes to find them and dig out an airway to them before they asphyxiate. This will be one of the most stressful and frightening 10 minutes of your life. If you don't have the right equipment for the job, you may never get over it.

There are three essential pieces of rescue equipment that work in combination:

1. **Avalanche transceiver:** Sometimes called a "beacon," avalanche transceivers are small digital devices that allow your partner (who also has one) to narrow down a large search area into a very small one. You can pinpoint someone's location using a transceiver and then know where to probe and dig. These are crucial lifesaving devices when someone is buried in an avalanche.

2. **Avalanche probe:** The probe determines a buried person's exact location and depth. When you shovel, you dig down beside the probe, which has been left in place. Climbers will want a lightweight (carbon) probe that collapses into small segments for packing.

3. **Shovel:** Have you ever tried to dig through hard avalanche debris with your helmet or your hands? It doesn't work. There are many uses for a shovel in winter climbing, but none more pressing than when your partner is buried in an avalanche. Carry a light, collapsible shovel that fits in your pack and is strong enough to withstand digging through hard chunks of debris.

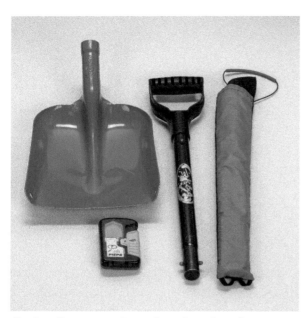

Avalanche transceiver, shovel, and probe.

Carrying avalanche rescue equipment adds weight to climbing packs, and for this reason it can be tempting to leave it behind, but instead try to think critically about where you might need it. It's easy to wear your transceiver every day, but sometimes you might only need to carry your shovel and probe to the base of the route. Other times you might want it all the whole way, or for the descent. Consider this equipment part of your essential climbing gear, know how to use it, and make plans with your partner ahead of time about who is going to carry what and where.

Conclusion

Good avalanche risk control skills are part of being a solid alpinist and waterfall ice climber. While climbing a great route feels awesome, climbing it in good style and doing everything you can to reduce your risk along the way feels even better. If your goal is to climb frozen waterfalls in the mountains, take the time to learn about avalanches, carry the proper gear, and respect the ever-changing conditions.

Risk Management

Ice climbing will present numerous hazards (sources of harm) throughout the day. Risk is defined as the probability or chance of being affected by those hazards. Risk management is ultimately about loss versus benefit, which in turn is based on balancing probability versus consequence. Probability is the chance of something occurring. Consequence is the outcome of an event, which could be either negative (injury) or positive (the top of a climb). The other important aspects of risk management are exposure and vulnerability. Exposure to a hazard can be in time (duration) or space (route finding), while vulnerability is our susceptibility to the hazard. It is important to understand these concepts because we assess risk through probability and consequence, but we control risk through exposure and vulnerability by setting margins or a buffer between us and the invisible line of too much risk.

An ice climber must be able to anticipate, recognize, quantify, and appropriately mitigate the hazards to decrease the likelihood of an accident or injury occurring.

Situational awareness is the ability to recognize and mitigate hazards before they become a risk. An ice climber must be able to step back and evaluate all the variables in a given situation, determine their interactions, and evaluate the potential for this to present a risk to you and your partners. Situational awareness is closely tied to experience, whereby more experienced climbers tend to more readily recognize the events occurring around them and be better equipped to recognize potential risks.

Closely linked to situational awareness is the ice climbing leader's ability to recognize hazards and then make an analysis to determine their probability versus consequence. Ice climbing is an inherently dangerous activity and therefore has some level of risk associated with it. Risk cannot be entirely eliminated, but rather the goal is to recognize the hazards and ensure that they are well managed, mitigated, or avoided. A key step in successful hazard recognition is consciously anticipating and discussing various potential hazards prior to the ice climbing outing.

Once hazards have been identified (anticipated and recognized), and their probability assessed and severity analyzed, you must determine an appropriate mitigation strategy to manage vulnerability and exposure, which is ultimately how we exert control over risk. In some instances, this may involve avoiding the hazard entirely or modifying the situation to decrease the probability or severity of the hazard, or it may involve acceptance of the hazard and continuing forward.

A four-step risk-management process is an ongoing, continuous loop:

1. Identification: identify your exposure to hazards

2. Analysis: determine the probability and consequence of an occurrence

3. Evaluation: compare your analysis to what you consider to be acceptable

4. Mitigation: take action to reduce your exposure and vulnerability

Ice Climbing Hazards

Winter ice climbing has many more hazards than summer rock climbing. Even single-pitch ice toproping can have multiple overlapping hazards that make site safety more challenging. A short two- or three-pitch ice climb can often be exposed to the same complex hazards as a major summer alpine climbing objective. Being able to identify (anticipate and recognize), analyze, evaluate, and mitigate hazards are the four steps in risk management. Some hazards are obvious and easily dealt with, while others are more subtle.

Ice Fall

Ice fall is the single largest hazard to an ice climber and one that is often underestimated or misjudged. Ice fall can occur from a climber's swinging and kicking, or naturally from temperature fluctuations or solar radiation. The pieces of falling ice can range from as small as a marble to as big as a car (and even bigger). A helmet obviously is necessary to protect an ice climber's head from the smaller pieces, but it offers very little protection against anything bigger than fist-sized piece of ice, which can inflict broken bones, concussions, bruises (or hematomas), lacerations, and internal damages. Therefore, the key strategies for mitigating ice fall hazard are avoidance, situational awareness, good movement skills, and minimizing exposure time (moving efficiently and using sheltered belays).

An ice climber's swings and kicks can knock off brittle bulges, dinner plates, hanging icicles, and even entire pillars. If an ice climber shouted "ICE!" every time they knocked off a little piece of ice, they would holler themselves hoarse, plus the repeated warning would become background noise, thus losing its effectiveness. Having said that, save the "ICE!" warning for unexpected larger pieces, and if possible, make sure nobody is below before actually knocking it off or trying to bust it into smaller pieces.

Natural ice fall typically occurs on a larger scale with free-hanging daggers, skinny pillars, or even entire climbs collapsing. Ice is fairly stable with consistent temperatures between -15°C (5°F) and 0°C (32°F) in the shade. Major temperature swings or intense solar radiation can cause fragile features to become unstable. Ice climbs are guaranteed to fall down at least once per year, which of course is due to warming temperatures.

In more southern or coastal regions where winter is fickle, an ice climb could fall down and re-form a few times throughout the winter season. Therefore, if there is an extended period (more than a week) of warm temperatures above 0°C

Climber-generated ice fall. Daniel Harro on the final pitch of the Sorcerer WI5, in Alberta Canada.

(32°F)—especially with a solar aspect—most ice climbs should be treated as structurally suspect.

The effect of the sun should not be underestimated either. The sun can provide intense radiation and the rock around an ice climb can conduct that heat, causing water to flow behind the ice and weaken its adhesion to the rock even in subzero temperatures.

Delaminated sun-exposed ice (before).

Delaminated sun-exposed ice (after).

Conversely, very cold temperatures (–20°C to –30°C [–4°F to –22°F]) make the ice extremely brittle, causing unsupported or barely supported ice features such as curtains, free-hanging daggers, and skinny pillars to be even more fragile, to the point that a climber's swing or kick could be enough to break the entire feature. These fragile ice formations can also collapse naturally during rapid swings from warm to cold temperatures because the ice is shrinking through sublimation, creating a lot of internal tension. Very cold nights followed by a rapid increase in temperature (primarily due to the solar effect) can be enough of a shock for the ice to cause it to spontaneously collapse.

Pillar affected by cold temperatures (before).

Pillar affected by cold temperatures (after).

Some indications that the ice is under a lot of tension are groaning or popping sounds. If these sounds are present, all fragile ice formations need to be avoided. Similarly, ice climbing under active glacial seracs should be avoided because they can collapse at any time of the day or year, since they are triggered by the pull of gravity.

MITIGATIONS:

- Always wear a helmet
- Drop your head if swinging at bulges
- Shout "ICE!" for larger unexpected chunks
- Break up larger chunks of ice into smaller pieces
- Use sheltered belays under rock overhangs or in ice caves
- Ground anchors for belayers so they can safely belay away from the ice fall drop zone

- Practice situational awareness at crags with other climbers above
- Climb diagonal pitches
- Climb shorter pitches
- Climb simultaneously when multiple topropes are set up
- Do not climb under other parties unless there are big ledges with deep snow to "catch" the ice fall
- Avoid routes with extended exposure to large, free-hanging daggers
- Do not climb under seracs

Avalanche

In the mountains, ice climbs and their approaches could be exposed to avalanche terrain. You must research to determine if your planned route is

An ice climber engulfed by an avalanche.
ALEX RATSON

exposed to any avalanche hazard, and if so, what is the suitable level of acceptable risk. This will depend on the terrain, avalanche danger rating, forecasted weather, and your experience. Many mountain waterfall ice routes are located in gullies that are threatened by overhead avalanche hazard. These climbs are often found in the runout zone or track of an avalanche path, directly below the avalanche start zone. Making the decision to climb one of these routes can be difficult. Exposure times can be long with ice climbing, and the longer you are exposed, the greater the chance of being hit and/or buried. Even a relatively small sluff can have major consequences, either by knocking climbers off a cliff or burying them in a terrain trap (gully, canyon, creek bed, etc.).

Most times you will never even touch the snow in the avalanche start zone that you need to assess, so conventional snowpack testing methods don't bear much relevance. You need to understand whether natural avalanches are expected or not, and what will trigger them. If the public avalanche forecast indicates a "considerable" avalanche danger, then natural avalanches are possible. "Moderate" danger means natural avalanches are unlikely, but still possible, especially if potential triggers are present such as heavy precipitation, temperature inversions, and sun and/or wind effect.

The default decision should be to not climb routes with significant avalanche terrain above unless you can assess with confidence that the snowpack is below threshold amounts (less than 30 cm) or that it has already completely avalanched without new snow loading and the weather is in a holding pattern (no snow, rain, wind, or increase in temperature).

MITIGATIONS:

- Avoid routes or approaches threatened by avalanche terrain
- Climb when snowpack is below threshold amounts (early season)
- Climb during periods of low avalanche hazard
- Use alternative venues or routes
- Carry and know how to use an avalanche transceiver, probe, and shovel
- Review and practice avalanche companion rescue
- Monitor avalanche and weather conditions
- Reduce extended exposure
- Rope up and belay across slopes
- Cross the top of slopes
- Cross slopes or threatened gullies one at a time
- Start and finish early on sun-exposed avalanche terrain

Weather

Winter weather conditions are a hazard that needs constant consideration. Cold temperatures can inflict frostnip, frostbite, and hypothermia. Sub -15°C (5°F) temperatures also mean ice climbers are usually wearing more clothes, bulkier clothes, and thicker gloves and dealing with cold hands and feet, which makes ice climbing movements more awkward and challenging. The ice itself tends to be more brittle and of harder consistency, making for trickier climbing and possibly more ice fall hazard.

Cold temperatures complicate dealing with an emergency or injury, increasing the risk to the whole group. A final consideration with cold temperatures is vehicles possibly not starting at the end of an ice climbing outing. For all these reasons, cold days below -20°C (-4°F) should be given careful consideration, and alternative options closer to the road and in the sun should be used.

In addition to cold temperatures, other winter weather hazards include wind, precipitation, and even, sometimes, overheating due to too many layers, low fitness level, warm temperatures, or a strenuous approach/climb.

MITIGATIONS:

- Warm, well-fitting layers
- Face protection (balaclava, neck tube, facemask, tape, etc.)
- Warm belay jacket and insulated belay pants
- Double boots
- Large, thick gloves or mitts
- Chemical hand and toe warmers
- Electric heated gloves and socks
- Choose south-facing routes
- Thermos with warm drink
- Late start and/or shorter day
- Routes close to the parking in case of cold-related injury or other emergency
- Sleeping bag and sleeping pad (for emergencies)

Sharp Equipment

A major hazard that is not present in summer rock climbing is all the sharp equipment. Ice tools, crampons, ice screws, and V-thread hookers can injure ice climbers and damage soft-goods equipment. Crampons can catch on rocks, roots, or irregularities on the ice surface, causing trips when walking. Falling with crampons on often results in the points catching on the ice surface, breaking the falling climber's ankle or leg from the sudden stop of the crampon. Crampons catching on the ice in a fall can also flip the falling climber upside down, causing head injuries. Crampons can also damage the rope if stepped on or kicked, and tear pant legs or cause puncture wounds to lower legs.

Ice tools can puncture the rope or pop out of the ice or off rock holds and hit the climber in the face, causing lacerations, eye injury, or broken teeth. Beginner climbers should be instructed to hold ice tools by the head when lowered off a route so they do not swing them into their lower legs. Ice screws hanging off the harness can jab into a climber's upper legs. V-thread hookers can rip soft goods

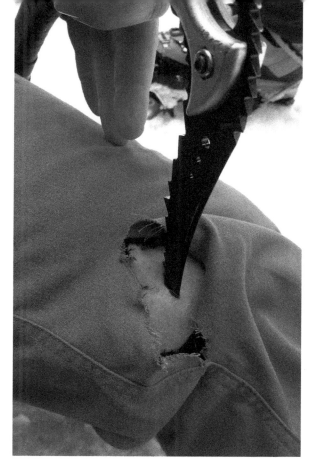

Ice tool pick stabbed into an upper leg from carelessness.
SEBASTIAN TABORSZKY

inside a backpack or catch on pant legs, causing a trip or stumble.

MITIGATIONS:

- Lower off ice climbs with ice tools holstered on the harness or by holding them by the head (not the grip) so picks cannot be accidentally poked into your legs
- Walk with wide feet and slow, deliberate steps when wearing crampons
- Do not jump with crampons on
- Rack ice screws pointing toward the back of the harness

- No adzes when mixed climbing or drytooling
- Maintain small, organized stacks of rope to avoid stepping on rope with crampons
- Keep tight topropes to avoid crampons hitting the ground or ledges
- Do not boulder with crampons on

Rock Fall

Even though rock fall is commonly considered more of a summer hazard, it can occur any season. Some rock types are naturally looser than others, but any rock type can produce rock fall. Typically, rock fall is more of a concern in the early ice season, before much snow has had a chance to accumulate and bury loose rock found on ledges and in scree bowls, or in the late season when longer days and warming temperatures melt the snow and ice holding the loose rock in place. However, it can occur anytime throughout the season, especially when mixed climbing and drytooling. Ice tools are effective crowbars and can easily pry off seemingly solid holds.

MITIGATIONS:
- Wear a helmet
- Shout "ROCK!"
- Use sheltered belays
- Minimize exposure
- Avoid very warm, rainy, or extremely windy days
- Avoid south-facing routes at the end of the ice season

Falling Ice Tools

In addition to falling ice and rocks, ice tools can also be dropped creating a significant hazard to climbers below. In a busy crag setting, especially at a mixed climbing venue, falling ice tools have more human targets to hit so maintaining situational awareness is of the upmost importance. It is easy to become distracted by all the "action" happening at popular mixed crags so if not climbing or belaying then observers should be standing away from the cliff watching from a safe distance. Some ice climbers choose to attach stretchy umbilical leashes from their harness to the bottom of their ice tools to prevent dropping if they accidentally let go of the tool or knock it off. While these might be a prudent choice for runout or serious long routes, they can be awkward toproping and following pitches since they often get twisted and tangled around the rope.

MITIGATIONS:
- Wear a helmet
- Situational awareness
- Do not stand under someone climbing
- Sheltered belay stances
- Use ground anchor for belayer
- Rest on the rope if getting too pumped to hang on to ice tools
- Umbilical leashes

Wet Ice

Low-angle ice can sometimes have water flowing over its surface, while steep ice and pillars can sometimes be a steady shower. Wet ice is a hazard in that it can lead to discomfort, which may ultimately progress to hypothermia and/or frostbite. Gloves, boots, and clothing can become soaked, which can present a major hazard. In addition, equipment such as ropes, slings, and carabiners can become frozen and stiff or even fully encased in ice, rendering them difficult to use. Rappel ropes can be difficult to impossible to pull if they freeze into the surface of wet, slushy ice. Avoidance is the main line of defense against wet ice.

MITIGATIONS:
- Avoid wet, dripping ice (especially on cold days)
- Avoid low-elevation, sunny ice late in the season
- Wear waterproof jacket and pants

Extremely wet ice should be avoided.

- Pack extra gloves
- Keep rope and other equipment out of puddles and away from wet ice

Open Water

Thin ice over water—whether on a creek, river, canyon, or lake—can pose a significant hazard on approaches and even the actual climb itself. The hazard can range from punching a foot through and getting a soaked boot (potential frostbite) to an ice climber's entire body being submerged, resulting in hyperthermia or even drowning. Thin ice is an increasing issue with climate change. There have been accidents involving ice climbers breaking through thin ice in river canyons and disappearing under the ice. For lake ice, a thickness of 15 cm is considered safe. This can be confirmed by drilling an ice screw into the lake ice.

Average daily air temperature is key to ice growth. Seven days of -7°C (19°F) creates roughly 15 cm of ice in still water. Shell ice is thin with water running behind. High-volume waterfalls often do not freeze completely, resulting in a thin shell of ice with a raging waterfall behind. These create a serious hazard that is challenging to mitigate. If the ice climber misjudges the strength or thickness of the shell ice and breaks through, falling into the gushing cavern behind, they will most likely freeze or drown.

MITIGATIONS:

- Minimize creek crossings to avoid getting wet feet
- Belay if unsure of integrity of canyon ice
- Check depths of lake ice with ice screw
- Avoid potential weak areas where flowing creeks enter lakes
- Avoid shell ice with a high volume of flowing water behind
- Retreat if unsure of thickness and strength of shell ice

Open water poses a significant hazard both on the approach and the climb.

Cornices

Cornices can develop over ice routes depending on the terrain above and aspect to the prevailing winds. Cornices are usually composed of very hard snow, which poses a considerable overhead hazard if they fail. Ice climbers must take care when negotiating a cornice, with the belay safely out of the way in case chunks fall off or the whole structure fails. Natural triggers include increased load either from wind-transported new snow or precipitation in the form of snow or rain, or from extreme temperature swings. If the cornice is sagging, dripping, or cracked from warm temperatures, it should be treated as suspect. Conversely, very cold temperatures can cause cornices to become brittle and possibly fracture more easily.

MITIGATIONS:

- Do not climb under large cornices
- Use sheltered belays
- Avoid during very warm, very cold, or very windy weather

Snow Mushrooms

Snow mushrooms are similar to cornices in that they can collapse, causing a significant overhead hazard. They are formed by a combination of snowfall building up on ledges or wind swirling and eddying the snow into dollops that cling to corners or chimneys. These formations can become very large and dense as the winter season progresses. They are not just a threat on larger-scale alpine ice climbs but can form in below tree line canyons and crags. The primary triggers are climbers and warm temperatures.

MITIGATIONS:

- Minimize exposure by avoiding time under snow mushrooms
- Be sure nobody is below if rappelling or lowering over a snow mushroom

- If possible, knock them off while on rappel or lower as long as nobody is below and the ropes are not exposed to being hit
- Do not climb under snow mushrooms on very warm days or with intense solar radiation

Short Days

Winter days are short, meaning less daylight for driving, approaching, and climbing. Short winter days need to be managed so an ice climbing outing is completed well before dusk. Spending an unplanned mid-winter's night out in the open without proper camping gear due to a late start, slow climbing, or an injury is a serious prospect and needs to be avoided. In the event of an emergency, darkness greatly complicates the rescue, and helicopters cannot fly at night.

MITIGATIONS:

- Choose shorter routes with shorter approaches for the darker months around the winter solstice
- Save longer or more remote objectives for the end of the ice climbing season when the days are longer

Be prepared for short winter days with an appropriate turnaround time and a headlamp.

- Start early
- Plan a turnaround time at least a couple of hours before last light
- Pack a headlamp, fire starter, and emergency shelter like a lightweight tarp

Wildlife

Wildlife encounters can occur any time of the year. The obvious one is bears early or late in the season on either end of their hibernation, but ice climbers have been known to stumble across dens and wake bears midseason. Cougars, coyotes, wolves, wolverines, and even elk and moose can pose a threat. Ravens are less of a hazard and more of an annoyance, as they are known to open zippers of packs left at the base of routes and rummage through packs. This becomes a hazard if they steal your vehicle keys or other crucial items. Tick season can overlap with the end of ice climbing season in late winter and early spring.

MITIGATIONS:

- Carry bear spray
- Make noise
- Be aware of your surroundings
- Be able to identify tracks and scat
- Heed all wildlife closures
- Do not leave important items at the base of ice climbs
- Hide or secure packs under rocks or snow if ravens are present
- Check body, hair, and clothing for ticks

Approach Trails

Slips and trips on approach trails or at the base of ice climbs can result in varying degrees of injury. Approach trails to popular ice climbs can become very slippery as they get packed down with foot traffic. Rain or warm temperatures can glaze trails

with a layer of ice. Creek crossings can present verglased rocks and logs. Lake or canyon ice may be free of snow covering and therefore very slippery. Slips can result in injuries such as sprains or breaks. Slips can also turn into slides, which become a more serious hazard if there is a potential to slide over a cliff edge or into rocks or trees.

MITIGATIONS:

- Wear crampons (but this increases the hazard of tripping or puncturing one's own leg)
- Wear micro spikes
- Leave the trail to walk in snow on the side
- Use a trekking pole for balance for creek crossings
- Find alternative approach routes
- Use hand lines or fixed lines to protect exposed sections of trail

Winter Driving

Winter road conditions can be a major non-climbing hazard. Winter storms can make roads slippery, cause poor visibility, and make the day overall move slower. Be sure to check online for road conditions and road closures.

MITIGATIONS:

- Find an alternative ice climb with better road conditions or less driving
- Use a four-wheel-drive vehicle with winter tires
- Keep an emergency kit in the vehicle that includes shovel, chains, tow rope, sleeping bag, and battery booster pack

Human Factors

Human factors are decision-making patterns that can lead to increased risk taking and increase the probability of accidents. It appears that when certain psychological cues are present, people find it difficult to heed more objective cues about hazards.

These psychological cues have very little to do with conditions and a lot to do with our unconscious assumptions, biases, and habits.

FACETS is an acronym developed by Ian McCammon listing the human factors (described below). These heuristics are often poorly applied simple rules that may affect decision making. In the FACETS test, you simply run through the list and see which cues are present. Depending on your experience, group size, group experience, etc., each cue may have a different level of influence on your objectivity. But in general, the more cues that are present, the more difficult it will be for you to objectively assess the danger.

Familiarity

The familiarity heuristic relies on our past actions to guide our behavior in familiar settings. Rather than go through the trouble of figuring out what is appropriate every time, we simply behave as we have before in that setting. Most of the time, the familiarity heuristic is reliable. However, when the hazards change but the setting remains familiar, this rule of thumb can become a trap.

Acceptance

The acceptance heuristic is the tendency to engage in activities that we think will get us noticed or accepted by people we like or respect, or by people who we want to like or respect us. We are socialized to this heuristic from a very young age. One of the more familiar forms of this heuristic is gender acceptance or engaging in activities that we believe will get us accepted (or at least noticed) by the opposite sex.

Consistency

Once we have made an initial decision about something, subsequent decisions are much easier if we simply maintain consistency with that first decision. This strategy, known as the consistency heuristic, saves us time because we don't need to sift through all the relevant information with each new development. Instead, we just stick to our original assumptions about the situation. Most of the time, the consistency heuristic is reliable, but it becomes a trap when our desire to be consistent overrules critical new information about an impending hazard.

Expert Halo

Sometimes leadership is based on knowledge and experience, but it can also be based on simply being older, a better climber, or more assertive than other group members. Such situations are fertile ground for the expert halo heuristic, where an overall positive impression of the leader within the party leads others to ascribe skills to that person that they may not actually have.

Tracks (Scarcity)

The scarcity heuristic ("tracks" is derived from competitiveness for first tracks in skiing) is the tendency to value resources or opportunities in proportion to the chance that you may lose them, especially to a competitor. Competing with another group to be first on a route or being forced to a more difficult or hazardous route due to overcrowding is an example of this heuristic in action.

Social Facilitation

Social facilitation is a decisional heuristic where the presence of other people enhances or attenuates risk taking. When a person or group is confident in their skills, they will tend to take more risks using those skills when other people are present than they would when others are absent. In contrast, when a person or group isn't confident in their skills, they will tend to take less risk with those skills when other people are around. A practical example is that climbers tend to climb better when they know others are watching them climb.

Morning Checklist

A morning checklist is an important risk management tool. By systematically going through and addressing all preparations, the checklist ensures that nothing is left to chance. Formatted protocols like this may seem contrived but are key in helping develop mountain sense—an elusive skill that can indeed be learned. It is an opportunity to go over equipment, conditions, hazards, and travel considerations with your climbing partner(s), which will assist in deciding if the chosen route is a reasonable objective and making sure all essential equipment is remembered.

- **Objective**—Discuss route conditions and any information gleaned from research efforts from the day before. At least one alternative route should also be researched in case the first choice is not available due to other users, increasing avalanche hazard, bad ice conditions, poor road conditions, or changing weather.

- **Weather**—Make note of the current weather including cloud cover, air temperature, precipitation, new snow amounts, and wind speed and direction, and also acknowledge the weather forecast for the day with importance placed on any major forecasted changes or anomalies like temperature inversions.

- **Hazards**—Discuss anticipated hazards specific to the route as well as big-picture, general ice climbing hazards along with appropriate mitigations. Research the current avalanche forecast for the specific region in which the route is located as well as any relevant snowpack discussion notes that the forecast contains. Also, research the ATES rating for the proposed route and all alternative routes.

- **Emergency response**—Determine the name of the area's rescue agency along with the phone number and/or radio frequency. Ensure that emergency equipment is accounted for. This includes first-aid kits, tarp, splinting material, and communication devices (cell phone, radio, personal locator beacon, satellite phone, etc.).

- **Equipment**—Initiate a thorough discussion on personal and group climbing equipment to make sure that all required gear is packed. This includes personal gear like helmets, harnesses, boots, crampons, ice tools, anchor material, rack, and ropes.

- **Travel considerations**—Research road conditions and note any potential closures or poor winter driving alerts that should be avoided. Make sure the vehicle is fueled and has appropriate park permits, if required. Make note of the travel distance and time and where to park. Approach beta, including estimated time, should also be determined and discussed.

- **Turnaround time**—Set a turnaround time or departure time from the route or crag to ensure there is enough daylight to descend the route and return to the vehicle. Also, keep in mind that rescue efforts are much more complicated at night and that helicopters cannot fly an hour before dusk.

- **Reevaluate plan**—After going through and discussing all the above topics, reevaluate your plan given the information you discussed to make a final decision on whether the planned objective is feasible and if the risk is manageable. If not, then decide on one of the discussed alternative routes or maybe even the possibility of canceling the day if factors are overwhelmingly obvious that the route should not be climbed.

Near Misses

A near miss is an unplanned and undesired event that has the potential to cause injury in varying degrees from minor to catastrophic. These incidents may have been caused by a human error or an act of god, but harm was prevented by other

Near miss with falling ice.

considerations and circumstances. Near misses are very important to acknowledge, analyze, and discuss so that learning can occur to hopefully avoid similar situations and become aware of our own biases that could possibly contribute to a near miss or actual accident.

The Five Whys

The Five Whys is a debrief technique used to explore the contributing factors and root cause of a near-miss incident. These are determined by repeating the question "Why?" Each answer forms the basis of the next question. This technique may help you understand why the incident happened. Five "Why" questions are often (but not always) needed to get to the root cause. Start with the incident first and keep asking "why" until you feel you have determined the root cause of the incident.

EXAMPLE:

1. I almost fell off a belay stance on a multi-pitch climb. Why?
2. My clove hitch was not tied properly. Why?
3. Checking the knot was not done properly. Why?
4. I felt very comfortable with the situation. Why?
5. I had climbed the route many times, leading to overconfidence.

Biases

Was there a bias that led to the contributing factors and root cause identified by the Five Whys?

- **Availability bias**—A bias toward a quick recall of similar situations that is inherently limited by your own experiences, especially recent experiences. Example: "I have never imagined someone falling on such low-angle ice before and had not even considered placing ice screws where the fall occurred."

- **Adjustment and anchoring bias**—This is where a decision has been made but additional information is not given enough credence and plans are not changed in accordance with the new information. Example: "The weather forecast was for warmer temperatures, but at the parking lot our car thermometer showed −25°C (−13°F). When we arrived at the climb, we decided that groaning and popping sounds emanating from the pillar were not a concern."

- **Overconfidence bias**—The tendency for people (especially more experienced climbers) to be more confident than the evidence or their own experience should lead them to be. Example: "I have ice climbed in this area for ten winters and had never seen an avalanche come down over that climb."

- **Motivational bias**—In some ways this is the most insidious bias in climbing. This occurs when we have a personal stake in the outcome of a decision and choose to ignore or downplay objective hazards. Judgments can be intentionally manipulated to achieve some kind of goal. Example: "All the other ice climbs will be crowded, and Professor Falls probably won't avalanche this morning."

Emergency Response

Despite solid preparation, the best-laid plans can sometimes go awry. Hazards can be missed or wrongly evaluated, resulting in accidents and injury. With this in mind, it is foolhardy to adventure without some first-aid supplies, a communication device, and the knowledge of how to use them.

First Aid

Each member of an ice climbing team should carry a small first-aid kit containing essential trauma supplies. This would include latex gloves, pocket mask, antiseptic wipes, adhesive bandages, sterile non-stick pads, triangular bandage, elastic bandage, steri-strips, second skin, moleskin, medical tape, compact moldable splint, and small scissors. The list of possible injuries that can occur while ice climbing are vast, including wounds, fractures, hematomas, and concussions as well as sprains, strains, and dislocations.

Common minor injuries include blisters, bruised toes, and small facial lacerations. Prevent blisters with proper fitting boots and dry socks, and by paying attention to developing hot spots so they can be attended to with moleskin or second skin before they turn into blisters. Bruised toes happen frequently among novice ice climbers from misguided or hard kicking. Proper fitting boots help somewhat, but precise footwork is the main prevention tactic. Facial lacerations often appear more serious than they actually are due to the bleeding. Flying ice chips are sharp like mini razors and easily inflict cuts to the cheeks and nose. Like bruised toes, climbing technique is the prevention. Aiming ice tools at depressions instead of bulges reduces the amount of ice breaking. Also, a quick drop of the head exactly when the pick strikes the ice will protect your face. Companies have tried designing visors for helmets as shields for face and eye protection, but they have not caught on despite seeming like a good idea—most likely because they are difficult to see through if they get splattered with water or fog up.

Communications

In this day and age, it is irresponsible to be climbing without some type of communication device. Cell phones are the obvious choice, but 911 networks do not work in all areas due to limited connectivity; therefore climbers should carry either a programmable VHF radio, personal locator beacon (PLB), satellite messenger, or satellite phone.

Programmable VHF radios allow two-way communication but are limited to areas that have repeater towers like Canadian national and provincial parks and heli-skiing operations. Plus, users are supposed to be trained and registered with an operator's license. PLBs send an SOS signal to rescue agencies along with your location and avoid subscription fees. A satellite messenger (SPOT or inReach) is like a PBL but offers two-way communication options. PBL and satellite messenger brands don't all use the same satellite networks for SOS signals; all networks work fine in the United States and Canada, but reach can vary internationally. Satellite messengers are making satellite phones obsolete since the network plans are less expensive and the devices are smaller in size.

Rescue

If near the road or outside rescue is not available, then a self-rescue needs to be attempted. However, do not get caught in the idea that you need to self-rescue, especially if trained rescue personnel are available. Sure, you may opt to limp out with a sprained ankle, but do not hesitate to initiate an outside rescue if the injuries are more severe or unknown (internal damage, concussion), or if there is a chance of spending the night out. A cold, unplanned bivouac with a minor injury can quickly turn into a more serious situation, such as frostbite and hypothermia.

If self-rescue is deemed unpractical or impossible, then outside rescue resources will have to be called on. You must know what your rescue options are for the area you are climbing in. Many national parks have professional in-house rescue staff, the cost of which may be covered with your park pass. Other areas may rely on volunteer search and

NEED RESCUE?

YES   **NO**

PARKS CANADA

rescue organizations. If near a road, local fire and police services may be involved.

Have rescue phone numbers or radio frequencies preprogrammed so they are readily available. The most important bit of information to convey is always location: "We have an emergency and we are at . . ." That way if you lose coverage, drop your communication device, or the batteries die, at least the dispatch knows where you are. Beyond that, the dispatch operator will prompt with questions like:

- Exact location of the patient
- Caller's name and phone number
- Nature of the accident
- Number of patients
- Severity of the injuries
- Time of the accident
- Local weather conditions
- Size of the group
- First-aid actions that have been initiated

If a helicopter is to be used for the rescue and can land, some safety considerations must be followed due to risk of fatal injury from both the main and tail rotors:

- Watch the helicopter land
- Only approach from the front
- Keep control of all loose objects
- Wear eye protection
- Remain stationary
- Stay low

In the case of a technical cliff-side rescue with long-lining capability, everyone should be attached to the anchor with releasable tethers (a piece of climbing rope or doubled cordelette attached to the anchor with a tied-off Munter hitch) so the complications of having to unclip from an anchor are eliminated.

Survival Skills

If the day does not go according to plan due to either inefficient climbing or an accident, a forced bivouac may become a reality. Winter nights are long and cold, increasing the chance of hypothermia or frostbite, and should be avoided. Starting early, proper time management, and strict turnaround times should hopefully prevent an unplanned bivy. However, if unforeseen circumstances necessitate a night out, then emergency shelters and fire lighting are two important survival skills.

In the event of an unplanned bivouac or an accident, an emergency shelter must be constructed. Emergency shelters must protect from precipitation and wind and hopefully trap some heat. Look for overhanging boulders, caves, large trees, and natural features that provide protection. If possible, select a site on rock. The go-to emergency shelter is a tarp. It should be used in conjunction with some form of wind block. This can be the lee side of a wind-exposed ridge or boulder, or a wall constructed from rocks or snow.

Helicopter sling rescue by Parks Canada.
PARKS CANADA

Snow shelters—such as quinzees, snow caves, and igloos—can also be fabricated. A shovel will dramatically accelerate the construction process, but gloved hands, helmets, and ice axes, while inefficient, will work. A huge amount of energy may be needed to construct an adequate shelter. To move the least amount of snow possible, look for wind scoops, tree wells, or ice caves.

When at tree line or below, fires are an additional resource to provide warmth and/or psychological comfort in the event of an emergency. Proficient fire lighting is an essential skill that will increase the comfort level in an emergency situation. If it appears that you will be spending the night out in an emergency situation, sufficient wood must be gathered to sustain the fire through the night. Although starting fires with natural materials is an essential skill, it is prudent to carry some form of fire-starting material on remote outings. Small strips of bicycle inner tube are a lightweight and compact fire starter.

The Approach

Approaching ice climbs can be a significant part of the overall outing. In fact, on some days, more time will be spent walking to and from the route than actual time spent climbing. There are many factors to consider when approaching an ice route, including navigating, approach times, mode of travel, avalanche terrain, pacing, transitions, and crampon walking technique.

Navigation

Getting to an ice climb might be as simple as following a well-traveled, packed trail with the actual route in sight the entire time. It could be equally as simple as following a previously recorded GPS track. But it could also be as complicated as spending hours of tedious navigating with a map and compass.

An approach may need more advanced navigating if it is remote or obscure. Above tree line, approaches can become complicated if weather moves in causing a whiteout. Whiteout navigation in winter can feel like being stuck inside a Ping-Pong ball with little sense of knowing which way is up or down, let alone right or left. Similarly, greenout is a lack of visibility due to thick forest cover. Approaching in the darkness of predawn can also have the same disorienting effects.

Learning how to use navigation tools is an essential mountain skill set that all climbers should understand. Modern smartphone apps like Gaia or route apps with downloadable tracks can take much of the sting out of tricky approaches. However, an overdependence on technology can lead to folly—batteries die, screens get damaged, devices get dropped. When using a smartphone for challenging navigation on committing approaches, a backup battery charger should be packed as well. Despite technology, the basic skills of knowing how to use a map, compass, and altimeter are still important and should not become a lost art.

Approach Time

If the guidebook does not list the suggested approach time, then calculating approach time will help in the overall planning of an ice climbing day. Consult a map or even Google Earth and note the approach distance and elevation gain, which will be used to help calculate an estimated approach time. There are many variables that can influence time estimations, such as fitness, mode of travel (walking, ski, snowshoe, etc.), density of forest, visibility, pack weight, snow depth, and avalanche terrain rating (simple, challenging, or complex). There are, however, a few rules of thumb that can be used to roughly estimate how long a particular approach may take.

Jon Walsh high up above the Icefields Parkway in the Tabernac Bowl leads Whoa Whoa Capitaine (WI6, 80 m), Banff National Park, Alberta, Canada.

The approach to an ice route can be a major part of the overall day.

HORIZONTAL TRAVEL:

- Approximately 4 kilometers (2.5 miles) per hour on a well-packed trail
- Approximately 5 kilometers (3.1 miles) per hour on a dry road
- 3 kilometers (1.9 miles) per hour with light trail breaking (boot top)
- 1 kilometer (0.6 mile) per hour with deep trail breaking or breakable crust

ELEVATION:

- Approximately 1 hour for every 300 meters (1,000 feet) of elevation gain
- Descending is often slightly faster than horizontal travel; subtract 10 minutes for every 300 meters of elevation loss.

OTHER CONSIDERATIONS:

- Add 10 to 15 minutes for each transition (putting on crampons and harness).
- Add approximately 10 minutes of break time per hour.
- It is typically faster to travel through simple avalanche terrain versus complex avalanche terrain.
- Travel through relatively open forest is faster than through dense forest.
- Poor visibility (whiteout or greenout) requires a slower rate of travel to maintain accurate navigation than travel in good visibility.
- Walking in crampons is slower.
- Skiing is usually the same speed as walking uphill but significantly faster downhill.

Avalanche Terrain

Some approaches may be exposed to avalanche terrain. As discussed in Chapter 3, determining if your proposed ice climb is threatened by avalanche terrain is part of the planning process. If the approach does indeed travel through avalanche terrain, an ice climbing day is much more complicated. Snow stability and avalanche hazard ratings for the area must be researched and terrain must be analyzed. Avalanche rescue equipment including a transceiver, shovel, and probe needs to be carried by you and your partner(s), and everyone needs to be trained and practiced with these tools. If daytime warming is a factor in decreasing snow stability, an approach through avalanche terrain that might be fine in the morning could become very hazardous in the afternoon on the return trip. In that case, an early start and careful time management should be incorporated. Good travel habits should be employed, too, such as spacing out when crossing avalanche paths, avoiding terrain traps like tight valley bottoms or deep creeks, and vigilant route selection like working ridges and thick timber.

Approach Equipment

Depending on the length, steepness, difficulty, terrain, and condition of the approach, various equipment might need to be considered to make the approach quicker, more efficient, and even safer. Popular approach trails can become very slippery, necessitating adding traction to boots like crampons or micro spikes. The snowpack can be faceted (rotted from cold into a sugary consistency) or isothermal (saturated from heat thus losing strength), resulting in deep post-holing without snowshoes or skis. There could be creek crossings requiring trekking poles for balance.

Trekking Pole

An adjustable trekking pole or ski pole not only can be used for support and balance but also can assist in uphill propulsion. If the trail or terrain is steep, be sure that people are spaced out far enough (at least a few steps behind the person in front) so if a pole slips out, it doesn't poke or stab the person behind. A pole greatly helps during slippery creek crossings; in fact, two poles are even better to offer stability on slick rocks. A trekking pole can also be used to knock fresh snow off tree branches to prevent getting wet.

Crampons

A key transition occurs when the surface becomes hard enough to warrant crampon usage. The transition to and from crampons is a critical decision. Sometimes you can easily walk to the base of an ice climb with just boots and then gear up at the base. If the approach becomes steep, slippery, or icy, crampons should be worn to avoid slips and tumbles. Even a small slip on flat ice could result in injuries like broken wrists, sprained ankles, or twisted knees. Always look ahead and evaluate the probability and consequences of your feet slipping. It can be tricky anticipating this transition, but it is important to not do it too late, thus forcing an awkward transition. Try to use spacious, flat areas—free of exposure to slipping or falling, or overhead hazards—for putting crampons on before moving into steeper, slippery terrain.

If the approach is short and icy, it may be decided to wear crampons right from the parking lot but be careful of too much unnecessary walking in crampons. It not only can be jarring on the knees but also bears its own set of hazards, including tripping, tearing clothing, and/or puncturing one's own leg. It should be noted that whenever it is decided to transition into crampons that harnesses, and most likely helmets, should also be donned.

Micro Spikes

If the approach is a popular winter hiking trail, it will most likely be packed down to the point of being slick. It may be possible to walk in less slippery snow off to the side of the trail, but it may be better to consider using micro spikes, which are snow-hiking cleats that attach to boots. These offer enough traction to not slip on slightly inclined

Micro spikes for slippery approach trails.

packed snow. They are less awkward to walk in than crampons and, more importantly, there's less chance of tripping or spiking oneself. However, they are not a replacement for crampons if the ground becomes ice.

Snowshoes

Most popular ice climbing routes have well-packed trails to their base, but in areas of less popularity, high snowfall, or cold, faceted snowpack, snowshoes may be a better option than the tiring chore of deep post-holing. They are also fairly straightforward for first-time users to figure out how to use.

Skis

Skis are an efficient tool for mountain travel but can also be quite the opposite if the user is not well versed in skiing in variable snow conditions with a heavy pack. Skiing also means carrying ice climbing boots in your pack to switch into once at the base of the climb. Some older-style ski touring bindings will accept a climbing boot, but skiing in climbing boots is an advanced skill due to the lack of support. The other option is to ice climb in ski touring boots, which again is not ideal but can work on certain routes. Regardless, skis definitely add another layer of complexity to an ice climb.

Open Water

Some ice climbing approaches may involve dealing with open water and its associated hazards, namely drowning and hypothermia from cold-water immersion. Any open water or thin ice over water should be treated with a fair amount of caution. Even getting a wet boot can end a day of ice climbing before it starts.

Creek Crossings

Since many ice climb approaches follow valley bottoms, you may need to negotiate creeks with open, flowing water. Ideally, avoid crossing creeks by staying to one side or the other, but this is not always possible. As the winter progresses, creeks may have snow bridges spanning them or be fully covered by a deepening snowpack or avalanche debris. However, early season often means open, flowing water. Find a shallow or braided section to cross. Modern ice climbing boots are fairly waterproof, so step in shallow sections of water with slow movements instead of leaping from higher rocks or boulders. Avoid jumping from rock to rock, as this often results in uncontrolled falls. Uncontrolled jumps can lead to bigger slips and falls, as opposed

Care needs to be taken around open water.

to calculated, precise movements. Be particularly aware of rocks poking slightly above the surface of the water, since they will most likely be glazed with invisible ice and thus more slippery than stepping on rocks just under the surface. Having a trekking pole will greatly help with balance during creek crossings.

Sometimes climbers will set parallel logs across creeks to facilitate crossing. These too can become glazed with ice, so consider donning crampons. High log crossings should be avoided since a slip would result in a more serious fall into the creek. Come spring, be aware of thinning snow bridges over creeks, which can collapse similar to a glacier crevasse fall.

Canyons

Many ice routes form in canyons. These canyons often have water running through them, ranging from trickling creeks to raging torrents. Be mindful of thin ice shelves over moving water. If the ice collapses, a climber can be swept under the ice sheet.

For canyons with lots of water, it is usually best to wait until later in the season or after a lengthy cold snap to allow the ice to thicken and the snow to build up. It is not unheard of for unsuspecting early season ice climbers to break through ice in canyons and submerge themselves up to their armpits.

Water levels can also drop throughout the winter, creating suspended ice shelves of varying or unknown thickness. If the ice you are stepping on sounds hollow, it should be treated as suspect and avoided. If it needs to be crossed, proceed one at a time, stay low (even crawl), and rope up so suspicious sections can be belayed.

Lakes

If possible, avoid lake crossings by following the shore. If a frozen-over lake needs to be crossed, check the thickness of the ice with an ice screw. In still water, 15 centimeters (6 inches) is considered a safe thickness. Average daily temperature is key to ice growth; for example, -7°C (19°F) over seven days straight creates roughly 15 centimeters of ice

Test lake ice for thickness with an ice screw.

in still water. Everyone should have their backpack waist belt undone as well as their harness on with an ice tool in hand. Avoid potential weak areas such as where streams or rivers enter and/or exit and along the edge near the shore.

Tides

Along coastal sea cliffs, high and low tide times need to be researched when approaching ocean-side ice climbs. Some ice routes may only be accessible during low tide, with high tide cutting off retreat. Tides can also wash away the lower sections of ice routes, making them unclimbable or more challenging.

Pacing

Pacing is a mechanism to manage energy for an entire day. In general, the pace should be set for the slowest member of the group. The term "guide's pace," though, doesn't necessarily mean walking slow. It means walking steady at a rate that can be maintained without having to stop to catch your breath. Pacing promotes fluid and in-control steps, reducing the chance of slipping or tripping, both of which are a waste of energy.

If the temperature at the start of the approach is cold, you may start with several warm layers on to ensure overall comfort, but plan to take a layer break shortly to ensure not overheating and possibly perspiring too much. Everyone warms up differently, so close monitoring and management of personal layers when approaching will be important for comfort during the day.

If you arrive at the route soaked from sweat, you will most likely be cold for the rest of the day since the damp base layer will pull heat away from your body. For long or strenuous approaches or for people whose engines tend to run warm, it is a good idea to pack an extra upper-body base layer to change into after the approach. A dry shirt should help keep the chills away.

Pacing conserves energy for the climb ahead.

Plan transitions in appropriate places and use them as part of your rest or snack time strategy during approaches. Planning breaks with transitions will ensure a good flow to the approach and overall day versus a day that feels choppy. Planned breaks reduce the number of cascading stops that may otherwise occur.

Step Kicking

The reason for step kicking in snow is to build a platform that will support you and your partners. Consistency is the key. If you are taller than your traveling companions, make the distance between the steps with shorter people in mind. The step kicking method will depend on the hardness of the snow. In soft snow, plunge your foot down into the snow to pack a platform. In harder snow, use the side of your boot and the serrations on the sole to carve a platform. All following team members work on improving the track by pressing, kicking, or carving a better platform. Steps should angle into the slope.

Duck Foot

In soft snow, it may also be possible to kick your toes straight into the slope, thus creating a staircase of steps. However, as the slope steepens, open up your stance and splay your feet out. This will allow you to kick and press your feet into the slope. This is known as duck foot or by the original French term, *pied canard*.

Flat Foot

When it is no longer possible to proceed with a duck walk, transition to a rising diagonal line. This is called flat-footing (*pied à plat*), where the feet are level (i.e., flat) and parallel. The box step is an efficient method of progression.

- Gain elevation with the uphill foot, creating a balanced position.
- Move forward with the downhill foot, creating a less balanced position.
- On lower-angle terrain, it may be possible to cross the downhill foot over the uphill foot, thereby gaining both horizontal and vertical distance.

Walking in Crampons

Ice (and hard snow) movement skills with crampons are an extension of the skills learned by step kicking on softer snow. The crampon can be stomped straight down or sliced into the hard snow or ice by swinging the foot from the knee like step kicking with boots. Care must be taken, though, when walking in crampons because, for the uninitiated, it is easy to trip over the points or catch points on pant legs—both of which can result in a stumble or fall. A lack of crampon-point awareness can also result in injury, such as puncturing your own leg or stepping on someone else. Picture your partner kneeling to tighten their boots or put on their crampons as you carelessly stumble and step on their hand. It is not a pretty image, but one that can

Duck foot with feet splayed outwards so weight is on the heels.

be easily avoided by giving other climbers a buffer of personal space.

Every step in crampons needs to be deliberate and focused. Your head should be constantly alternating between looking down for your next step and looking up to see where you are going. Depending on the surface you are walking on, steps might need to be aggressively stomped. Feet should be shoulder width apart to avoid snagging pant legs or crampon straps. Try to walk bowlegged like an old-school cowboy to maintain enough separation between your feet.

The surface underfoot can be a variety of mediums including ice, snow, dirt, scree, or rock slab. Learning how to walk in crampons in each of these is important. Ice often requires aggressive stomps, while snow might require kicking. Dirt is fairly straightforward but be conscious of possible tree roots to trip over. Scree will take patience since it is loose and unstable. Rock slabs offer very little to no purchase and therefore can be unpredictable and slippery. Always quickly inspect the bottom of your crampons when transitioning between different surfaces. A small rock could be wedged between the bottom points after walking on scree, or a plug of snow might be balled up underfoot. Both of these examples could prevent the points from biting into ice later, resulting in a slip or fall.

Crampon Flat-Footing

Duck foot on ice is essentially the same as duck foot on snow, with feet splayed so that all the bottom points of the crampon are in contact with the ice surface. Like duck foot, flat-footing follows the same principle except both feet point in the same direction instead of angled outward in opposite directions. The ankle of the lower foot is rolled to maintain contact with the outer crampon points. However, because the upper ankle does not flex well to the inside, the knee must be turned to point downhill slightly so all the bottom points engage in the ice surface.

Flat-footing in a rising diagonal makes use of a modified box step. On lower-angled ice it is possible to cross over and gain both horizontal and vertical distance with every step. As the terrain steepens, it becomes increasingly difficult to keep the outside crampon points of the uphill foot in contact with the ice. The tendency is to roll this foot up and lose full contact. The danger is that the edging that occurs will cause the crampon to pop. If the ice surface is wet and soft, the bottom crampon points will bite much better than if the ice is dry and hard. In the case of cold, smooth ice, scuff the bottom points into the ice by swinging your foot from the knee to create a bit of a divot to step into, thus lessening the angle that the ankle needs to roll.

Your ice axe becomes a third point of contact in the uphill hand. If one foot slips, the other foot and the axe will provide stability. This necessitates a change in the natural rhythm of walking to a three-step process (foot, foot, axe, foot, foot, axe . . .). When walking or climbing with an ice axe, it is

Flat foot with ankles rolled downhill so all the bottom crampon points are in contact with the ice.

Do not edge since it is unstable and only half the points are in the ice.

Hold the ice tool by the head in the uphill hand for stability.

For increased stability, front point with both knuckles on the ice.

important to know where the pointy parts are facing, as an inadvertent movement or swing of the arm may place the tool into your flesh or somebody else's.

Front Pointing

Front pointing makes sense when ice becomes too steep for secure flat foot technique but not steep enough to warrant full-blown two-tool ice technique. It might be tempting to simply stand upright and front point up this angle of ice using ice tools as canes (holding the head and with the spike on the ice) but depending on the angle and the softness of the ice, it might be better to "knuckle" the ice. Take small steps with crampons directly under your body (like walking up stairs) but with your weight forward, holding a tool in each hand but only the knuckles against the ice for stability. As

the ice steepens, this will smoothly transition into swinging the ice tools.

Alpine Position

The most comfortable and efficient position for going straight up classic 30- to 40-degree planar ice and hard snow is the alpine position, or third position (*pied troisième*). It is a blend of flat-footing and front pointing, combining the upward efficiency of front pointing and the energy efficiency of flat-footing. One foot is flat and one is front pointing.

1. Step up on the front point foot.
2. Place the flat foot above the front point foot and stand up.
3. Fully straighten the flat foot leg to a locked position.
4. Move your axe.

Alpine position uses a combination of flat-footing and front pointing.

5. Repeat for twenty to thirty steps, then switch feet.

Descending in Crampons

Descending low-angle ice with crampons always feels much harder and steeper than ascending; therefore, more conservative techniques need to be employed. If the angle is low enough (20 to 25 degrees), walking straight down with bent knees and forward-facing flat feet will work. Be sure to stomp the crampons straight down for purchase and take small steps, coming to a full stop with each step, to avoid gaining momentum and tripping forward. The climber's hips need to be directly over the feet, and as the angle steepens, a deeper knee bend is required. From a side profile, it should appear as nose over knees over toes in a vertical plumb line. An ice tool held by the head like a cane will assist with balance. Once the angle becomes too steep to stay in control, it is better to turn and face in on all fours.

Nose over toes! When descending, bend knees to keep weight over the feet.

Descending Snow

Descending snow can be fun, but it also carries some risks. In softer snow the plunge step can be very effective. Face out and plunge your heel into the snow dynamically. This works best when each climber makes their own track. Stay out of the up track so as not to destroy the steps, since the track may be useful to you or others on subsequent days. If wearing crampons, keep your toes up to avoid tripping over the front points. Also, be very aware of maintaining wide feet to reduce the chance of putting a crampon point into your own calf.

Snow surfaces can become very hard from sluffing, melt-freeze cycles, or repeated foot traffic. If the snow that you are descending is both hard and

Plunge step: keep toes up and feet wide.

steep, it may be necessary to face into the slope and use the front points of your crampons for traction.

Glissading is descending snow slopes by way of sliding, either standing on your feet like skiing or sitting (bum sliding). Glissading can be a fun, efficient, and quick method for descending snow slopes, but precautions must be taken since it is possible to lose control, possibly resulting in injury. Some considerations when glissading are:

- Do not glissade with crampons on.
- Wear a helmet.

- The snowpack needs to be deep enough that all rocks are well buried.
- Have an ice axe in hand to rudder and, if need be, self-arrest.
- The runout at the bottom must flatten with no obstacles to hit (like trees or boulders).
- There should be no cliffs below to slide off.
- The snow should be soft and deep enough to control speed.
- Go one at a time to avoid collisions.

Technical Systems

Technical systems are a major part of ice climbing. Some of the systems are similar to what one would use when rock climbing, but there are many others that are unique to ice climbing. Arming yourself with as much knowledge as possible about strengths, limitations, and applications of various working components of ice climbing technical systems will make you not only a more efficient climber but also, ultimately, a safer climber. This chapter will cover topics such as ice screws, V-threads, anchors, belaying, lowering, and rappelling.

Ice Screws

Ice screws are the primary protection when ice climbing. An ice climber needs to carry a variety of lengths for anchors, lead protection, and V-thread construction. The strength of an ice screw is found in its threads (i.e., pull-out strength). On average, slow pull and drop tests averaged around 10 to 11 kN for mid-length ice screws, meeting CE testing requirements of 10 kN. In dense, well-supported ice, some tests have resulted in 19 kN. However, screws tested in aerated, chandeliered ice are, as expected, much weaker and well below 10 kN. Therefore, the most important factor to consider in placing ice screws is the quality of the ice. For comparison, a 3/8-inch Hilti Kwik bolt has about 24 kN in shear strength and slightly higher in tension (pull out).

Placing Ice Screws

Often, but not always, the surface of the ice needs to be prepared by clearing off bad ice (snowy, slushy, or sun baked) or dinner plates in order to get down to better quality ice. Choke up to the upper grip on an ice tool and use the pick to chip at the ice to clean off the surface (work away, not toward yourself to minimize the hazard of hitting yourself with the pick). Striking a convexity at a 45-degree angle can result in shearing off the bulge to often reveal a perfectly smooth, planar surface for an ice screw placement.

Do not place screws in convexities. Screws test strongest in slight depressions but avoid the back of deep concavities since that will prove awkward to turn the hanger.

Use two hands to drill the screws—one to push and turn the screw and the other to stabilize it by loosely gripping the shaft near the ice. After a handful of clockwise turns (righty tighty), the screw should not wobble anymore. At this point, the crank can be flipped out so the screw can be spun all the way in until the hanger is flush with the ice surface. However, do not overtighten screws because this stresses the threads. It is better to turn an ice screw back a half or even three-quarter turn than over-tighten it. A good analogy is overtightening a wood screw with a screwdriver or cordless power drill. If you overtighten, the threads can strip and lose holding strength.

Brent Peters rappels the last pitch of the Sorcerer (WI5, 190 m) in the Ghost River Wilderness, Alberta, Canada.

A continuous core signifies solid ice devoid of air pockets.

Be sure to get into the habit of always flipping the crank back into its closed position as soon as the screw is all the way in. It is important to not leave the crank flipped out because ropes or carabiners could possibly get hooked on the protruding crank. This becomes even more of a concern when lead climbing.

Signs of a quality ice screw placement include:

- Continuous core
- Full depth (but do not strip the threads by overtightening)
- No cracking or fracturing
- Flat, planer ice surface or slight depression (not into a convex bulge)
- At least 30 centimeters (12 inches) away from the edge of the ice
- Ice is bonded to rock behind

Removing Ice Screws

To remove ice screws from the ice, simply reverse the steps mentioned above. Flip the crank out and use it to spin the screw counterclockwise (lefty loose-y) while loosely holding the shaft with the other hand to grab it when it fully releases from the ice. Flip the crank back into its closed position.

The ice core inside the shaft will often fall out on its own, especially in dry ice. However, if the ice is moist and the air temperature is cold, the ice core could stick inside. It is crucial to remove stuck ice cores immediately or they can freeze inside the screw, rendering them unusable. The best tactic for removing a slightly stuck ice screw ice core is to turn the screw upside down, grip it by the threaded part of the shaft, and shake it up and down. If this doesn't clear the core, the next step is to hit the end of the shaft straight down on the head or hammer of an ice tool. It is okay to be aggressive and hit the screw hard to knock out the stuck core, but it is important not to strike the side of the shaft or any threads or teeth, since these need to be kept in pristine condition.

Remove frozen cores by hitting the hanger-end of the tube straight down on a hammer.

There are some commercially available V-thread hookers made with stiff plastic shafts that are specifically designed to push stuck ice screw ice cores out. If the core freezes into the inside of the screw and cannot be shaken, pushed, or hammered out, try putting the screw inside your jacket to warm it up and hopefully loosen the frozen, stuck core.

Lengths of Ice Screws

Use mid–length 13 to 17 cm ice screws (yellow and blue) for lead protection and longer 16 to 22 cm ice screws (blue and green/purple) for anchors. Be sure to always save a 21 to 22 mm ice screw (green/purple) for V-thread construction. Tests show that the strength difference between 16 cm and 22 cm ice screws is minimal because it is the first few threads that provide most of the pull–out strength. However, stubby 10 cm ice screws (red) tested noticeably less strong, therefore should only be used for thin–ice lead protection. If an ice screw is too long for the thickness of the ice, then use a shorter screw. Do not tie off an ice screw's shaft with a sling, as the sling could possibly cut on the threads or hanger.

Ice Screw Angle

Ice screw angle has been well tested and documented (see appendices). A positive angle of about 15 degrees (105 degrees to the direction of pull) provides the strongest orientation because the load is better distributed around the entirety of the threads. Ice screws are notably weaker at a negative angle and provide very little leverage strength. Rightfully so, there is often confusion with the terminology *positive* and *negative* angle. Mistakenly, climbers tend to "tent peg" the ice screw angle with the teeth lower than the hanger. This is negative angle and therefore weaker. A positive angle is when the teeth are higher than the hanger. It is important to remember that the ice screw's angle is determined by the direction of force and not with regards to the surface of the ice, so predict the

Angle ice screws at a 15-degree positive angle (teeth higher than hanger).

vector for the load and increase that angle by 105 degrees. An exception to this rule would be ice of very poor quality, which might benefit from a slight negative angle (tent pegging).

Re-Bored Screw Holes

Re-bored ice screws (i.e., using existing holes) have tested stronger than expected and can be nearly as strong as freshly drilled ice screws, but results are variable. If the ice is "Swiss cheesed" from over-use, use a slightly longer screw in an existing hole instead of further weakening the overall integrity of the ice by adding more holes to it. In addition, modern, aluminum-shaft ice screws have a larger tube diameter, so use them in re-bored placements. Using a smaller-diameter stainless shaft ice screw would be too loose if placed in an existing hole

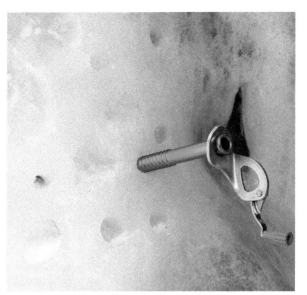

Ice screws with aluminum tubes should be used when re-boring due to their larger diameter.

Stainless steel ice screws will be too loose in the old screw holes.

that was made by a larger-diameter aluminum shaft screw.

V-threads

V-threads—aka Abalakovs (named after the Soviet climber, Vitaly Abalakov)—are used in anchors, including rappel, toprope, multi-pitch, and rescue anchors, as well as lead protection points. They are constructed by boring an equilateral triangle tunnel (all three angles at 60 degrees and all three sides of equal length) in the ice through which a 1.5-meter (5-foot) length of 7 mm cord is threaded and tied as a protection point. Tested strengths of V-threads in good quality ice have averaged around 11 kN. Vertically oriented V-threads—known as A-threads—test stronger, at an average of 14 kN, because most of the force is on the upper hole, placing more total surface area in compression in a single vector rather than in multiple vectors.

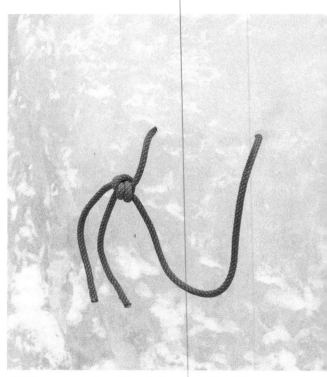

A V-thread made with a 1.5 m length of 7 mm cord and tied with a flat overhand knot that is dressed, is cinched tight, and has 15 cm of tail.

V-Thread Construction

The longest ice screws (21 to 22 cm) need to be used for making V-threads so they can be as robust as possible. They should enter the ice at a 60-degree angle to the horizontal plane (30 degrees to the vertical axis), creating the equilateral triangle so the V-thread is as deep as it is wide. The easiest method for ensuring the two tunnels connect is to stare down the first hole with one eye closed and sight the angle of the second screw with peripheral vision. In cases where the holes are filling with water and cannot be sighted down, leave the first screw halfway in as an angle guide. However, this is trickier to line up, because now you are projecting two lines through the ice instead of eliminating one variable and just sighting one line into the ice. If the holes are a full 22 centimeters (9 inches) apart, the chance of them not connecting is very high. Set the second hole about 18 centimeters (7 inches) from the first one.

Do not over drill the second hole. Stop when they meet. This makes getting the cord through easier.

After the first hole is drilled, sight down the hole to get the correct angle for the second hole.

V-threads are equalateral triangles so ice screws need to bore the holes at a 30-degree angle to the vertical axis.

A V-thread hooker is used to snag and pull the cord through the hole.

Cord is pulled through the holes with a V-thread hooker. 7mm cord is the minimum diameter that should be used, and webbing tests even stronger. This has nothing to do with the strength of the material but everything to do with surface area of the material spreading the load over the back of the thread—thin 5 mm cord is literally slicing through the ice. Webbing tests the strongest due to its wide, flat surface area. The 7 mm cord should be tied with a fisherman's knot or flat overhand knot. A flat overhand is fully acceptable and strong enough, but it must have enough tail (15 cm/6 in), be dressed (no twists), and be cinched tight by pulling on all four opposing strands. Many fisherman knots are incorrectly tied and do not have enough tail.

Existing V-threads

Popular ice routes will often have many existing V-threads from past ascents. Upon careful inspection and assessment, they can be included as a protection point in an anchor. Check that the sheath of the cord does not have any obvious wear or friction

burns from pulling rappel ropes through it. Also, be sure to check that the knot is tied correctly with enough tail. If the knot of the V-thread has been covered over by ice and cannot be inspected, it should be regarded with suspicion.

If you come across a random V-thread that does not seem to have any specific purpose other than as a onetime retreat anchor, it is worth taking the time to untie and remove it. This helps reduce unnecessary nylon garbage littering the bottom of the climb after the spring melt.

Anchor Protection

An ice climber needs to know how to construct anchors with a variety of protection options including ice screws, V-threads, bolts, rock protection, and natural protection. It is necessary to know how to assess each of these options for strength.

Ice Screws

Ice screws apply a radial stress zone on the ice, so with this in mind, ice screws need to be no less than 30 centimeters (12 inches) apart in anchors—double the cone of force, in engineer terms. Of course, they can be farther apart than 30 centimeters, but then longer anchor material will be required to equalize them together. At 30 centimeters apart and slightly staggered from one another by about 10 to 20 degrees (from vertical alignment), they can almost always be joined with a standard 120 cm sewn sling and have a minimal angle at the masterpoint knot.

There is a myth that ice screws in anchors should never be placed at the same level for fear that ice fractures horizontally. In terms of anchors, this is not true. Of course, pillars often fracture horizontally at their top attachment point, but that is not relevant. Anchor screws can indeed be placed at the same horizontal level, but staggering is often more optimal simply to decrease the sling angle at the master point.

Ice screw anchors must consist of at least two ice screws that are at least 30 cm apart.

V-threads can be incorporated into anchors.

Ice screws can rapidly melt out and loosen with warm temperatures and/or direct solar radiation (even on cold days). Mitigate this by choosing shady aspects for ice screw anchor placements and/or using V-threads instead of ice screws for one or all anchor points. If anchor melt-out is a major concern (late season sun and warming temperatures), choose routes with bolt, rock, or tree anchors.

V-Threads

As with any anchor protection point, V-threads should not be used as a single-point anchor, but always need to be backed up or doubled for redundancy. Since they are made from cord as opposed to metal, they do not melt out as quickly as ice screws, so should be used in toprope (and sometimes even multi-pitch) anchors for one or both anchor protection points if warm temperatures or solar exposure is anticipated. (It is shocking how quickly ice screws can melt out, especially when under tension in a toprope context.)

During warm temperatures or direct sun exposure, V-threads are preferred to ice screws for anchor points due to quick melt-out.

Bolts

Bolts come in a variety of types, including self-drive, expansion, and glue-in, as well as materials like carbon steel and stainless steel. Modern 10 mm stainless steel expansion bolts in good rock check in at about 24 kN. Bolted anchors on ice routes may be exposed to a lot of moisture and therefore can corrode, so inspect bolts carefully if they look rusty. When assessing the integrity of bolts, the following criteria should be considered: size (length and diameter), age, quality of the bolt, quality of the rock the bolt is placed in, quality of the bolt placement, and any potential multiplication of force that could be exerted on the bolt once it is loaded.

Rock Protection

Rock protection such as nuts, cams, and pitons can be used to protect ice and mixed routes as well as construct anchors. Be sure that cracks are well scraped out and not icy. Camming devices do not work well if the sides of the crack are frosty or glazed with ice. Nuts can be seated into cracks with the pick of an ice tool, but this will often deform and damage them. All fixed pitons suffer from corrosion as well as the loosening effects of melt-freeze cycles, so they should be tested thoroughly with the hammer of an ice tool.

Natural Protection

There are many natural anchors that an ice climber can use to set up both toprope or multi-pitch anchors as well as lead protection. These include trees, boulders, horns, and threads. Single-strand cord is sufficient for low loads and the absence of sharp edges. If in doubt, use webbing or double the cord. Fixed slings around natural features should always be carefully inspected for fading, fraying, and cuts. The knot of fixed cord should also be inspected to make sure it was tied correctly.

Anchors

A well-constructed anchor is one that is able to withstand all potential forces, is efficient to construct, and requires a minimal amount of equipment. An ice anchor should be able to hold 20kN to be considered full strength, which is a two-times margin of safety for maximum potential loads that could be experienced in high-force climbing load. Two mid-to-long ice screws in good ice (dense and zone of compression) is considered an adequate anchor for most general ice climbing applications including toprope, multi-pitch, rappel, and rescue. However, sometimes the quality of ice or anticipated load might dictate using three ice screws for an anchor. These situations may include thin ice, lower-quality ice, exposed multi-pitch belay, team of three, or high-advantage raising systems. There are various acronym mnemonics (IDEAL, SERENE, E(A)RNEST) that can be used as an anchor checklist, but the overall quality of a constructed anchor can be assessed by ensuring it meets all the following criteria:

The angle between anchor points should be less than 60 degrees to minimize vector forces.

- Longer screws are better (16 cm or longer)
- Screws minimum 30 cm apart (double the radial stress zone)
- Equalized for anticipate load
- Master-point angle should be 60 degrees or less
- Incorporates redundancy
- Minimizes potential for extension
- Efficient use of gear (and time)

Anchor Configurations

Multi-point anchors can be configured in a variety of manners. They can be either pre-equalized and directionally focused with a tied master point (figure-eight, girth-hitch, or series) or self-adjusting to equalize with a moving load (sliding-X or quad). They can also be unidirectional or multi-directional. The most important consideration with all anchor configurations is that the actual protection points are of the highest quality and that you understand the strengths and limitations of each configuration and their various applications.

> Locking carabiners are not required on the actual protection points since there is already redundancy by being doubled, and they are noncritical attachment points (i.e., there are two of them if one fails).

Figure-eight Anchor

The figure-eight anchor is the classic multi-point, directionally equalized configuration constructed by connecting anchor material—static rope, nylon/Dyneema sling, or 7 mm accessory cord—to two or more independent protection points. The material is aligned with the anticipated direction of load and a master point is created by tying a figure-eight on a bight. A secondary shelf (for an auto-braking belay device) is located between the strands above the

Figure-eight configuration for a directionally focused, two-point anchor (120 cm sling).

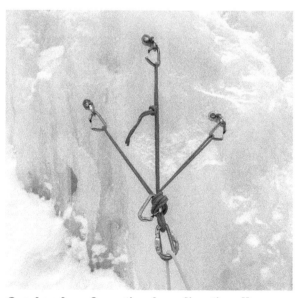

Overhand configuration for a directionally focused, three-point anchor (5 m x 7 mm cordelette). Note the use of a carabiner clipped through the overhand knot to help loosen after it has been loaded.

master point's figure-eight on a bight. An overhand on a bight could also be used but should be avoided since it is often much more difficult to untie, especially after being loaded, due to the round nature of the knot (as opposed to the figure-eight on a bight, which is a longer knot with more bends and therefore much easier to untie). If you have only enough material available to tie an overhand, then clip a carabiner through the knot itself to help with loosening after being weighted.

If building large anchors from trees that are far back from the lip of the cliff, a length of static rope should be used as anchor material. Attach one end of the static rope to a tree with a basket hitch, and then use a clove hitch to adjust the slack on a second basket-hitched tree. The static rope will need to be folded back on itself prior to tying the figure-eight on a bight to create two loops at the master point for redundancy. The closed tail should also then be passed over the master point to capture it. A single length of static rope (40 to 60 meters) can be used to create side-by-side figure-eight anchors using the W-method construction, with clove hitches on locking carabiners at the shared anchor points to adjust equalization.

Girth-Hitch Anchor

The girth-hitch anchor is a multi-point, directionally equalized configuration constructed by girth hitching a locking carabiner as the master point. In a toproping application, a second locking carabiner needs to be added with its gate opposed through the girth hitch. The value in the girth-hitch anchor is its ease to undo, especially after being loaded. This makes it a useful anchor for extended toproping situations. The girth hitch also uses less material compared to the figure-eight, allowing protection points to be farther apart without increasing the angle past 60 degrees.

Girth-hitch configuration for a directionally focused, two-point anchor (120 cm sling).

Girth-hitch configuration for a directionally focused, three-point anchor (180 cm sling).

Series Anchor

A series anchor is yet another multi-point, directionally equalized configuration constructed by placing two protection points in series using a clove hitch to adjust equalization. Adjusting the clove hitch can sometimes prove finicky, and true equalization cannot usually be attained, but this configuration works well in conjunction with a figure-eight or girth-hitch anchor to make three-piece anchors.

Series configuration combined with figure-eight configuration for a directionally focused, three-piece anchor (180 cm sling).

Series anchor is also used to construct a bowline anchor, which can be used for fixed-point lead belays. The bowline configuration uses a bowline on a bight (or double-loop figure-eight, aka bunny ears figure-eight) to create a doubled loop as the master point for multi-pitch top belaying as well as the fixed point for lead belaying on a multi-pitch. This bowline on a bight loop is clipped to the lowest anchor screw with a small locking carabiner, then the sling is equalized in series with a clove hitch to the upper screw (clip the tail into the carabiner to close the

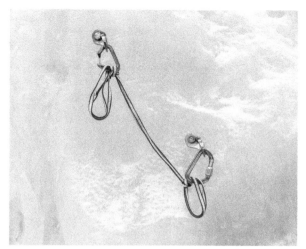

Bowline configuration using a bowline on a bight equalized with a clove hitch (120 cm sling).

hitch). The benefit of the bowline on a bight is that it is very easy to untie after being loaded.

Sliding-X Anchor

The sliding-X anchor is a self-adjusting, two-point configuration that may be used in certain

Sliding-X configuration for a self-equalizing, mulit-point anchor (60 cm sling).

applications, such as a quick "soft" anchor to clip personal tethers into while rappelling. To construct a sliding-X anchor, connect a sewn sling to the hangers with non-locking carabiners and place a single half twist in one strand of the sling, creating a loop. To create redundancy and limit extension, overhand knots can be tied into each of the anchor arms in such a manner that the anchor's self-adjusting properties are not restricted. All knots need to be removed from the sling after each use so that they do not become permanently seized, thus weakening the material.

Quad Anchor

The quad anchor is another type of self-adjusting configuration that offers redundancy and distributes force better than a sliding-X and offers two separate clip-in points. To tie a quad anchor, double a quad-length (240 cm) sewn sling and tie overhand knots in both ends about 10 to 12 centimeters (4 to 5 inches) from each end. Clip each of these bights to anchor points (two bolts or two ice screws). There will be four independent strands at the center

Quad configuration for a self-equalizing, multi-point anchor (240 cm sling) set up for top-anchor belaying.

between the overhand knots. Any two strands can be used to clip into for anchoring. As mentioned above, all knots need to be removed from the sling after each climbing outing so that they do not become permanently seized, thus weakening the material.

Unidirectional Anchors

Unidirectional anchors can only be loaded in one direction, typically downward. Examples of unidirectional anchors are ones consisting of all (or mainly) nut placements or slung boulders or horns. Unidirectional anchors can be used for toproping, rappelling, rescue from above, or multi-pitch belays only when the next pitch is not 5th-class climbing (i.e., must be either walking or easy scrambling).

Multi-Directional Anchors

Multi-directional anchors can withstand loads both downward and upward. Examples of multi-directional anchors include ice screws, bolts,

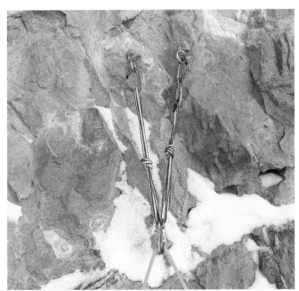

Quad configuration for a self-equalizing, multi-point anchor (240 cm sling) set up for toproping.

pitons, girth-hitched trees, and horizontal camming devices. If there is potential on a multi-pitch climb for the next pitch to produce a significant upward pull on the belayer if the leader were to fall (and possibly rip out a unidirectional anchor), a multi-directional anchor needs to be used. Multi-directional anchors are also required for rescue scenarios from below. Ice screw anchors are multi-directional.

Single-point Anchors

Anchor points such as ice screws, V-threads, bolts, and rock protection cannot be used as single-point anchors. They always need to be doubled for redundancy and strength. In some situations, large single-point anchors such as trees are appropriate. For a tree to be used as a single-point anchor, it needs to be alive, well rooted, and larger than your upper leg (minimal 15 cm/6 in. in diameter). A sling can be either basket hitched around the base or basket hitched and tied off with a figure-eight on a bight to create a master point and a shelf. Unlike multi-point anchors, the shelf on single-point anchors is

Single-point tree anchor with a figure-eight masterpoint (180 cm sling).

not between the strands but through all the strands together. If the tree is at least 40 centimeters (16 inches) in diameter, the sling can be placed higher up on the trunk. To prevent the basket hitch from slipping down the trunk, use a longer sling and add one full wrap around the tree so the sling grips and stays in place.

Toproping

Toproping is a great way to try out ice climbing. Leading ice should only be done after much experience is first gained under the security of a toprope. However, just because the rope is above your head, there are still many hazards associated with toproping ice, including ice fall, avalanche, rock fall, sharp equipment, falling tools, cold weather, wet ice, and the list goes on. In reality, a day at the crag toproping ice can be more akin in terms of risk management to a day of alpine climbing with multiple overlapping hazards. Most of these hazards can be mitigated or avoided, but it is still critical to maintain situational awareness at all times. It is all too easy to let your guard down while at a seemingly safe crag and become too lax in toprope situations.

Belaying

The movement for belaying a toprope on rock is the same as on ice, but there are a few differences that should be noted. Unlike rock belaying, there is constant overhead hazard from climber-generated falling ice and maybe even dropped ice tools tomahawking through the air. The belayer must be positioned so they are not exposed to ice fall. If you injure or knock out your belayer, then you have no belay. If the only non–exposed spot to belay is far back away from the climb, there is a chance the belayer could get yarded forward catching a fall or lowering. If that is the case, a ground anchor should be incorporated to help them maintain their position.

Cold temperatures can mean bulky gloves or cold hands, which could interfere with properly gripping the rope. Wet ice often results in icy ropes, which can be challenging to pull through the belay device.

Hitting the rope with an ice tool's pick is a real concern, but it can be avoided by keeping the rope tight and not pulling in slack when the climber is swinging. Direct strikes on ropes do not often result in a catastrophic sever, but damage can be inflicted to the rope's sheath and core that should be immediately examined. If a clean hole is found, the rope should still be okay to lower back down. The damaged section will need to be cut out of the rope before it is used again. Along the same lines, all climbers must be aware of crampon points so they do not step on rope that is stacked or lying on the ground.

Belay Checks

Self-checks and partner checks are a key risk management strategy to help avoid human error. Bulky clothing, gloved hands, and basic lack of focus are reasons that these checks are very important before any technical system is about to be engaged. For belaying, this means that after the climber ties in and the belayer sets up their belay device, the climber and the belayer initiate:

1. Self-check:
   - Climber checks harness buckle, tie-in points, knot, and crampons.
   - Belayer checks harness buckle, belay device, locking carabiner, and stopper knot in the end of the rope.

2. Partner check:
   - Climber and belayer face one another and each takes a turn to show the other what they checked in their self-check.

It is easy to become lax with both the self- and partner check and start to unknowingly "fake" the checks (i.e., going through the actions of checking but not truly checking). Be diligent about self- and

Always initiate a self-check and partner check before climbing.

partner checks. Have your partner pull up the bottom of their belay jacket to offer an unobstructed view of the harness, showing either their knot (clearly see it passing through both the tie-in points on the harness) or their belay device (see that it is threaded properly and the carabiner is locked). If someone needs to take off or loosen their harness to adjust layers or use the bathroom, then a conscious check of the harness waist belt and buckle needs to occur again.

Directionals

The use of directional protection points in toprope ice climbing can significantly increase safety and comfort. Almost any type of protection can be used as a toprope directional, including an ice screw, V-thread, tree, bolt, or rock gear. A directional not only helps keep the toprope directly over the line of ascent but is necessary for separating the two strands of rope (belayer side and climber side). In a rock-climbing context, the belayer's strand of rope behind the climber is simply annoying as it slaps the climber in the back of the head. However, in an ice climbing context, the climber can inadvertently snag the belayer's rope with their ice tool as they reach back to swing. Hooking the unseen belay rope while swinging can result in either a dropped ice tool or actually sticking the pick into the rope itself.

Properly placed directionals help:

- Keep the rope in line with the climbing route
- Keep the rope out of wet ice
- Prevent a pendulum swing or fall on routes that traverse
- Create two separate climbing lines from a single toprope anchor
- Keep the toprope away from fragile ice features (pillars, curtains, daggers, etc.)
- Keep the toprope climber away from the belay strand of the rope so they don't snag it with their ice tool as they swing
- Prevent swinging out away from the rock on steep mixed routes
- Prevent climbers from going higher than you want them to (over a bulge, too close to an ice anchor, out of sight, etc.)
- Decrease force on the actual toprope anchor

Top-Anchor Belaying

Top-anchor belaying occurs in situations where the toprope belay is being provided from above rather than below. In these instances, it is preferable for the belay to be provided directly off the anchor with an auto-braking device instead of the belayer's harness. The comfort of the belayer should be considered when determining the positioning of the anchor. Ideally, the anchor is placed high enough so the belayer is chest-to-eye level with the anchor's master point.

Common top-belay situations include:

- Toprope climbing from above because the bottom of the climb is inaccessible (canyon, sea cliff)

Use directionals when toproping to maintain separation between the climbing strand and the belay strand.

- Toprope climbing from above because the pitch is longer than half a rope length
- Toprope climbing from above because overhead hazards (hanging daggers) threaten belaying from the base
- Single-pitch lead climbing with a walk-off descent
- Multi-pitch climbing

Auto-Braking Belay Devices

Auto-braking belay devices are attached directly to the anchor and used to belay one or two ropes from above in auto-brake mode (formally called auto-blocking, which is confused with auto-block hitch for rappel backups, and sometimes called guide mode). When a force is applied to the active rope(s), the device automatically brakes (locks). Although braking is automatic, the device requires constant management (hand on the rope or backup knot) since slippage may occur. They are one-way devices so they can be problematic to reverse (pay out rope and lower). They are often multipurpose devices and can sometimes be used as manual- or assisted-belay devices and for rappelling. Auto-braking belay devices can also be used as a progress capture in rescue or raising scenarios.

Considerations for top-belaying with an auto-braking device:

- Most devices are designed to be used only with specific rope sizes.

- It is possible for the rope to slip though the device if not used in accordance with manufacturers' recommendations, particularly in situations where one rope is weighted and the other is not.

- Slippage may also occur with wet or icy ropes, small-diameter ropes, slick ropes, and when two ropes of different sizes are belayed.

- The brake strand needs to be managed at all times (i.e., not hands free).

- It can be very difficult to move the second rope if one rope is weighted.

- Device positioning is important, and they tend to work most effectively when attached to an anchor at waist height or higher and do not contact the rock.

- For more efficient rope movement, use a round-radius locking carabiner.

Auto-braking belay device set up through the shelf of the anchor for top-anchor belaying.

Auto-braking devices are not hands free. Use an overhand on a bight to back up the device if fully letting go.

- Rope diameter and texture will influence ease of movement through the device, generally lower-diameter, slicker ropes will require less pull effort than larger, rougher-textured ropes.

Lowering with an Auto-Braking Device

Lowering and feeding out slack with auto-braking devices can be problematic. To feed slack on an unweighted rope, pull back on the locking carabiner and pull on the climber's strand while maintaining a hand on the belay strand. For short lowers with an auto-braking belay device that cannot be unweighted, ratchet the loaded locking carabiner up and down to "walk" rope out through the device.

For longer lowers—where again unweighting the device is impossible—use the nose of a carabiner in the release hole to leverage the device open. For this method, a backup needs to be employed. Ice climbing is rife with overhead hazards like ice fall, dropped ice tools, sluffs, avalanches,

Always use a third-hand backup hitch if using the leverage hole to release slack or lower short distances.

To feed slack, pull back on the braking carabiner while still maintaining a brake hand on the rope.

and snow mushrooms, all of which are good reasons to back up lowers. The simplest method for backing up a lower is with a "third hand" friction hitch from the belay loop onto the brake strand of the lowering rope. This can be done similar to a rappel backup using 7 mm cord as a three-wrap prusik, or a Hollowblock as a four-wrap auto-block hitch.

If the climber can unweight the ropes, then use the Load Strand Direct method:

1. Add a third hand friction hitch from your belay loop to the belay strand as a backup.

2. Clip a carabiner (either locking or non-locking) to the loaded strand of rope in front of the auto-braking device.

3. Ask the climber to unweight the rope so the carabiner can be clipped to the same place on the anchor (master point or shelf) that the auto-braking device is clipped to (with the other hand holding the belay strand).

4. Climber then re-weights the rope and lowers.

Always use a third-hand backup hitch when lowering with the Load Strand Direct method.

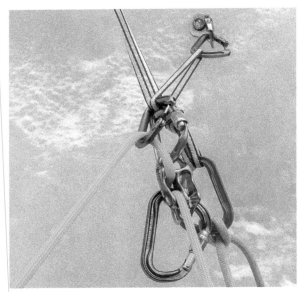

Load Strand Direct works well for lowering into climbs from above. When the climber unweights the rope as they start climbing, unclip the rope from redirected carabiner (blue non-locker) to enage auto-braking mode.

The Load Strand Direct method is an effective lowering system for ice climbs in canyons like Ouray Ice Park. A climber can be lowered to the bottom of the canyon from an anchor at the rim with this method. When they start climbing and slack is introduced to the rope, the redirected carabiner of the LSD system can be unclipped, allowing the auto-braking belay device to operate as per normal. Be sure to use a third-hand backup for the lower (prusik or autoblock hitch).

Cleaning Anchors

Cleaning anchors by threading the rope through the fixed hardware so your anchor setup can be retrieved is a fundamental single-pitch crag technique that requires a methodical approach. Lowering is often preferred over rappelling in single-pitch situations since it is faster, more efficient, and can be safer. Your belayer must keep you on throughout the entire process, never releasing their brake hand.

Lowering on a Figure-Eight on a Bight

If the anchor is Fixe rings or large quick links and can accept a bight of rope, then:

- Clip into the anchor with a tether or even a single runner like a quickdraw (appropriate in this situation because the belay is always active).
- Call for "Slack!"
- Pull up slack rope to pass a bight of rope through the rings.
- Tie a figure-eight on a bight knot.
- Clip the knot into the harness's belay loop with a locking carabiner.
- Untie from the original figure-eight follow-through knot.
- Pull loose end of rope through the rings.
- Execute a visual check.

- Holler "Take!" to weight the rope to complete a physical function check.
- Remove tether and clean the anchor.
- Lower back down the route.

Lowering on a Figure-Eight Follow-Through Knot

If the anchor is a small chain link that doesn't have enough room for a bight of rope, then:

- Clip into the anchor with a tether (clipping in with just a runner is not appropriate in this situation because the belay is inactive while untied to thread the anchor).
- Call for "Slack!"
- Pull up some slack on the rope and clove hitch it to a gear loop on the harness.
- Untie from the figure-eight follow-through knot.
- Pass rope end through the anchor's metal links.
- Retie in with figure-eight follow-through knot through the tie-in points of the harness (as per normal).
- Undo the clove hitch.
- Execute a visual check.
- Holler "Take!" to weight the rope to complete a physical function check.
- Remove tether and clean the anchor.
- Lower back down the route.

When threading anchors for cleaning and lowering, do not say "secure" (Canada), "off belay" (USA), or "safe" (UK). These commands mean "take me fully off belay," which is not the desired intention. In fact, the climber threading the anchor does not need to say anything other than maybe "slack" and then ultimately "take" when they are ready to be lowered after threading. By sticking to this principle, you can avoid accidentally being dropped.

Rappelling

If a route cannot be lowered and/or does not have a way of walking off from the top, it must be rappelled. For whatever reason, rappelling accidents are sadly commonplace, but they do not need to be. Accidents usually occur because of an incomplete understanding of the rappel systems. Unlike the actual climbing where the rope and anchors may never be loaded, rappelling systems are loaded every single time. We commit all our weight to the anchor, ropes, and rappel device. For this reason, rappel systems need to have backups in place. By shortcutting the backups, we leave ourselves exposed to the very real possibility of not only human error but also overhead hazards.

Any manual-braking device can be used as a rappel device as well as most auto-braking belay devices in manual mode. Assisted-braking devices that accept two ropes work well too, with the added bonus that a backup is not required.

Joining Ropes Together

Single ropes should always have the halfway point well marked when rappelling so there is no doubt that middle is at the anchor. The middle point could be a black band from the factory, or it could have a pattern or color change in the sheath, or it could be added with a rope marker. If executing double-rope rappels, the standard knot for tying two ropes of somewhat similar diameter (no more than 3 mm difference) together is the flat overhand knot. Critical components of the flat overhand knot are enough tail (30 cm/12 in.), dressed (no twists), and tight (pull on strands to cinch).

If using skinny 5.5 mm static Spectra cord as a tag line, the Reepschnur method should be used. The tag line should always be the pull line because its smaller diameter will feed through the rappel device faster than the thicker single rope, causing the ropes to creep through the rappel anchor. Interconnected figure-eight knots or another suitable bulky joining knot should be used to attach the

Many accidents occur while rappelling so a solid understanding of the systems and backups is key.

The flat overhand knot is used for joining two ropes together for rappelling.

The Reepschnur should be used when joining a skinny tag line with a single-rated climbing rope (diameter difference greater than 3 mm).

single rope to the 5.5 mm Spectra cord. Due to the rope creep caused by the different diameters, a big knot is necessary to jam against the anchor rings or quick link, but unfortunately, this may also be more prone to snagging. A locking carabiner needs to run from the tag line to the lead rope in case the joining knot squeezes through the rappel rings (unlikely but an important backup).

Personal Tethers

When threading an anchor for rappel, securing to the anchor can be completed using a personal tether. For this application, the simplest tethering system is girth hitching a 120 cm sewn sling through the harness tie-in points, and then using a locking carabiner to connect the sling to the anchor's master point. It is also suggested to tie an overhand knot about 20 centimeters (8 inches) from the harness to create a shelf for extending the rappel device. Simple sling tethers can be shortened easily enough by pulling up the excess slack above the locking carabiner and tying an overhand knot to eat up the slack.

Commercially sold tethers like PAS (Personal Anchor System) will obviously also work but are somewhat limiting since they only have one use, as opposed to a multipurpose sling. Other tethers like the Petzl Connect or a Purcell prusik (self-made from a cordelette) are both easy to adjust and somewhat shock absorbing but tend to be bulky.

Whatever tether system you decide to use (personal preference), it should *not* be permanently fixed to your climbing harness since that increases clutter and can cause focused wear on the harness and the sling material. Keep the tether stowed on the back of the harness and attach it to the harness tie-in points when it is needed (e.g., top of a climb when transitioning to rappel mode).

Due to the low elongation (static) properties of sling material, it is important to keep personal tethers tensioned at all times with little to no slack. A 2-meter (6.5-foot) fall on a 1-meter (3.3-foot)

Using a 120 cm sling as a tether. Shorten by pulling up the slack through the carabiner and tying an overhand knot.

Using a PAS as a tether. Shorten with another carabiner.

tether is a factor 2 fall creating a potential 10-12 kN of force, which could be enough in certain circumstances to break the tether and/or do serious physical harm to the climber (e.g., break bones, internal organ damage).

Rappel Backups

Rappels should *always* be backed up with either a friction hitch (aka "third hand") or firefighter belay. The auto-block hitch (aka French prusik) with a 13.5-inch Hollowblock has streamlined using a rappel backup, making it simple and fast, so there is really no excuse not to use one. A traditional prusik hitch can also be used but is more time consuming to attach. A minimum of a three-wrap auto-block hitch or two-wrap prusik is recommended for normal threaded or double-rope rappels in which two strands of rope are placed through the rappel device. Single-strand rappels (fixed line rappels) require an extra wrap (four wraps for auto-block hitch and three wraps for prusik hitch) since less rope surface area is available for friction. Regardless of which

A "third-hand" rappel backup with an auto-block hitch (aka French prusik).

friction hitch you decide to use, it should be connected to the belay loop of the harness with the rappel device extended.

The past method of attaching the rappel device directly to the belay loop on the harness is quickly being replaced by the more modern method of extending the rappel device. The main reason for extending the rappel device away from the harness is so there is enough separation between the backup hitch and the device. This is critical so that there is no chance that the hitch could possibly slip by contacting the edge of the rappel device.

The method of attaching the backup friction hitch to the leg loop has proved ineffective because it is difficult to get the required separation between hitch and device. Even if there appears to be enough distance between the two, an unconscious climber will invariably sag backward with their legs raised enough that the hitch would most likely come into contact with the device and subsequently slip.

Firefighter Belay

The other method for backing up rappels is the firefighter belay. A climber below holds the rappels ropes, ready to pull hard on them to halt the descent of the climber on rappel above. The hands of the firefighter belay act as replacement hands for the climber rappelling if they were to lose control of the brake. Easing off on the tension will continue the lower. This rappel backup technique only works if full attention is focused on the climber rappelling. The climber providing the firefighter belay must not be trying to multitask. They should be looking up with hands above their head on the ropes ready to apply tension.

Unlike normal toprope or lead belays, where if a climber falls there is direct and immediate feedback to the belayer (upward movement and load on the rope) even if they are not fully watching, with a firefighter belay, if the climber on rappel loses control of their descent, there most likely will

A firefighter belay is also a suitable rappel backup but requires a partner and constant attention.

Pulling on the ropes replaces the rappeller's hands and stops the descent.

not be any change to the way the ropes are reacting from below.

V-thread Rappels

V-threads are used for rappelling on ice when fixed anchors like bolts or trees are not present. Like any anchor, redundancy is important, so rappelling from two equalized V-threads might make sense in some situations. These can be equalized to a master point or simply in series where one takes the load while the other exists as a backup. Unfortunately, this would also mean leaving behind a lot of cord that ultimately becomes garbage. With experience, it is acceptable to rappel off a single V-thread, but *always* implement an unweighted backup anchor clipped loosely to the rappel rope for the first person(s)

A properly backed up V-thread rappel for the first climber to descend, therefore testing the V-thread. Note that the locker draw is clipped to the rappel rope but does not take any weight.

Do not clip the backup to the actual V-thread.

Do not have the backup too tight.

Do not have the backup too loose.

Case Study: Spray River Falls Rappelling Fatality

On December 12, 2000, three ice climbers reached the top of the four-pitch Spray River Falls on Sulphur Mountain in Banff. The terrain on top was relatively flat ice, so the climbers unroped and prepared to rappel the route. They discovered a small loop of 7 mm cord poking out of the ice. It was a previous V-thread that they assumed had frozen over, covering the knot. They threaded their rappel ropes through the existing V-thread and gave it a yank to test it. The first climber began rappelling while the other two stood waiting their turn.

As the first climber leaned over the edge and committed his full weight to the ropes, the anchor failed, and he fell 140 meters (460 feet) to his death. The cause of failure was that the loop poking out of the ice was in fact not the actual V-thread but only the end of the tail of the V-thread knot. When the rappel ropes were fully weighted, the tail popped out of the ice, resulting in the climber falling with the ropes, leaving his two partners stranded on top.

This accident could have easily been prevented by backing up the V-thread with a sling clipped loosely to an anchor. The tail still would have popped, but the backup would have caught the ropes. This is also why V-thread backups are clipped to the actual climbing rope and not the V-thread cord. The lesson learned is to *always* inspect existing V-threads and *always* back up single-point rappel anchors.

down to fully test the V-thread. The last person to rappel removes the unweighted backup.

The V-thread backup must be clipped to the rappel rope and not to the V-thread cord. A locker draw is very useful for the backup as long as the length is satisfactory. It also must be slack enough that it does not take any weight, but not so slack that if the V-thread were to fail there would be a major shock load to the backup anchor.

No-Threads

No-threads—also called zero threads or naked threads—are V-threads where the rope is fed directly through the bored holes, eliminating the need for leaving cord behind. As ice climbing attracts more and more participants, ice climbers must increase awareness of their environmental impacts. All V-threads ultimately become plastic garbage in our watersheds. In light of this, bolted anchors on popular routes are far less impacting than numerous V-threads throughout the season. As an ice climbing community, it would be valuable to organize summer cleanups to access the bottom of often-used ice climbing areas to gather old V-thread cord.

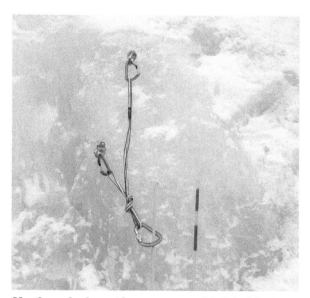

No-threads do not leave any cord behind but also need a backup for the first person down.

Even though the environmental benefits are obvious, no-threads should be avoided in very wet ice combined with cold temperatures to avoid the rappel ropes freezing in. On popular routes that are not re-forming, it might make more sense to set a good V-thread instead of a no-thread, because repeated no-threads will Swiss cheese the ice with numerous holes, rendering it weaker.

In addition, some climbing ropes have a hard plastic casing at the ends. These can make it tricky to snag the end with a V-thread hooker. No-threads also need to be tested with an unweighted backup in the same way as for standard V-thread rappels.

Stacked Rappels

Stacked rappels—in which both climbers pre-rig themselves on the rappel ropes—are crucial for ensuring that all rappel systems are set up correctly and checked. Originally a guiding technique, it is surprising that more climbers do not use stacked rappels. It is standard practice to execute partner checks when belaying but then all too common to leave your partner (often the less experienced one) at the top of climb to set up their rappel without any partner check. Stacked rappels are actually not only safer but also more efficient because both climbers set up their rappel devices on the ropes at the same time. Then it is a simple matter of unclipping and rappelling when your turn comes to go down. Stacked rappels can be executed with as many climbers as need be.

To make stacked rappels more comfortable for the second (and even third rappeller), an extended rappel device (as described above) is necessary. The device can be either clipped into a loop on the tether or a separate sling (60 cm should sling) basket hitched through the tie-in points of the harness. The first person down uses a friction hitch for their rappel backup, then provides firefighter belays for the other(s). If it is decided that the second person to rappel will use a backup friction hitch as well, it can be placed on the ropes but not clipped to the belay loop until it's their turn to rappel. This will help minimize being yanked by the tensioned ropes while the first climber rappels.

A stacked rappel. All rappel devices are pre-rigged so partners can complete checks together.

Extended rappel device prevents the stacked climber from being pulled toward the tensioned ropes.

Stopper Knots

As with toprope belaying, stopper knots in the end of the ropes must be present when rappelling to close the system. The knot of choice for this application is the double overhand, also called a barrel knot. It is essentially half of a double fisherman's and is a suitable blocking knot in the end of the rope because it is large and stays tight. A properly tied double overhand knot should create an X pattern in the rope, be tight on itself, and possess a minimum of 20 centimeters (8 inches) of tail.

Stopper knots are *always* required when rappelling to eliminate the chance of rappelling off the ends of the rope. Even if the ends of the rappel ropes can be seen touching the ground, still always add knots so the practice becomes habit. There is simply no good reason to not have knots in the ends. Some climbers may argue that there is a chance of the knots getting stuck or even

Stopper knots ALWAYS need to be tied in both ends of the rappel ropes.

maybe forgetting about them when pulling rappel ropes. Neither of these rationales are better than the alternative (falling to your death), and both of these pseudo issues are easily avoidable.

If the concern is the wind blowing the rappel rope far off to the side and the knot possibly getting stuck, then saddlebag your ropes by coiling and clipping the coils with a sling to both sides of your harness. If the concern is forgetting to untie the knot when pulling rappel ropes, then always clip the free end of the rope that is going up through a quickdraw on your harness. This is a great habit regardless to keep control of the loose end, with the added bonus that the knot in the end or any other unforeseen tangles will catch on the carabiner of the quickdraw.

System Checks

Before committing to a rappel, a series of visual checks needs to be completed to ensure that all systems are set up properly. This can be done from the top down starting at the anchor:

- Check all anchor protection points for integrity.
- Check fixed webbing, cord, and chain for wear or damage.
- If a single-rope rappel, check that the rope's middle marker is at the threading point.
- If a two-rope rappel, check that the flat overhand is dressed, is tight, and has 30 centimeters (12 inches) of tail.
- Check that all rappel devices are oriented and threaded properly.
- Check that locking carabiners are locked.
- Check that the backup hitch is set up correctly with the appropriate number of wraps.
- Check that stopper knots are tied in the end of both strands.

A J-loop closes the rappel system and maintains control of the ropes.

Function Checks

Visual checks are always required to ensure everything is set up correctly before loading technical systems such as anchors, belays, and rappels. The idea behind a function check is to actually test any new system before fully and singularly committing to it. This is particularly important when rappelling as we are constantly moving back and forth from one technical system to another (from our personal tether to a rappel device then back again to the tether).

To execute a function check before rappelling, suck up as much slack as possible through the rappel device and third-hand backup hitch so body weight is fully loading the rappel device while you are still clipped into the anchor with the personal tether. If all works as it is supposed to, then you have just confirmed your visual check with a real load. Then you can unclip your tether with confidence knowing your rappel and backup are set up properly.

At the bottom of the rappel, clip into the next anchor with your tether and feed out rope through the rappel device so the ropes above have enough slack that you fully load the tether (function check) before dissembling your rappel rigging.

J-loop

On multi-pitch rappels, close the rappel system with a J-loop. After the first climbing rappels, before undoing the rappel device, pull up a few meters of slack from below the device and tie an overhand on a bight to clip into the anchor. This not only closes the system but also maintains control of the rope ends so that they can't accidentally swing out of reach. Once the J-loop is clipped into any random point on the anchor, the ropes can be removed from the rappel device.

Ice Movement

Refined and precise technique is paramount to climbing frozen waterfalls. Solid movement skills are the foundation of not only efficiency but also safety. This includes being able to get solid ice tool and crampon placements, climb all angles of ice with fluidity, rest and recover while climbing steep ice, and apply various strategies to advanced ice features.

Magazines and climbing equipment advertisements often show ice climbers high-stepping, stemming wide, or doing some other "fancy" move to make it more exciting. The reality, though, is that ice climbing movement is very boring to watch since it is repetitive and stable looking. The foundation for good ice movement is achieving solid pick and crampon placement from stable body positions.

Crampon Placements

Solid crampon placements may be the single most important component of ice climbing technique—even more so than solid ice tool placements. Secure feet that can be trusted ultimately means more relaxed movement and less strain on arms. The concept is the same for both dual and mono front points. When first learning to use crampons, dual front points can feel more stable than the single mono-point. However, with practice, mono-points

A well placed crampon with a level foot and a buried front point supported by engaged secondary points.

tend to work better because they are more precise and displace less ice.

Front points (or point) need to be engaged with secondary points adding stability. A solid crampon placement means that no part of the front point is visible sticking out of the ice. To achieve this, the crampon must be kicked slightly upward into the

Manoah Ainuu styles Bingo World (WI6, 35 m) in Hyalite Canyon, Montana, USA.
AUSTIN SCHMITZ

The heel is too high levering out the front point.

The heel is too low disengaging the front point.

ice by lifting the big toe and pressing it to the top of the inside of the boot. This angle of attack is crucial so the very tip of the point strikes the ice. If the kick is aimed downward instead of upward,

the angled front edge of the front point will hit the ice instead of the tip. More important than kicking with force is kicking with precision. Like swinging an ice tool, the kick must stop as the points strike the ice. If you kick too hard, the points will often simply bounce off and the risk of bruising toes will increase.

When the ice is featured with holes from previous ascents, there is a temptation to place crampons deep in the hold. Instead, aim slightly lower (only a centimeter or two) for the very front of the holes. This will allow the front points and secondary points to properly engage and will make the ice feel a few degrees less steep.

Ice Tool Placements

Most people have one arm that is stronger than the other, but with practice and repetition, your swing can become equally strong with both arms. Think of swinging an ice tool like throwing a dart, in that quick acceleration needs to be achieved over a short distance with a snapping wrist motion. Shoulder, elbow, wrist, and head of the tool all need to be stacked in alignment. If these components are not aligned and the elbow is sticking out (chicken winging), the swing will be weak.

The goal is to accelerate the head of the ice tool with a well-timed wrist flick at the end of the swing. Some initiating force is generated with the elbow, but most comes from dropping the head of the tool far back with the wrist. Make sure your hand is at the bottom of the grip with pinky against the pommel so as not to choke the swing. Also, swing the tool with a relatively loose grip, only clenching your grip at the moment of impact. This loose grip with a well-timed clench will assist in "flinging" the head of the tool through the arc of the swing.

Aim for depressions and concavities in the ice. These are supported features, whereas convex surfaces are under tension and almost guaranteed to

Swinging an ice tool requires accelerating the pick by dropping the head back with the wrist and elbow.

A well placed ice tool with the pick solidly engaged in a concaved depression.

crack and break unless the ice is very soft. Choose a depression, concavity, or divot in the ice's surface at just less than full reach (slight bend in the elbow). Set the pick on the chosen spot to help with aim and also to provide quick information as to how much force you will need to swing. If the spot you are aiming for already has been used (i.e., a previous pick placement), then less swinging force will be required.

Removing Ice Tools

Ice tools sometimes get stuck and can be difficult to get out, requiring more energy to remove the tool than getting the placement in the first place. It is a fine balance between having solid tool placements that do not wobble and over-driving them too deep. The goal is not to get them stuck in the first place. The more you climb, the more you will get a feel for how hard you have to swing. Stuck tools happen for several reason reasons, including:

- Over-driving the tool by swinging too hard.
- The pick on the tool may be dulled in a way that makes it hard to remove.
- Ice features jam the head of the tool in place.
- The top of the pick has teeth (often found on mixed picks).

To remove ice tools, pull back aggressively on the grip so the top of the pick cuts up into the ice, thus disengaging the teeth. This levering action of pushing the grip inward and then pulling back on it might need to be repeated a few times to create enough room for the teeth of the pick to slide out of the ice. Be cautious when yarding back on the tool so that it does not suddenly pop out of the ice and hit you in the face or, worse, knock you off balance.

Sometimes it is necessary to grab the tool by the head to yank it out. If so, after freeing the tool, hook the pick over your other thumb so you can re-grab the grip without having to awkwardly shuffle your hand down the shaft.

If the tool cannot be removed by pulling back on the handle, then slide your hand up the shaft to lift it out.

Make sure you don't torque the pick laterally by twisting the tool from side to side, since it is possible to bend or break the pick. If the tool is stuck behind an ice feature, you may have to break the ice surrounding the stuck tool to free it. Placing a screw for protection while you free the tool may be required in extreme circumstances. You might even have to hang on the screw and tap the stuck tool out with your other free tool.

Ice Climbing Movement

An ice climber's main source of security, especially when leading, is not necessarily the ropes, anchors, and protection but deliberate and efficient technique. The idea is to make every move secure and smooth so the chance of falling off becomes almost nonexistent. This means solid ice tool and crampon placements need to be achieved with ease and with as little energy as possible.

There are two basic body positions for climbing ice that work from low-angle WI2 all the way up to WI6: the swinging position and the kicking position. By adhering to these two positions with minimal deviation, ice movement will become more efficient, and achieving solid ice tool and crampon placements will become easier. Of course, specific terrain features might require breaking the regimented movement described below, but for the most part, this framework should be the rule, not the exception.

Many ice climbers have heard of the saying "swing like you screw, kick like you poo." This is a simplistic way of describing these two fundamental body positions for ice climbing: the swinging position and the kicking position.

Swinging Position

The swinging position is a triangular stance (A-frame) with the two crampons forming the

The swinging position. Note that feet are slightly wider than shoulder width and also level and parallel to one another. The lower tool is centered between shoulders creating an A with feet.

The swinging position. Note that knees and hips are stacked directly over toes with a very slight bend at the knee joint. Back is arched so chest is away from the ice, and the hand of the lower tool is between chest and neck height.

Reaching too far stretches the body out and results in heels rising up.

Chest too close to the ice results in a poor swing.

lower two corners of a triangle and the planted tool as the triangle's apex. The fist of the gripped ice tool should be in the center of your body. If you place the tool off to one side or the other, then move your body with a series of foot movements so you are situated directly under the tool. Once in this triangular tripod stance, concentrate on keeping your heels low, hips in, and back arched. It is important to keep your upper body away from the ice so your elbow can be in front of you for swinging. If your chest is too close, it forces your elbow out to the side (chicken winging) resulting in an ineffective swing.

Locked knees force the hips away from the ice resulting in a rigid, unstable position that stresses the calf muscles.

Too high on the lower tool results in more strain on the bicep and chest too close to the ice.

Not being in the A-frame (feet on either side of the lower tool) results in the elbow sticking out (chicken winging).

Feet too wide is awkward and reduces reach.

Toes splayed outward means weight is not directly over front points resulting in wobbly crampon placements.

Feet too close together is very unstable.

Staggered feet force the hips outward and chest inward resulting in a poor swing. Unlevel feet also put more stress on the lower calf muscle.

The following are key components of the swinging position, described from bottom upward:

- Both feet at the same horizontal level
- Both feet parallel to each other (so heels rotate outward)
- Feet slightly wider than shoulder width
- Knees unlocked and over toes, so legs are slightly bent
- Hips also vertically aligned over knees and toes
- Core engaged by squeezing glutes together
- Planted tool centered at the midline of chest
- Hand of planted tool between chest and face level

It is crucial to maintain a "quiet" body while swinging. This means that the only part moving is the arm doing the swinging. The rest of the body should have zero movement. Engage the core muscles by intentionally squeezing your glutes together with each swing. This stabilizes the entire body so all energy is directed into the swinging ice tool and not lost on hips floating back and forth.

Kicking Position

The kicking position has your hips sticking out with your body away from the ice so you can look down at your feet and place them appropriately. All the while, tools are staggered, with the top arm straight. Place your feet just wider than shoulder width and at the same horizontal level. Kicks should be angled upward into the ice with the big toe pressing up against the top of the boot. Once crampons are set, stand up in a single fluid motion, pushing hips in, and reassume the swinging position.

The following are key components of the kicking position, described from top down:

- Loose, open hand with thumb off the grip

The kicking position. Note that most of the weight is on the straight upper arm while the lower arm is key in pushing the hips away from the ice. Both knees are bent at 90 degrees with hips slightly higher than the knees. Head is looking down at feet.

- Straight-arm hanging off the upper tool
- Bent arm pushing outward off the bottom tool
- Head bent looking down at feet
- Hips away from the ice
- Knees bent no more than 90 degrees, so knees are never higher than hips

Many novice (even intermediate ice climbers) find it challenging to keep their upper arm straight while placing crampons. The straight arm is very important, though, to gaining quality crampon placements. By keeping you low and away from the ice, it allows you to see your feet better, thus better able to evaluate each crampon placement. It also makes it much easier to kick "up" into the ice. Finally, a straight arm is more efficient as opposed to a bent (and thus flexed) bicep muscle.

The kicking position. Note that the upper arm is straight and the knees are as wide as the feet.

Hips are lower than knees resulting in feet being way too high.

Upper arm is bent and body is too close to the ice resulting in kicking down and hitting the toe of the boot instead of the front points.

Ice climbers will find it easy enough to maintain a straight arm while kicking the foot on the opposite side but feel like their body will collapse into the ice when they try to kick the foot on the same side that they are hanging on the straight arm (e.g., if right arm is straight, right foot feels awkward to kick). They inefficiently resolve this by committing weight to the opposite foot and standing up. This causes a bent, flexed arm, which is tiring and ultimately rushes the same-side crampon placement. It also makes it slightly more challenging to elevate if the feet are truly level. The solution is to push off slightly from the ice so your hanging body is like a pendulum. As your body swings back toward the ice, a well-timed, light kick will set the crampon because the force of your entire body helps drive the points in.

Upper arm is bent and head is not looking at feet. Knees are not bent at the same angle.

Transition Between Positions

The transition between the kicking and swinging position is the key to fluid movement. Once satisfied with your crampon placements (feet level and parallel, all front points and secondary points engaged), bring your knees in over the toes and slide your hips up, pushing with the legs. It's important that the body from just below the knees down does not move at all. The lower legs and feet are isolated and immobilized, so they are static through this transition.

Staggered Tools

Always stagger tools. The old X-position with tools side by side is not only highly inefficient compared to the A-frame but also potentially dangerous. Placing tools wide and out to the side is very out of balance and promotes barn dooring (picture a barn door slowly opening). Planting tools at the same horizontal level or too close together risks breaking one or the other out of the ice. Ideally, if climbing straight upward, tools will be staggered a tool length apart (50 cm/20 in.) and stacked almost vertically above each other with about 10 to 20 centimeters (4 to 8 inches) of horizontal separation. The simplistic breakdown of the movement is to place one tool then move both feet up; place the other then move both feet up. Essentially it is tool, foot, foot, then other tool, foot, foot and repeat.

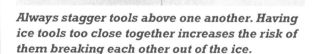

Always stagger tools above one another. Having ice tools too close together increases the risk of them breaking each other out of the ice.

Avoid the X-position with tools out to the side. It is not only very inefficient but also extremely out of balance.

Ten Common Ice Movement Mistakes

1. Feet not at the same level

2. Feet not wide enough

3. Feet not parallel to each other

4. Core not engaged when swinging

5. Too high on ice tools

6. Bent arm while kicking the second foot

7. Not kicking "up" at the ice

8. Tools not staggered

9. Knees locked straight when swinging

10. Reaching too far when swinging

Triple Kick Footwork

A variation to the footwork movement described above is the triple kick. Even though it is more efficient to make one move with each foot, sometimes the terrain dictates making multiple foot moves, especially if stemming wide. The triple kick uses a third auxiliary kick directly under the center of the body before separating the feet into a level, wide stance.

When hanging in the kicking position, the three kicks are:

1. Move one foot directly under the tool you are hanging off

2. Set the other foot wide

3. Set the last foot level

Low-Angle Ice

Low-angle ice is less strenuous than steep ice but can feel fairly awkward sometimes. The key is to maintain proper ice-movement fundamentals using the swinging and kicking positions, but not reach too far for tool placements. Like slab rock climbing, the body's center of mass (the hips) must be over the feet. If you reach too far forward on low-angle ice for a tool placement, the hips will no longer be vertically aligned with the feet. This can cause heels to rise and crampons to lever out of the ice.

Bulges

Bulges—where the ice goes from steep to low-angle—can often be a distinct crux of an ice climb. The key to surmounting them efficiently and confidently is a well-refined kicking position. The upper arm must be fully extended so the hips can have maximum separation from the ice in order to see the feet and kick upward into the ice. Also, making shorter tool placements (not reaching as far) will assist in not becoming too stretched out over the bulge.

A very well refined kicking position is key for clearing bulges. Note that the tools are only staggered by half a tool length so as not to reach too far and stretch the body out over the bulge.

Steep Ice

Steep ice requires very refined technique so as not to get pumped. If technique is even off a little, it will become more strenuous, requiring muscle strength as opposed to good movement skills. Ideally, try to climb corner features like shallow grooves or between two pillars. On dead vertical ice, level feet are very important. If they are off even a bit, it will force your hips away from the ice, which results in the chest going into the ice to compensate for the outward shift in center of mass. With the chest close to the ice, the swing suffers due to a lack of alignment with the shoulder, elbow, and wrist. On vertical ice, try hard to have hips into the ice and chest away from the ice. The position should feel similar to an upward dog pose in yoga.

Resting and Recovering

Learning how to rest and recover is an important strategy for ice climbing at any grade. Ice climbing needs to be done in a controlled manner and allowing yourself to get pumped is a loss of control. Movement technique tends to fall apart once a pump sets in, which unfortunately is when solid movement is needed the most. Taking time to get solid crampon placements with wide, level feet will pay off in the long run by keeping more weight on stable feet and off the arms.

Try to maintain an open, loose grip on the ice tools. One trick is to constantly remind yourself to keep your thumb up. If your thumb is up and off the handle, it is almost impossible to over-grip. Force yourself to let go of your tools and do a quick shake of the hand. Do this right from the start of a pitch—do not wait until your arms tire. This not only keeps the pump at bay but also helps keep hands warmer by shaking new blood back into them. A quick shake out every move forces recovery.

If you forget to shake out frequently and find your forearms fatiguing, then establish solid feet

Learn how to rest by shaking out almost every move to recover hands and when possible finding features to step sideways on to relieve calf strain.

and take some time to alternate shaking out on one tool, swapping hands between the lower and upper grips. Remember to breathe while doing this. It will not only expedite recovery but also calm the mind.

Calf muscles can also get pumped ice climbing, especially on lower-angled slabs of ice. When front pointing, calves are flexed and can tire quickly. Making sure feet are level will even out the load so both calves share half the body's weight. Whenever flat features like small ledges in the ice present themselves, take advantage of them by setting your foot sideways so all the weight is on the heel. This uses the skeletal system instead of flexed muscles and can relieve cramping calves.

Traversing

Traversing on ice can feel very awkward. It is much better to anticipate a traverse and angle gradually rather than moving horizontally. On a gradually angled traverse, swing your tool over to the other side, then unwind your arms by swapping hands, using the upper grip, while the tool remains in the ice. Try to move feet sideways in incremental steps. If forced to cross your feet, lead with the heel of the foot as you pass it over the other foot placement.

Traversing: plant ice tool to the side.

Traversing: remove other tool and hook over shoulder (or place in thumb) then grab the upper grip to match.

Traversing: grab tool from shoulder (or other thumb).

Traversing: plant ice tool to the side again and repeat.

If tools need to be swapped between hands and cannot be left hanging in the ice, use either the thumb catch to swap (described on page 185 of Chapter 8) or, if using umbilical leashes, the shoulder hook. Avoid placing a tool over your shoulder if not using umbilical leashes since it might slip off and be dropped.

Snow Ledges

Topping out on snow ledges can feel insecure, especially if the snow is deep. On well-packed ledges, solid sticks may be achieved if the snow is hard enough. If loose powder snow, swing hard into the snow to try to get a stick in underlying ice. There may be no ice under the snow, but frozen dirt, moss, roots, and grass can all offer secure placements. Since it is not possible to visually inspect the placement with the snow masking it, yank downward on the tool to get a feel if it is solid. If it feels like it is merely cutting through the snow, either reset it or try a different spot. Since tool placements might be less secure in snow, try to keep as much weight on the feet as possible, taking small steps. This will help you avoid fully committing to the tool placements.

Movement Drills

With any movement-based activity, there needs to be exercises and drills to break down and isolate key components of the skill. The following exercises will assist in helping beginner, intermediate, and even advanced ice climbers improve and refine their ice-movement skills. These exercises only work if they are executed correctly. The old adage "practice makes perfect" should actually be "perfect practice makes perfect." If done wrong, it is "practice makes permanent," thus engraining bad habits. All of these exercises should be done either on toprope or barely 30 centimeters (12 inches) above flat, even, snowy ground. Do not "boulder" high off the ground with crampons on, since even short falls can often result in broken ankles or tib-fib fractures due to the rigidity and traction of crampons and ice boots.

The Pendulum

Skills learned: maintaining a straight arm while kicking, relaxed grip, kick timing, kick precision

Place two ice tools in the staggered position directly above one another so feet will be just off the ground while hanging straight arm. While in the kicking position, alternate pushing off with the

The Pendulum (A).

The Pendulum (B).

feet and kicking crampons, constantly penduluming back and forth. As soon as one crampon hits the ice, the opposite one comes off.

The One Tooler

Skills learned: level feet, hanging straight arm, kicking position, crampon placement, triangle body

position, surmounting bulges

Toprope WI2–3 ice with only one tool. When hanging in the kicking position with a straight upper arm, use the knuckles of the free hand to push off against the ice to keep the hips out. Make sure participants' switch hands occasionally so both arms are used.

The One Tooler (A).

The One Tooler (B).

The Tool Traverse

Skills learned: triangle kicking position, hanging straight arm, open grip, transition from kicking to swinging position, traversing

Set a traverse line of pre-placed ice tools horizontally and close to the ground. The ground needs to be even and flat for this, with no edge hazard to fall off of. Be sure to over-drive the tools so they are 100 percent solid. Traverse from one side to the other, moving between the swinging and kicking positions. Only switch hands on the one tool that is at the center of your triangle and only while completely standing in the swinging position.

The Tool Traverse (A).

The Tool Traverse (B).

The Tool Traverse (C).

The Tool Traverse (D).

The Tool Traverse (E).

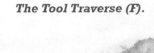

The Tool Traverse (F).

The Shake Out

Skills learned: resting, letting go of tools

A key skill for steep ice and for leading is being able to rest and recover but also feel confident to let go of tools and leave them in the ice. For this exercise, once the upper ice tool placement has been set from the swinging position, do not immediately drop into the kicking position. Instead, let go of the lower tool and do a quick shake out while maintaining the swinging position (weight over the feet and hips in with core engaged). After shaking out, re-grab the lower tool and cycle through the kicking and swinging position to repeat the shake out on the opposite hand. Repeat this process on every move for a whole toprope pitch of climbing.

The Ninja

Skills learned: reading the ice, hooking, efficiency, being gentle, stabilizing ice tool and crampons

The Ninja climb exercise is basically toproping a pitch of well-traveled, hooked- and stepped-out ice with zero swinging and kicking while maintaining perfect ice climbing technique every move, including wide, level feet, straight upper arm, staggered tools, triangle, etc. This is easier said than done; it is easy enough to just "drytool" up pegboard ice with haphazard, random moves, but the purpose of this exercise is to consolidate the movement framework while learning the intricacies of reading ice and being delicate. It will force you to potentially use small features for your front point(s), which will require focus to keep them stable (trick: engage your core by squeezing glutes together).

The One Hitter

Skills learned: efficiency, precision, visualizing

The idea of the One Hitter exercise is that the climber is only allowed one swing per ice tool and one kick per crampon. This means taking extra time to choose the correct spot to swing and kick, and consciously trying to remember all the subtle nuances of how to swing and kick before actually doing it. It will help you be more efficient, focusing on doing everything right so the first swing or kick counts. The exercise helps refine movement and eliminate unneeded moves, therefore conserving energy and ultimately climbing faster.

A fun game can be made out of the exercise by keeping track of the number of times that extra swings or kicks are used. The goal, of course, is to reach the top with a score of zero; even more important is to achieve solid tool and crampon placements. Climbers must be honest with themselves if placements are not completely solid, and if not, then they need to swing or kick again.

Advanced Ice Climbing

It's not until you begin to climb steep ice that the climbing begins to feel a bit more like rock climbing. Some ice climbs form three-dimensional features that require techniques beyond the basic ice movement. Stemming, chimneying, backstepping, twist locking, heel hooking, and drop kneeing are all rock climbing moves that may be applied to advanced, steep ice features.

Ice that used to be considered too thin, or pillars that were too skinny, are now being pursued by those looking to push the limits, but it's a delicate balance of climbing safely while discovering what's possible. When ice grades go up, the availability of protection tends to go down and the commitment required is higher. Ice screws can be a wasted effort to place since the ice they are in is often too fragile to hold a fall. The boundary between pushing technical difficulty and luck on difficult ice routes is a thin line.

Moving Faster

Learning to climb efficiently and securely is paramount to moving faster. The goal is to flow over the terrain with an economy of movement. Rushing does not equate to climbing faster. In fact, rushing often results in getting pumped or, worse, falling

Advanced ice climbing is steeper and the actual ice features are often more fragile.

off. Falling is only fast in one direction. The saying "slow is smooth, smooth is fast" holds very true for ice climbing. Taking extra seconds to make sure footwork is perfect gains minutes in the long run. If the ice is picked out, using the existing steps is definitely quicker, but always maintain the fundamentals of footwork with level feet that are shoulder width apart.

Training yourself to take your time to achieve solid tool placements with one swing and solid crampon placements with one kick is a huge time saver as opposed to swinging and kicking multiple times. The One Hitter drill described on page 127 is a great exercise to help develop this skill.

As a follower with the rope above you, drafting the leader's pick holes by hooking instead of swinging speeds things up significantly, but don't be too careless, since even toprope falls are a time eraser. The Ninja drill described on page 127 will help you become more comfortable with hooking and stepping instead of swinging and kicking.

Choking Up

Choking up on the upper grip of an ice tool helps you gain height for reachy moves. It also is a way to rest so the other hand can let go of the lower grip. If a tool placement is lower than desired, choking up can open up more options for the next placement with the other tool. However, do not get into the habit of choking up every move. Despite seeming like it might be more efficient to creep up the tool for more reach, often it just stretches out your body too much. You need a bit of bend in your arm so there is slack to get your hips away from the ice

in order to kick properly from the kicking position. Also, never choke up higher than the upper grip. Grabbing the shaft higher than the upper grip puts too much outward force on the pick, increasing the chance of it suddenly popping out.

Pillars

Pillars are free-standing columns of ice that can be some of the most aesthetic and compelling structures to climb. It can also be very dangerous, however, to even be around these features depending on the conditions. Recognizing when a pillar is safe to climb can take years of experience, and still catches even experienced climbers by surprise from time to time.

Choking up to the upper grip can help extend reach but be careful about over-extending.

Free-standing pillars are beautiful features to climb but require experience to evaluate.

Pillars are formed by water dripping off overhanging rock—a vertical plumb line of ice. They can form many meters away from the rock behind them, creating caves between the ice and rock. The ice often forms in both directions—a hanging icicle reaching down to a pedestal of ice building upward.

As time passes and if conditions permit, the dagger and the pedestal will connect, forming a continuous structure of ice.

There are two attachment points that are important to the strength of a pillar: the top where it pours off the rock and the bottom where it stands

A cracked pillar signifies that tension has been released. They can reheal to be solid or on the verge of falling over.

on its pedestal. When pillars break, they tend to break just below the main upper attachment point, where the stress on the ice is greatest. If the pillar has a solid base, it will help support the weight of the freestanding ice.

One of the most important things to consider with pillars is the temperature—not only the temperature the day you are going to climb, but also the temperature in the days leading up to it. The colder the temperatures, the more the ice contracts and the higher the chance a pillar will fracture. After a period of very cold temperatures, it is not uncommon to find pillars shattered on the ground. It is not only extreme cold temperatures that affect ice; also pay attention to extreme temperature swings while the ice adapts to the new temperature.

Pillars will often sport cracks, often near the top but also sometimes near the base. Cracks release the tension of the ice contracting and expanding and can re-heal, offering a bit of added confidence, but they should still be treated as suspect. If a pillar does not have a crack, the climber might just be the catalyst that pushes the pillar past its breaking point.

Even the most experienced climbers have been surprised when a pillar snapped and collapsed underneath them. The obvious danger in a pillar collapse is taking a big fall, but also consider the weight of a pillar crushing you and/or your belayer. Another thing to keep in mind is that if you have just led a pillar and, in immediate retrospect, felt it was not the best decision because it seemed fragile, do not expose your second to the same hazard. Rappel the pitch and clean your screws. If for whatever reason the pitch absolutely needs to be followed, then pull your rope up through the ice screws and drop it back down, so if the pillar does break while seconding, the follower will not get flossed off the end of the rope by the mass of falling ice. Of course, these situations should be avoided in the first place by choosing the right conditions and with careful assessment.

Realistically, if you are reading this book for advice on climbing pillars, you probably shouldn't be climbing them, as it takes years of experience to judge them correctly.

Climbing pillars also requires very solid technique. Pillars may be straightforward enough to climb with standard steep ice technique. However, if the ice is extremely featured or narrow, advanced moves like stemming, twist locking, flagging, and heel hooking around the column might be required. The best conditions for climbing a pillar are when the ice is soft and plastic. This not only makes getting tool placements easier but also means the actual pillar has more elasticity to it. Brittle ice is unforgiving and under a lot of tension. If a pillar has been climbed a lot and is picked out, it may be a simple hook up.

Twist-locking technique (I-beam, as opposed to standard A-frame) on narrow ice features like pillars.

Sometimes a heel hook around the pillar will help maintain balance instead of barn dooring.

Some things to take into consideration before climbing a pillar:

- What is the current temperature?
- What were the overnight and previous days' temperatures?
- Is the ice plastic or brittle?
- Are there signs of a horizontal crack in the ice?
- Is the pillar well connected to the pedestal for support?
- Is the top attachment point thick ice?
- Has the pillar fractured and re-healed?
- How much of the pillar is attached to the rock?
- How "free standing" is the pillar?
- Is the pillar plumb or is there a slight lean?

Overhanging Ice

Though rare, ice can sometimes form overhangs. These can be umbrellas formed by wind and updrafts, or large cauliflowers formed by dripping water, or horizontal roofs formed by pillars snapping off, or spray ice formed by water freezing to overhanging rock. Some ice climbers even seek glacial ice caves, but that is beyond the scope of a waterfall ice book. Regardless of the type of formation, all overhanging ice is extremely strenuous and requires advanced movement skills to surmount.

Ice umbrellas like at the top of the famous Canadian Rockies route, Wicked Wanda (WI4+), are intimating features both for their obviously strenuous climbing and for their equally obvious overhead hazard. Luckily, they can often be bypassed on one side or the other by more-vertical paths.

Cauliflower ice is large petals and fins at the base of steep pillars. It is formed by dripping water splattering, creating a cone-like pedestal on which the pillar stands. Depending on how the

Cauliflower ice formed around a pillar's pedestal is often overhanging but well featured.

petals form, they can be relatively small and make for good footholds for crampons, or they can be large and formed in a fashion that it takes one or two overhanging ice moves to get over each layer. Swinging can often break them, so sometimes hooking the top of the petal works better, albeit is less secure.

When pillars snap off from temperature changes, they leave in their wake horizontal ice roofs. These roofs are more problematic than a hanging pillar because nothing is left to stem to. Sometimes these ice roofs can be a couple of meters long, requiring advanced maneuvers like Figure-4s.

Spray ice like found at Helmcken Falls in central British Columbia is pushing overhanging ice standards, with WI13 being claimed. It is formed by the mist from the massive, high-volume waterfall freezing to the nearby overhanging rock. So far, it has proved difficult and dangerous to protect these spray climbs with normal ice protection like ice screws. Most spray ice routes are protected by bolts in the rock, so it ends up being sport ice climbing.

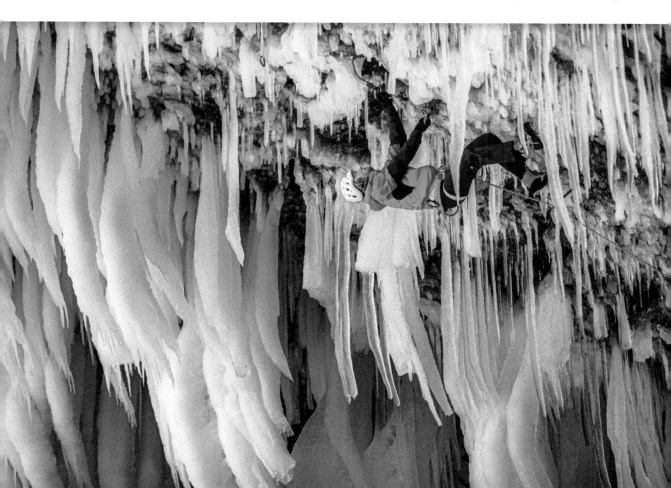

Spray ice offers the steepest pure-ice challenge.
JON GLASSBERG

Horizontal ice roofs form when a dagger or pillar breaks.

Thin Ice

Thin ice is more akin to mixed climbing than pure ice climbing. It is categorized by typically being less than 10 centimeters (4 inches) in thickness. Protecting thin ice can be more challenging than climbing it. Often the protection is rock gear to the side if it is too thin for 10 cm stubby ice screws.

Thin ice climbing demands well-refined technique so as not to destroy the already minimal ice. Forceful swinging will only cause picks to bounce off the rock underneath. Deliberate, well-directed taps are the strategy of choice. Chipping a divot in the surface of the ice to hook is a good option.

Placing your thumb on the back of the grip instead of wrapped around it helps aim and control the swing to achieve precise blows. It is important to make every swing count. Multiple strikes at the same spot will only break away more ice than necessary.

New, fresh ice is better bonded to the underlying rock than late season ice. Porous or highly textured rock like limestone or conglomerate tends to offer a better bonding surface than smooth, hard rock like granite. As the season progresses and the ice undergoes warming and cooling trends, it will sublimate, or shrink, and usually detach from the

Thin ice is not only challenging to climb but can also be challenging to protect.

rock behind. Detached, thin ice can be very hazardous since it is unsupported and can easily shear away.

Verglas is ice so thin that it typically will not accept a pick placement. It is basically a slick glaze over rock. In this case, attempt to drytool rock features under the icy coating.

Thin ice is usually thicker on edges and small ledges over which it flows. These "ice-brows" can be twice as thick as the ice on a vertical plane only inches above or below. Not only are ice-brows thicker, but the pick is less likely to shear through because the ice is better supported by the rock underneath. The back of corners and cracks typically offers a thicker buildup of ice, too.

Small icicles that may appear too frail can sometimes be hooked. If you must swing, aim for the ice at the bottom supporting the icicle. On thin curtains find naturally occurring holes to slot your pick through or tap lightly to make your own hole.

Gentle, precise taps are required in order to not destroy thin ice.

Ice blobs are splatterings stuck to the rock from water dripping above. These bulbous features are fragile due to their convex nature. They can range in size from a tennis ball to a beach ball; both of which are usable for pick placements. Peck gently at them so they do not break. Hard swinging will surely knock them off.

On thin ice routes that have already seen previous ascents that season, search for preexisting pick placements in the ice instead of making your own. This is not only more efficient but will preserve the already minimal ice for future repeats.

Footwork on thin ice is just as demanding. Kicking will undoubtedly destroy what ice there is, so approach thin ice footwork like climbing rock. Gingerly place your front points on features. Monopoints can be drafted in your pick holes, eliminating the need to kick.

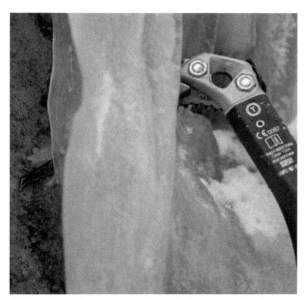

Chipping a hole to hook is the best method to deal with fragile thin-ice features.

CHAPTER 7

Leading Ice

Leaving behind the safety net of a toprope and tying into the sharp end of the rope to lead is a big step in an ice climber's progression. Solid, efficient movement is an ice leader's first line of defense. Movement skills should be so dialed that the chance of falling off becomes almost zero. So in that case, why bother placing screws? Why not just solo? The answer is because we are human and we make mistakes. Also, gear like crampon bails or ice tool picks can possibly break, and the abundance of overhead hazards means that there is always a chance something out of your control could make you fall.

Leading ice is a serious endeavor and should only be undertaken if a climber has:

- Ice-movement skills that have been consolidated and refined

- Taken a course on leading ice

- Seconded many pitches of ice while removing ice screws

- Executed a number of mock leads with no issues (physically or mentally)

- Chosen easy routes with good quality ice well below toprope ability

The Leader Must Not Fall

There must be absolutely *no* falling while leading ice. Unlike rock, the ice protection is more spread out, the medium is less predictable, the terrain tends to have more ledges, and an ice climber has too many sharp points attached to themselves (which can catch on the ice or stab body parts). Even on short falls, crampons can snag the ice, causing either broken ankles and legs or being flipped upside down—or both. Plus, a lead fall can endanger the whole climbing team.

Place lots of ice screws. There is no good reason to run it out on ice. Modern ice screws are light and place within a matter of seconds. Ice climbing falls are always bigger than anticipated, so stack the cards in your favor for the unexpected by placing screws every couple of body lengths. Also, choose routes with good quality ice and below your toproping limit so there is a broad margin of safety. If ice quality becomes poor or the climb feels too steep, be prepared to downclimb and/or rappel off from a V-thread. Downclimbing is a necessary leading skill that should be practiced on toprope before actually leading.

If you feel your hands becoming too cold or arms too pumped, then place a screw and hang on it. It is far better to rest and recover to re-group than pushing past your safety margin of grip strength and technique. If you find yourself hanging on screws regularly, you are probably trying routes that are too difficult for your ability and fitness. Your leading technique should be practiced and refined to the point that you can always at the very least place an ice screw with energy to spare. If not,

Samira Samimi leads the last pitch of Urs Hole (WI3, 150 m) in Banff National Park, Alberta, Canada.

The leader must not fall! If hands are cold or a bit pumped, then it is much better to place an ice screw and hang to recover (or retreat) than take a lead fall.

then more technique training on toprope or mock leads is required.

Some ice leaders will clip into their ice tool to hang for a rest, but this tactic should be avoided unless the situation is dire. If you do find yourself needing to hang off your tool, be aware that some clip-in holes on the bottom of ice tool grips are not rated for even body weight.

The low-angle ice often found on aprons at the bottom or at the top of steeper pitches must be treated with respect. It can be easy to fall into complacency and not move with as much focus as on the steeper sections or place less protection, but do not be lulled into a false sense of security. Gear can break, ice can fall on your head, crampons can skate off cold, hard ice—all of which could result in a fall. Leading ice is serious, and as an ice climbing leader it is your responsibility to choose routes well within your limit so not to unwittingly increase the overall hazard to the group. Leading ice climbing outings is done for the goals of the participants and not for the leader to push their own personal climbing agenda.

Dropped Tools

Dropping an ice tool while climbing on toprope is no big deal because you can just say "take" and lower back down. Of course, you might lose your tool in deep snow or hit someone below with it, but at least there is no lead-fall hazard. However, a dropped tool while leading can be a major issue. If the ice is good and your body position is stable, place an ice screw and lower back down to retrieve the tool. Or make an anchor so you can secure yourself, then lower down a loop of rope to pull your tool back up.

Bottom line, though, it is best to not drop ice tools, so prevention is key. Be aware of your ice tools at all times, and make sure that if you are letting go of one to shake out or place an ice screw, it is well planted in the ice. Despite being a somewhat popular technique, avoid hooking a tool over your shoulder when ice climbing. It is too easy for it to slip off your shoulder, so save this technique for low-commitment bolted mixed routes. If you cannot place the tool in the ice, then use a thumb catch by hooking the pick over the thumb of your other hand. This way you always have control of it.

Umbilical leashes can help prevent losing ice tools while leading.

Some ice climbers choose to use umbilical leashes that attach to the harness belay loop with a carabiner and have two lengths of bungee cord that clip into the bottom of each tool. This prevents losing an accidentally dropped tool but poses its own set of unique hazards. Leashes should not be used for single-pitch or toprope mixed climbing due to the hazard of them being flung toward the climber in a fall. When less experienced ice climbers second multi-pitch ice, umbilical leashes should be clipped to the rope and not the climber's harness, so if they fall the tools are not yanked out of the ice and rocketed toward the climber's head. Having said all that, umbilical leashes are indeed a benefit on more serious, runout thin ice or mixed terrain.

Mock Leads

When learning to lead ice, always practice by doing mock leads first. Mock leads are lead simulations

Mock leads are a great progression for practicing leading.

while on the security of a toprope. The simplest way to set up a mock lead is to tie into both the actual toprope as well as the bottom of the rope, which will become the mock lead strand for clipping into protection placed while toproping. Upon reaching the top of the mock lead, you can say "take" and lower on toprope. You will have to remove the protection (or at the very least unclip the mock-lead strand from the protection) or the belayer will run out of rope to lower. Another option instead of tying into the bottom of the rope is to bring an extra rope to use as the mock rope.

Fall Forces

Impact force and fall factor are two important concepts in the physics of climbing falls. To understand a climbing fall, it is important to recall a basic law of physics: When an object falls, it stores energy. It is important to understand the difference between forces on an anchor, whether it is a toprope belay, top-anchor belay, lead belay, or rappelling. If a climber (1 kN) simply hangs on a toprope, there will be twice their force on the toprope anchor (2 kN) due to the fact that the belayer's weight must equalize the equation from the belay side. Having said that, toprope forces can be higher due to slack belays or pendulum swings increasing forces as much as two and a half times. In a top-anchor belay though, a simple hang is a 1:1 ratio since there is no pulley effect multiplying the forces on the anchor. The same is true with rappelling; it is just the climber's weight on the anchor with no multiplication of forces. That is why slow, smooth rappelling is a much better practice than jumping with spurts of acceleration, which increases the climber's weight, thus putting more force on the rappel anchor.

The fall factor is often used to quantify the severity of a lead climbing fall. It can have a value between 0 and 2 in climbing. The fall factor is the ratio of fall length to rope length. In theory, the higher the fall factor, the higher the forces generated. The concept of severity as a function of fall factor is useful only with a dynamic rope. The more rope in play means the more energy it can absorb. This theoretical fall-factor model is rather simplistic; therefore it is more useful to talk about the actual fall factor.

Three factors that work together to absorb force in a fall are rope stretch, belay device slippage, and belayer displacement. Rope drag created by the friction of the rope running through quickdraws prevents the rope from stretching over its entire length. Thus only a part of the rope will absorb the energy of the fall. This is called effective rope length. It is clear that if a climber does not take the necessary steps to avoid rope drag, the actual fall factor can quickly increase. In this case, the fall will be more severe for the climber and put more force on the top protection point. The type of belay device is also a crucial component in reducing fall forces. Assisted-braking devices that lock automatically can put up to 30 percent more force on the top protection point due to their lack of rope slippage. The final energy absorber is belayer displacement. In sport climbing falls on summer rock routes, an experienced belayer will "jump" up with the fall (depending on differences in weight) to produce a "soft catch" (i.e., absorb force). In the ice climbing context, though, where ground anchors are often used to protect the belayer from falling ice, falling ice tools, getting yanked violently forward, and/or exposure to the crampon points of a falling climber, the belayer-displacement component is eliminated.

Ice Quality

The quality of ice is an important factor when placing ice tools, crampons, and screws. An ice climber must know how to identify and deal with various types of ice conditions. Conditions on even a short single-pitch route can change within a few moves from straightforward, secure climbing with ice screw placements wherever desired to challenging climbing with poor options for screws. Ideally, most types of ice will have been experienced to some degree on toprope before leading. It is much safer to learn the intricacies of chandeliered, delaminated, or sun-baked ice while on the security of toprope rather than the seriousness of lead.

Plastic

Plastic ice is the most user-friendly type of ice to climb because it willingly accepts ice tool picks and crampon front points with little force. It refers to ice that is soft but not very wet and goes by other pseudonyms such as "blue goo," "hero ice," and "one hit shit." It usually occurs during spells of warmer temperatures or on solar-facing routes. It is often deeply hued in color due to being moist and dense, unlike more aerated types of ice like chandeliered or sun baked.

Wet

Wet ice is a progression of plastic ice in that it is usually soft in texture but sometimes has become too saturated. Picks and crampon points penetrate easily. However, if the ice is too wet it can become slushy, making weaker ice screw placements.

Brittle

Brittle ice has been subjected to extended periods of cold temperatures and therefore is insecure to climb because tool and crampon placements take more effort to penetrate the hard surface, and the ice cracks and breaks more. Bulges, thin ice, and pillars are more fragile since the elasticity of the ice has been reduced.

Picked Out

Picked-out ice—also known as pegboard ice—occurs on popular, well-traveled ice climbs simply from overuse. The ice gets riddled with pick holes and steps, which can make it easier to climb, but at its extreme can be so pocked that the ice becomes fragile and tricky to find solid ice screw placements.

Picked-out ice is caused from many ascents.

Chandeliered

Chandeliered ice is essentially newly formed, unconsolidated icicles. It is not only difficult to get secure ice tool placements but also challenging to find solid, non-aerated ice for ice screw protection. Chandeliered ice can be either dry and brittle or wet and slushy, both of which are not great for climbing. Having said that, crampon placements can be satisfactory since they often break open large holes as footholds, despite ice tool picks feeling like they will shear.

Chandeliered ice is fresh, unconsolidated icicles.

Sun Baked

Solar-aspect ice, especially later in the season, will become sun affected, meaning the surface recrystalizes and bleaches white, almost becoming snowy in texture. This outer layer can sometimes offer easy ice tool placements since it is often soft, but if it is particularly rotten, it will have to be cleaned off to get to better ice beneath. The surface of sun-baked ice can also be quite unpredictable. Be wary that some placements might feel solid but can suddenly shear off large plates of ice that are not well bonded to the colder, denser ice below.

Snow Covered

Low-angled ice that is covered in snow is challenging to climb due to the fact that the snow needs to be tediously cleared away in order to sight pick placements. The insulating snow also creates a temperature gradient promoting sublimation, which degrades the quality of the ice surface. Onion skin is formed by water dripping on snow ledges, creating a hollow shell of thin ice over snow. It is fragile and can collapse easily.

Onion skin is formed by water dripping on snow ledges.

Delaminated

Delaminated ice means it is not bonded to the rock behind it and can be quite fragile since it is unsupported. Delamination can happen from temperature swings, solar radiation, or poor bonding with hard, smooth rock.

Swiss Cheese

Obvious rest stances and belay ledges on popular routes can develop Swiss cheese ice, which is ice riddled with holes from too many ice screws being drilled in a small area. This ultimately weakens the ice and makes finding new ice screw placements tricky. The best protection strategy in Swiss cheese ice is to use existing holes (re-bore) with large-diameter, aluminum-shaft ice screws.

Placing Ice Screws

There is no reason to run it out on ice climbs unless the ice quality is poor, but that is the realm of very experienced leaders. Modern ice screws are light and place quickly, so protect a pitch for the worst-case scenario. When first learning to lead, bring more than enough ice screws to put one in every body length. This will help ease the mental game of leading. As you become more comfortable with leading, stretching out the spacing to a couple of body lengths might seem reasonable. Regardless, place screws!

Racking

Racking strategy is critical for successful ice leading. Ice screws, quickdraws, and anchor gear must be organized and easily accessible. In some situations a shoulder-style gear sling may make sense, but usually all ice gear is racked on the harness's gear loops. This keeps the weight balanced at the body's center of gravity and also prevents the gear from annoyingly hanging in front of your body on lower-angled ice.

An ice climbing harness needs to have four gear loops on the waist belt and slots for adding racking clips (aka ice clippers), which are flat plastic, carabiner-like devices for carrying ice screws and ice tools. A harness should be equipped with a minimum of two racking clips (one on each side), but for leading ice it is advisable to have three or four total (two on the dominant side or two on each side). Racking clips should be located at your hip bones—not too far forward (screws jab into your thigh) and not too far back (can't easily see or reach them). Some climbing manufacturers now make racking clips that can be fitted onto a harness without slots, which allows better placement of the clip. Most racking clips have a flat shelf on top for temporarily setting a screw up and out of the way when a different screw length underneath is needed.

Screws should be racked with similar lengths together and with the teeth pointing behind. The forward two gear loops on each side of the harness should be reserved for runners (quickdraws and alpine draws), while the back two gear loops are where anchor, belay, and rescue gear is stowed.

Racking clips are necessary for racking ice screws on the harness.

Two racking clips on each side of the harness allow similar length screws to be racked together.

Of the back two gear loops, choose the one that is more easily reachable for the gear you will need continuously for each belay (belay device, anchor package, locking carabiner). Put the gear that you do not need at every belay (cordelette, rappel prusik, V-thread hooker, personal tether) on the less reachable back gear loop.

A standard ice rack may look something like this:

- four 13 cm screws
- eight 16 cm screws
- two 19 to 22 cm screws

If the route is thin or it is early season, it would be wise to swap some 16 cm screws for more 13 cm screws and even bring a few 10 cm screws. A longer 21 cm or 22 cm screw should be carried by each climber as personal equipment for making V-threads.

Prepping the Ice

The ice must be evaluated and sometimes prepared before placing an ice screw for protection. Ice screws not only need to be placed in dense ice of high quality to be strong, but flat, smooth surfaces also make spinning them in more efficient. Depressions, bumps, and ridges of ice can interfere with the hanger. Before grabbing an ice screw, identify where you want to place it and make sure the area is appropriate—a 20-centimeter (8-inch) diameter circle of planar ice is ideal. Such features often exist naturally, especially on rolling, low-angle ice flows. However, steeper sections of ice might have an irregular surface and need to be prepped. This can be as simple as chipping off small bumps with the pick of your ice tool, or it can require knocking off larger chunks or dinner plates. Regardless of the amount of cleaning needed, be sure to chip and swing *away* from your body. This is important so you do not accidentally miss and swing the pick into your stomach or leg (see photo on page 55). Choking up on the upper grip of the ice tool helps control the cleaning action.,

Swing and chip away from your body when prepping the ice surface for a scew so not to accidently stab yourself with the pick.

Before placing an ice screw, move the ice tool up and out of the way.

After prepping the ice surface for a screw, it is a good idea to plant the tool up and out of the way. Even if prepping is not required, it is still a good idea to move that lower tool out of the way so as not to inadvertently knock it off. It is not unheard of to have the tool too close and be hyper-focused on spinning the screw, then accidentally send the tool flying when your hand smacks it out of the ice.

One-handed Placements

Placing ice screws with one hand while hanging onto an ice tool with the other hand can be strenuous. Luckily, modern ice screws that are well maintained will place very quickly.

Remove the appropriate length screw by grabbing the tube and rotating the hanger against the gate of the racking clip so it snaps off. Adjust the screw in your hand by placing your index and middle finger around the tube near the hanger with the end of the screw against your palm. Place the screw somewhere between chest and waist height and close to your body so you can push solidly. The key to getting the screw started is cranking your wrist as far counterclockwise as possible, then pushing hard and turning slowly so the teeth bite in that first half to three-quarter turn. If it does not bite and grab on the first try, re-crank your wrist and do it again, ensuring that you are pushing hard and turning slowly—push hard, turn slow is the key to making it stick. Another trick is to put a bit of downward pressure on the screw while turning, so the threads grab.

The screw needs to bite securely into the ice so you can let go of it to re-crank your wrist for another turn. This first half to three-quarter turn leaves the screw vulnerable to falling. One way to prevent it from falling is to maintain constant contact with the screw by clasping the tube near the hanger with your index and middle finger as you reset your wrist for another turn. Repeat this process four or five times, or until the screw is 3

Start the screw at waist to chest height by pushing hard and turning slow while holding it between your index and middle finger.

Keep your index and middle finger around the tube to prevent dropping it as you reset your wrist for another turn.

After about four to six turns, the screw should be steady enough to spin it the rest of the way in with the crank knob.

to 4 centimeters (1.2 to 1.6 inches) in the ice and not wobbling. At this point the crank knob can be flipped out and the screw spun in until the hanger is flush with the ice. Always flip the crank knob back in immediately after placing a screw. It cannot be left flipped out because the rope could catch on it.

It is important to be able to place ice screws equally well with either hand. Of course, most climbers have a dominant hand, but the weaker hand can be trained. Be sure to practice placing screws on your weaker side on toprope or mock leads. The goal is to become ambidextrous, because even though you might be predominantly right-handed, the good ice for placements could easily be on the left side of the line you are climbing.

Clipping

Clipping refers to attaching a quickdraw or other type of runner to an ice screw, then clipping the rope into the bottom carabiner. The gates of both carabiners on a quickdraw need to face the same way, away from the direction of travel. This prevents the gates from being pushed into ice features with the tension of the rope and accidentally nudged open (thereby reducing their strength by a third).

Clipping a quickdraw into an ice screw hanger is trickier than one might think. Since the gates of the quickdraw need to be facing away from the direction of travel, the ice screw usually spins a bit

The pinch clipping technique works best with gloves on.

Be sure the gates of quickdraws are facing away from the direction of travel.

when a carabiner gate is pushed into the screw hanger. The solution for this problem is to push the carabiner gate downward onto the hanger instead of sideways. This will prevent it from spinning. Of course, this is a non-issue with left-handed placements, because when the carabiner gate is pushed against the hanger, it is tightening the screw into the ice (righty tighty).

Clipping the rope into the quickdraw is similar to rock climbing except with the added bulk of gloves. There are a few different techniques for clipping, but the pinch clip seems the most appropriate for ice climbing since the gates are almost always facing away. With the rope in your palm, place the thumb on the spine and the middle finger on the nose, using the index finger to roll the rope against the gate.

Front-Point Stance

There are two main stances for placing ice screws: the front-point stance and the side-step stance. Of course, there can be slight variations of these two, but in most instances, one of these two stances should be used. The front-point stance is for steep or featureless ice and tends to be the default of the two stances.

The front-point stance is essentially the swinging position discussed in Chapter 6 but taking the extra time to fully ensure that all the components of the swinging position are exact, including wide, level feet, hips in, and arm directly over the head with a slight bend at the elbow. Also, it is prudent to kick out the crampon placements a bit more than normal and plant the tool a bit deeper, so all attachment points to the ice are 100 percent solid. Before placing a screw, remove the unused ice tool and use it to clear away and prepare the ice for a screw, then place the tool high and to the side. This facilitates two things: 1) It is out of the way and can't be mistakenly knocked off, and 2) it is available to shake out on if the main gripping hand gets fatigued.

The front-point stance for placing/removing ice screws.

Side-Step Stance

The side-step stance is mainly for lower-angled ice with ledges and pronounced features. Use it when a large enough flat surface is present to place one foot on sideways, thus taking the strain off the calf muscles. It works well on ledges, bulges, and mushroom features. Kick out and improve the hold with front points so it is level (not angled), then place the foot sideways on the hold with the inside of the foot against the ice. Straighten the leg; all your body weight should be standing on your heel. The opposite hand to the foot that is sideways should be gripping an ice tool directly above and in vertical

The side-step stance for placing/removing ice screws.

takes experience to judge. An ice flow may be narrow and only present one reasonable line to climb, but more often than not, a frozen waterfall will offer a variety of possible lines of ascent. As a novice ice leader, it is critical to be able to choose the easiest line on a given flow of ice. There are a variety of factors that contribute to what makes a line easier or harder. Just because an ice climb is assigned a WI grade doesn't mean there can't be a wide range of possible difficulties within that given grade.

Slab versus Steep

Lower-angled slabs of ice are less physically strenuous than dead vertical pillars. A wide flow of ice will often present both low-angle and steep lines to choose from. Despite low-angle ice sometimes feeling awkward, it is often easier since pretty much all of a climber's weight will be on their feet. Of course, calf muscles take more of the brunt, but legs will always be stronger than arms.

Grooves versus Arêtes

Inside corner features (grooves) are easier to climb than outside corners (arêtes) because they feel less steep. Even shallow grooves allow hips room to move inward, putting more weight on feet and less on arms. Outside corners are not only awkward for crampon placements but also push hips outward, forcing more weight onto arms.

Wet versus Dry

Wet ice is generally easier to climb than dry ice because it is softer to penetrate. Dry, cold ice is often hard and brittle, causing cracking and breaking and often requiring more swinging to achieve solid pick placements. However, wet ice can often become too wet, to the point that pick placements can shear through wet chandelier icicles. Also, very wet ice that is flowing with water will soak your rope, gloves, and even your whole body. The ideal ice to climb is what ice climbers call plastic ice— soft but not soaking wet.

alignment with the sideways foot, creating a balanced stance. If the right foot is sideways, then the left hand is gripping a tool directly above your head. The non-sideways foot can be lightly placed behind the back of the sideways foot but should not take any weight. This allows your body to be 45 degrees to the ice, and you now can easily place ice screws from a balanced and restful position.

Line Selection

Choosing an appropriate line to climb on a frozen waterfall, whether you are toproping or leading,

Picked Out versus Fresh

Ice generally becomes easier to climb with more travel. Bad quality ice gets knocked off, snow on the surface gets cleared, pick placements form, and steps for crampons become big and obvious. Fresh ice, especially if it is cold, dry, and brittle, takes much more energy to climb, requiring more swinging and kicking. Popular ice climbs often get to the point where you can climb them without any swinging or kicking. This hooked-out ice is called pegboard. Unfortunately, some well-traveled ice can become so pegboarded that it is tricky to find good ice for ice screw placements.

Protection Strategy

The primary protection when leading ice climbs are ice screws, but you could also encounter traditional rock gear, slung ice features, V-threads, bolts, and trees. Be sure to rack up with enough screws, including enough for the anchor (if required) and in case some get dropped or frozen. Ice screws should be placed with the following considerations:

- Space evenly (one to three body lengths apart)
- Protect the cruxes (bulges, technical sections)
- Use natural rest stances (ledges, mushrooms)
- Take advantage of good ice

Placing ice screws about one to two body lengths apart is a good spacing for novice ice leaders. And remember to always protect the bulge.

Runners

Runners are made from nylon sling material of varying lengths with two non-locking carabiners for connecting lead protection to the rope. Options for runners include:

- **Quickdraws:** These are the main type of runners used when leading ice for ice climbing. They are light and efficient for easy clipping with gloves on.

- **Alpine draws:** Unlike traditionally protected rock climbing, an ice climbing leader needs very few of these since rope drag does not tend to be an issue on ice routes. It is still a good idea to have a few, though, for changes in direction, changes in angle, and off-line placements (behind a pillar or under a curtain).

- **Double-length slings:** Long 120 cm slings with two non-locking carabiners can be used in the same way as alpine draws for off-line placements that could potentially cause rope drag. They are also good for slinging trees and chockstones as lead protection.

- **Load-limiter draws:** These can reduce peak force in the event of a high fall factor by 1 to 2 kN. They tend to be more bulky than regular quickdraws but having a few is prudent for protecting the anchor and first couple of protection ice screws until enough rope is in play.

- **Locker draws:** One locker draw should be carried for critical protection points. These are the same as quickdraws but have locking carabiners on each end.

Rope Management

Managing the rope is an important aspect of leading a pitch of ice. It is easy to be overly focused on looking up (route finding) but looking down is almost equally critical to ensure that the rope is running how you want it to. Every time an ice screw is placed for protection, the ice climbing leader needs to look down and make any adjustments by flicking the rope and setting it where it needs to be. Once you are above the new protection, it will be much trickier to adjust the rope below it.

Some considerations for rope management include:

- **Ice screw:** Be sure the rope is not hooked on the ice screw hanger, and the crank knob is flipped in so the rope cannot catch on it.

- **Footwork:** The rope should never be behind the leader's leg or ankle. If the leader were to fall, they would be flipped upside down.

- **Dry ice:** Try to keep the rope running over dry ice and away from wet ice.

- **Protecting the second:** Consider the second following the pitch and be sure to protect traverses adequately.

- **Anchor position:** Choose a belay stance for the anchor that allows for easy rope management at the belay (and not exposed to falling ice on the next pitch). When standing on the belay ledge, the anchor's master point should be positioned at chest level.

Be sure that the rope is never behind your leg when leading.

Rope Systems

There are three main rope systems to choose from for leading ice: single rope, half ropes, and twin ropes. There is no one system that is perfect for every route. All three have pros and cons and understanding their merits will help you choose which one will serve you best. Most experienced ice climbers will own both a single rope and a double-rope system, and choose which one makes the most sense depending on the objective.

Single Rope

Single rope is the simplest system because it is just one rope. It is suitable for cragging as well as multi-pitch routes that have walk-offs or short rappels. Two single ropes work well in a team of three in either linked caterpillar roping or split parallel roping (see page 165), since both following climbers need to be tied into a single-rated rope. Triple-rated ropes are lighter for the leader when parallel split roping but be aware of stretch.

If a team of two requires two ropes for rappelling, a skinny tag line can be trailed by the leader. This adds a bit more rope management but facilitates double-rope rappels. It also means the leader's pack can be hauled on more challenging pitches. If the tag line's diameter is within a 3-millimeter difference of the lead line, they can be joined together with a regular flat overhand knot. If using skinny 5.5 mm static Spectra cord as a tag line, the Reepschnur method should be used (see page 99).

Half Ropes

Half ropes are a double-rope system designed to be used in pairs. The strands should be clipped separately into alternating protection points throughout the route, because clipping both ropes into one screw increases the force on the protection point if a fall were to occur. A half rope system reduces rope drag on wandering routes, facilitates longer rappels, and provides redundancy on risky terrain. Half ropes can only be used as a team of two. They will not work for a team of three because a following climber needs to be tied into both ropes. They are not as popular for ice climbing but have some merit for traditionally protected mixed routes where the gear may not always be in a straight line.

Twin Ropes

Twin ropes are also a double-rope systems designed to be used in pairs but with both strands clipped together into every protection point. Think of them as one rope for going up and two ropes for going down. Like half ropes, the twin rope system also facilitates longer rappels and provides redundancy in case one of the strands is cut or damaged by a falling object, a sharp edge, or ice tools/crampons. Twin ropes can work well for multi-pitch ice climbing because they are lightweight and enable full-length rappels but can complicate rescue systems. Like half ropes, they will not work with a team of three since both climbers need to be tied into both ropes.

Lead Belaying

Lead belaying is a means of feeding the climbing rope through a belay device, which introduces slack into the lead climbing system and enables the climber to progress uninhibited by the rope. When lead belaying with either a manual- or an assisted-braking belay device, the friction-creating properties of the device are unchanged from those of a toprope belay. Friction is created by forcing tight bends in the rope or enabling the binding action of the belay device to properly engage. Depending on the type of belay device used, the belay pattern will vary. Similar to toprope belaying, the belayer's brake hand must maintain control of the brake rope at all times and be in the most mechanically advantageous position when slack is not being introduced or removed from the lead climbing system.

Manual-braking, tube-style devices often provide a smoother belay since slack is easily paid out.

Assisted-braking devices can be more finicky to pay out rope but will lock even if the brake hand momentarily lets go. One important detail to note with assisted-braking devices is that they place 30 percent more force on the top protection point in a fall due to the fact there is no rope slippage through the device.

Ground Anchor

Belayers should always assume a sideways, athletic stance ready to anticipate a load on the forward braced leg (opposite leg to the brake hand).

Standing facing forward with feet side by side can result in the belayer being yanked forward and potentially losing control of the rope. Ground anchors (aka back anchors) should always be considered for lead belays, because the belay will almost always be rendered ineffective if standing far enough away to avoid any overhead ice fall hazard.

Something to keep in mind, though, is that since ground anchors limit belayer displacement if a fall were to occur, more impact force will be put on the protection; therefore, assisted-braking belay devices should not be used when ground anchors

A ground anchor should always be considered for a lead belay on ice so the belayer can stand off to the side away from ice fall and crampons.

are incorporated. Also, the lack of belayer displacement can mean a harder fall for the leader, but this is better than the belayer getting injured and not being able to arrest the fall at all. Finally and most importantly, if using a ground anchor, be absolutely sure that the belayer is positioned out of the way of ice fall hazard, since they will be unable to move far. A common error is to miscalculate the extent of the icefall drop zone and "trap" the belayer in the line of fire. Ice always seems to fall and ricochet much farther than anticipated, so keep that in mind. If partway through a lead it becomes obvious that the ground anchor and belayer's position are exposed to the leader's ice fall, then the belayer must relocate to a safer stance. The bottom line is that a belayer must never be exposed to overhead hazard. If the belayer gets hit and hurt by ice fall, then there is no belay.

Considerations for ground anchors:

- Is the belayer exposed to ice fall or dropped ice tools by standing too close?

- Is the belayer exposed to being struck by the leader's crampons if they fall?

Do not ground anchor under a hanging dagger.

Do not belay far away without a ground anchor.

Do not belay directly below an ice leader.

- Is the belayer exposed to being yanked forward (especially with a low first protection point), smacking into the ice or rock?
- Is the belayer exposed to being pulled upward in an ice cave into hanging icicles?
- Is the belayer exposed to being pulled upward under a rock overhang and hitting their head?

Fixed-Point Lead Belay

Fixed-point lead belay (FPLB) is the method of belaying the leader from a fixed point directly off the anchor as opposed to from the harness belay loop. The technique has been in use in Europe for some time and, though slow to catch on in North America, is gaining momentum, especially for ice climbing. Force is transferred directly to the anchor in the event of a fall, and the belayer provides the braking action only. It is a very useful belaying technique for multi-pitch ice climbs where a fall factor 2 fall onto the anchor is possible. Exiting ice caves onto steep pillars is a prime example of a situation that benefits from a fixed-point lead belay. FPLBs do not work in every situation though, for example, if the belayer needs to extend themselves away from the anchor to be clear of falling ice.

Fixed-point lead belay with a Munter hitch from a bowline configuration.

FPLBs can use either a Munter hitch or a regular manual-braking device. The Munter hitch is more versatile for ice climbing because the brake is omni-directional so will work for both a fall factor 2 downward force (begins to slip at 3-4 kN) and an upward force (begins to slip at 2-3 kN). Learning how to allow the Munter to slip is the key to dissipating fall force. For a Munter hitch belay, use a triple-action, captive-eye locking carabiner with the gate facing toward the direction of travel. A manual-braking device can be used but only in combination with a redirect on the brake strand until at least two reliable protection points (e.g., solid bolts) are clipped by the leader. Since ice screws are challenging to assess, they are not considered fully reliable protection in this situation; therefore the redirected brake strand should always be kept

Fixed-point lead belay with a Munter hitch from a modified figure-eight configuration.

Fixed-point lead belay with a manual-braking device from a bowline configuration on bolts. Note the re-directed brake strand in case of a fall factor 2 fall.

in place with a manual-braking device, which can make the belaying awkward. As with all new techniques, training and practice is required for comfort and ease of use.

Consider using a FPLB when there is:

- Higher potential for a leader fall (difficult grade, bad ice)

- Potential for high impact force (high fall factor)

- Potential for a long leader fall (thin ice routes, runouts)

- Potential for harm to the belayer (icicles overhead)

- Problem maintaining the integrity of the belay (inexperienced, small or lightweight belayer, icy ropes, poor stance)

The anchor configuration and setup is slightly different, so you need to anticipate if you are going to use a FPLB while constructing the anchor. Considerations for anchor setup include:

- Use a modified figure-eight anchor configuration or a banshee belay (bowline on a bight equalized with a clove hitch) with a small (5 cm/2 in.) double-strand loop as the fixed point for the belay carabiner.

- Vertically oriented ice screws work best for the anchor.

- Dyneema, nylon webbing, or accessory cord (minimum 7 mm) can be used.

- Use a minimum of two multi-directional pieces of good quality (two ice screws, two modern bolts).

- Minimize fixed-point travel distance to 20 centimeters (8 inches) (fixed-point plus carabiner plus belay device).

- Anchor should allow for efficient rope handling (i.e., the fixed point should be about chest height).

Other considerations include:

- With most anchor-building materials (7 mm cord, 8 mm Dyneema), it is necessary to create a double loop (two strands of material) at the fixed point to achieve full anchor strength (about 20 kN).

- It is recommended to clip the fixed-point loop to the anchor with a small locking carabiner since there will be a lot of movement during a possible fall.

- It is recommended that with ice screw anchors, the belay carabiner be clipped through the fixed-point loop as well as the shelf to equalize load to both screws if a fall factor 2 fall were to occur.

- With a two-bolt anchor, there is no attempt to equalize the bolts. The fixed point is offset to just one of the anchor bolts (with the other bolt acting as a non-equalized backup).

- Avoid clipping the belay carabiner directly to a fixed protection (e.g., bolt hanger, ice screw hanger) because it can torque and twist, reducing strength.

Fixed-Point Lead Belay FAQ

Won't the Munter hitch twist the rope badly?

There is a common misconception that belaying with a Munter hitch (also known as an Italian hitch) will twist the rope. If used correctly the Munter hitch will not add twists. The key is to keep the brake strand and the climber's strand parallel to one another. This trick also holds true for lowering with a Munter. Be sure that the strand you are gripping enters the hitch parallel to the loaded lowering strand.

Won't all the force be on a single anchor screw in a lead fall?

Yes, the lowest ice screw in the anchor takes all the force of a lead fall, but it is important to keep in mind that the maximum upward force in a lead fall is approximately 4 kN onto a screw that should be able to withstand at least 10 kN. Also, the Munter hitch in an upward force orientation will begin to slip at 2-3 kN, thus reducing peak force on the screw. And finally, if that lower screw did fail, then the fall force comes onto the belayer via their clove hitch attachment to the anchor, therefore providing another 1 kN of ballast backing up the screw (2 kN if a team of three with two climbers hanging off the anchor).

Shouldn't you clip the highest screw of the anchor to prevent a factor 2?

The short answer is "no." In the worse-case scenario of a factor 2, it is better for the fall force to be arrested by two equalized ice screws than the two-times multiplication of force that would occur on the single clipped ice screw from the pulley effect.

Won't this make for very hard falls on the leader?

It shouldn't if rope is allowed to slip through the Munter hitch. The Munter hitch will begin to slip between 3 and 4 kN in its strongest orientation with rope strands parallel (i.e fall factor 2) and between 2 and 3 kN in its open position with an upward force.

How do I use double ropes with a FPLB?

Both twin- and half-rope systems can be use with a Munter hitch, but twin ropes definitely work better since the ropes feed out together as one unit. Using a manual-braking device simplifies double-rope systems, but the brake strand needs to be redirected until at least two fully reliable protection points are clipped by the leader, which is not always possible to achieve or evaluate with ice screws.

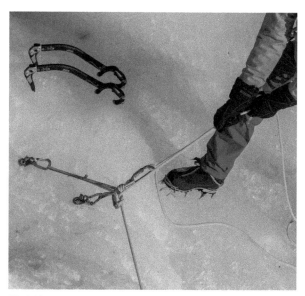

Holding a lead fall with a fixed-point lead belay.

- Clipping the belay carabiner to the welded ring on the Fixe ring anchor is okay though.
- Double-rope systems can be used with a Munter hitch but work best with a manual-braking device.
- Always wear gloves.

Multi-Pitch Systems

A multi-pitch ice route could be as few as two pitches all the way up to twenty and beyond. Multi-pitch ice climbing depends on a flow of well-refined systems and protocols. Longer ice routes are most efficiently completed as a team of two, but a team of three is manageable with solid rope management. Longer climbs can be more committing than single-pitch crag routes, where if something goes wrong, you can usually just lower back to the ground.

A multi-pitch outing also means bringing more gear that needs to be carried up a route. A leader should be solid enough that they feel comfortable carrying a pack with the essentials. A small pack (20 liters) is often ideal to carry extra gloves, belay jacket, snacks, thermos, and emergency gear like a first-aid kit and communication device. If the route is in avalanche terrain, a slightly larger pack (30 liters) will be required to carry a shovel and probe as well. It is rare to haul a pack on waterfall ice climbs, but sometimes a leader may also choose to not wear a pack on difficult and steep routes, especially if they are short (only a couple of pitches) and not in avalanche terrain. An alternative to carrying a pack is to clip various essentials to your harness. A belay jacket in a stuff sack, a first-aid kit, and extra gloves can all be clipped to the back of the harness. This takes the weight off your shoulders and places it at your center of gravity, which might feel less strenuous as long as you do not mind things swinging around from your waist.

Securing with a Clove Hitch

Securing to an anchor with a clove hitch on the climbing rope enables easy adjustments to the length of the tether. This is primarily used in the multi-pitch climbing context, as it allows the ice climbing leader and participants to position themselves comfortably for belaying. It is also full strength, uses minimal equipment (only one locking carabiner), and has some limited dynamic properties (small amount of stretch and tightening knots). To tether to the anchor using the climbing rope, the climber needs to be tied into the climbing rope with a figure-eight follow-through knot, with the

When constructing an anchor at the end of a lead, be sure to clip the rope to the first ice screw that you place with a quickdraw in order to protect yourself. This allows you to use two hands to place the second ice screw, equalize the anchor, and clip in with a clove hitch. If the first ice screw has two holes in its hanger, clip the upper secondary hole, leaving the lower hole for the actual anchor carabiner.

rope then connected to the anchor's master point (not the shelf) with a clove hitch on a locking carabiner.

Protocols

Belay commands are even more important in a multi-pitch context compared to toproping because the belayer and climber can be a full rope length away and fully out of sight. This can add to complications with communication. Be sure with each command to turn your head in the direction of your partner and take a deep breath to holler the command loud and clear. Small two-way radios can make this easier but are not a replacement for loud and clear commands since they can be dropped or batteries can die. Rope signals by way of tugs should be avoided since this can add to confusion. The best line of defense against tricky communication situations is a solid understanding of the protocols. If both the belayer and leader have a clear picture in their head of what the other is doing, even hard-to-hear commands will make better sense.

Belayer: "On belay!" Partner check is complete, the belay system is set up, and the lead climber may begin climbing when ready.

Leader: "Climbing!" The leader begins to climb from either the ground or the anchor (unclips).

Leader: "Secure!" After the leader constructs their anchor and secures themselves with a clove hitch into the master point. The leader then attaches their belay device in auto-brake mode to the master point or the shelf of the anchor so it is ready to be used. If the leader forgets to do this before pulling up the excess rope, it will be awkward to do one-handed since the other hand will be holding the weight of the rope.

Belayer: "Off belay!" Only say this after the rope is free from the belay device, since it is the leader's cue to start pulling in the excess rope.

Belayer: "That's me!" When the excess rope is all pulled up and comes tugging on the belayer's harness (on the ground) or clove hitch (at a

Secure, Off Belay, or Safe

There are a few different commands climbers use to announce that they have secured themselves to an anchor with a clove hitch or personal tether and therefore do not require a belay anymore. In Canada, we use "secure," but the United States uses "off belay" and the UK uses "safe." Different words that all mean the same thing: take me off belay. Regardless of the command you use, be sure to communicate beforehand with your partner what your preference is so there is no confusion.

multi-pitch anchor). This is the leader's cue to put the rope into the auto-braking belay device.

Leader: "On belay!" After doing a visual and physical check that the auto-braking belay is set up correctly. A physical function check is done by actually yanking on the belayer's strand of the rope to make sure it locks, then pulling on the brake strand to see that it slides.

Belayer: "Climbing!" Let's the leader know that the belayer is leaving the ground or multi-pitch belay stance after the anchor has been removed.

Belay Transitions

Efficiency is key to multi-pitch ice climbing in order to keep belay transitions smooth and quick. The entire transition should only take a couple of minutes if the leader and second understand the protocols and steps. Rope management to avoid tangles is the first step to efficiency. If possible, the easiest method is to stack the rope in a tight pile on the ground or ledge. If there is a chance that the piled stack of rope could slip off the ledge, it will need to be lap coiled across clove-hitched rope in even loops that just barely touch the ground. In addition, if the ledge is wet or if the rope is wet and the ledge is covered in loose snow, then also resort to lap coiling to keep the rope from getting too wet or caked in snow.

The following is a step-by-step description of the belay transition process for a team of two that is swinging leads (alternating the leader every pitch):

1. Climber A is the leader belaying up the second, who is climber B

2. As climber B nears the belay, climber A must decide what side they want climber B to be on. This will depend on which direction the next pitch goes. Climber B should be on the side that they will lead out on so that they do not have to climb over the anchor and expose the belayer to their crampons.

3. If climber B is approaching the anchor on the same side that they will also lead out on, then nothing needs to be done.

4. However, if climber B needs to be on the other side for the next pitch, then climber A must duck under the rope just before climber B reaches the belay.

5. When climber B gains the anchor, climber A ties an overhand on a bight on the brake strand as a backup so climber B can lean back on the rope and be secure.

6. Climber A hands over any extra ice screws and runners that they did not use on the previous pitch so that climber B (the new leader) has everything for the next pitch.

7. If a fixed-point lead belay is being used for the next pitch, climber A adds the Munter hitch to the fixed-point loop of the anchor to put climber B on belay. If a regular lead belay is being used, climber A takes climber B's belay device and puts climber B on belay from their belay loop.

8. A personal check and partner check must be completed at this stage. Harness buckles and tie-in knots should still be fine, but check that the belay system is set up properly and that the locking carabiner is indeed locked.

9. If using a fixed-point lead belay, the leader (climber B) can now undo the auto-braking device and take it with them for the next pitch. If using a regular lead belay, the leader (climber B) grabs rope behind the auto-braking device and clips a redirected quickdraw from the anchor's shelf to eliminate a factor 2 fall. Climber B then unclips their clove hitch from the anchor's master point.

10. Climber B immediately places an ice screw to protect the anchor from a direct factor 2 fall.

One trick for efficiency when swinging leads and using a regular lead belay from the harness belay loop is swapping belay devices at the transition (described in step 7). This saves climber B from the extra step of clove hitching into the anchor. It is much more efficient to simply lean back on the auto-braking device and add a backup knot (overhand on a bight) to the brake strand. Climber B then gives their belay device to climber A and takes climber A's device when they undo the auto-braking device and leave the anchor for their lead. Of course, with a fixed-point lead belay, there is no need to swap devices if the recommended Munter hitch is being used.

Multi-pitch transition (A): Place first anchor screw while holding onto ice tool.

Multi-pitch transition (B): Clip quickdraw into the first screw to protect yourself while placing the second screw with both hands.

Multi-pitch transition (C): Use sling to equalize the two screws to a master point.

Multi-pitch transition (D): Clove hitch (between harness and quickdraw) into the master point of the anchor with a locking carabiner.

Multi-pitch transition (E): Lean back on clove hitch to perform a function test before shouting "secure!"

Multi-pitch transition (F): Before pulling in excess rope, be sure to pre-place auto-braking belay device in shelf of the anchor.

Multi-pitch transition (G): When rope comes tight and belayer says "that's me!" remove the bite of rope from the quickdraw and put it in the auto-braking belay device.

Multi-pitch transition (H): Before shouting "On belay!" test that the auto-braking belay device is set up properly by yanking on the strand of rope going down to your partner to make sure it locks.

Multi-pitch transition (I): Belay partner up always maintaining a hand on the brake strand.

Multi-pitch transition (J): As your partner approaches the anchor, decide what side you want them on depending on which direction the next pitch goes. If you want them on the other side of you, then duck under the rope.

Multi-pitch transition (K): Tie an overhand on a bight in the brake strand so your partner is secured by the backed-up auto-braking device.

Multi-pitch transition (L): Make sure that the new leader has all the ice screws and runners for the next lead.

Multi-pitch transition (M): Put the leader on a fixed-point lead belay with a Munter hitch. If using a harness lead belay, then the new leader gives their belay device to the belayer and then takes the belay device that is in the anchor when they leave. The rope must also be clipped through the shelf of the anchor to prevent a potential fall factor 2.

Multi-pitch transition (N): Protect the anchor immediately with an ice screw.

Block Leading

Block leading is when one climber leads a block of pitches in a row. A block could be anywhere from two pitches to an entire route but tends to be about three to five pitches before the lead is switched. Block leading is more efficient because one person is in the lead zone. They get a rest while belaying the second and a chance to scope the next pitch, so are mentally and physically ready to lead again as soon as the second reaches the anchor. Block leading also helps keep everyone warmer because the second will arrive at the anchor warm from climbing before the leader begins to chill off.

Leading in blocks is essentially what guides do. They lead all the pitches for their client. The same holds true for a more experienced ice climber taking a novice up a route. The steps are the same except the leader brings the second into the side of the anchor opposite from the direction of the next pitch. Also, all gear including ice screws, runners, and anchor materials need to be transferred back to the leader.

When block leading, there is a slight variation to step 5 in the above-described belay transition. When climber B arrives at climber A's anchor after following the previous pitch, climber A grabs a locking carabiner from climber B's harness and clove hitches them into the master point. This way climber B can hang onto their ice tools while climber A feeds out some slack to make the clove hitch. The clove hitch should be made between climber B's figure-eight follow-through knot and the auto-braking device. It is always better for the person at the anchor to clove hitch their partner into the anchor because they know their own anchor, and also because it is better for the second (climber B) to be stable by holding onto their ice tools.

The stack of rope also needs to be readjusted so the leader is back on top of the stack. If it is piled on a ledge, scoop up the pile and give it a flip. If it is lap coils and they are fairly uniform, have the belayer move their hands out of the way and flip the whole lap coil onto their clove-hitched rope. If the lap coil loops are uneven or messy, have the belayer restack the lap coils themselves.

Protecting the Anchor

When an ice climber leads off from a multi-pitch anchor, their priority is to protect the anchor from a high-force fall (i.e., factor 2). The best strategy is to place multiple pieces of protection immediately off the anchor. A common but not recommended practice is to clip the highest screw in an ice screw anchor to prevent a factor 2 fall. While this is a suitable practice for bolted anchors, it is poor practice

ALWAYS protect the anchor by placing an ice screw right away to prevent a fall directly onto the anchor (fall factor 2).

for ice screw anchors. The reason is that in a worst-case scenario this clipped screw will be exposed to a 1.9 fall factor, which could theoretically generate as much as 14 to 15 kN on the single screw—ultimately resulting in it being ripped out and the entire team hanging on the one remaining anchor screw or, worse, total anchor failure. To prevent this, extend the belayer on their clove hitch and clip the master point or the shelf of the anchor as the first runner; better yet, use a fixed-point lead belay to belay the leader (and still place an early first screw).

Team of Three

Multi-pitch ice routes are more efficiently completed as a team of two. However, a team of three can be almost as efficient if everyone has solid rope management skills. Plus, a team of three is more social. It is way less lonely to share a cold belay with a partner than shiver on your own. And double plus, a team of three can be safer. If something goes wrong and one person gets injured or buried, there are twice as many people to perform a rescue.

A team of three requires more advanced rope management skills and efficiency. Route selection is also very important. Choose routes that are not too long and have decent-sized ledges and caves for belay stances. Block leading (one leader for a few pitches) on longer routes works best with a team of three because there are fewer prolonged periods of inactivity. Block leading also means rope ends only need to be untied and swapped around every few pitches rather than every pitch.

Ideally, the two seconds follow the pitches one at a time—to maximize experience and minimize hazards—with the middle climber trailing the second rope and clipping key directional points for the third climber. This is called caterpillar or linked roping. It can work well on a two-pitch climb where the first climber leads the first pitch, then the middle climber seconds trailing the other rope for the third climber. Once everyone is at the belay, the third climber becomes the leader and the

Caterpillar or link roping with a team of three.

caterpillar plays out in reverse. This eliminates the need for restacking ropes or untying to swap ends, but also means a lot of standing around for the first climber.

Split parallel roping with a team of three. Note that the two ropes come together through the final ice screw so they enter the auto-braking belay device parallel, reducing the chance of rope slippage if the ropes are weighted simultaneously in a fall.

ALWAYS use directional ice screws to keep the ropes separated so the two seconds never end up above one another. This dangerous situation exposes the bottom climber to not only falling ice but also crampon points if the upper climber was to fall.

> Multi-pitch climbing with a team of three needs to be completed with two single- or triple-rated ropes—one for each climber following. A seconding climber cannot be tied into only one strand of a half- or twin-rated rope system. Half and twin ropes are meant to be used together for a team of two where both climbers are tied into both ends of both ropes. A half or twin rope is too thin and has too much stretch to be used on its own.

Split parallel roping is when the leader decides to climb with both ropes and belay both seconds at the same time. This is definitely advanced multi-pitch technique and requires well-refined rope management as well as more advanced rescue skills if something goes awry. One trick for parallel roping is to clip the second trailing rope into your belay loop with a locking carabiner instead of tying in. This makes it easier to adjust for tangles. In parallel roping, separation between the ropes is crucial so the two seconds never climb in vertical alignment. This is important to avoid because the upper second could knock ice on the lower second. Also, if the upper second fell, with rope stretch their crampons could hit the lower second.

If placing directionals, both ropes should be clipped to a final ice screw before the anchor so the ropes are parallel when entering the auto-braking belay device to lessen the chance of possible unexpected rope slippage if simultaneously loaded from different angles. A locker draw is ideal for this last piece.

While belaying in two seconds from above, it might be tempting to try to separate and organize the ropes while belaying. It is challenging enough to offer a good belay to two climbers at once, so just stack or lap coil the two ropes together until the two seconds arrive, then separate and restack for the next lead when you have three sets of hands at your disposal.

Rope Rescue

Anyone climbing multi-pitch routes should be trained and well-practiced in improvised rope rescue techniques. Rope rescue skills should be learned from a course with a certified guide, reviewed through books and online videos, and, of course, practiced frequently. Emergency situations are stressful, so rope rescue skills need to be well-rehearsed so they are on automatic recall if an accident happens.

Rescue skills that a multi-pitch ice climber should have include rope ascension, escaping the belay, raising systems, lowering systems, and knot passes. Rescue rappelling systems like counterbalance rappels and tandem rappels should be avoided due to the obvious hazard of jostling and bumping into each other with crampons on. It is imperative to not create more injuries during a rescue.

There are many non-emergency situations that could potentially lead to causing an emergency or ultimately requiring a rescue. Below are four of the most common problematic non-emergency situations that an ice climber may encounter on a multi-pitch ice route. The purpose of this section is not to teach these rescue skills but to make you aware that they are possible.

Damaged Ropes

It is not uncommon for climbing ropes to get damaged by abrasion, rock fall, ice fall, or misplaced ice tools and crampons. If you suspect a damaged section or can visibly see core, tie off the section in question with an overhand on a bight with a long (20 cm/8 in.) bight/tail. To descend with a damaged rope containing tied-off section(s), use a jammed knot technique for a single-line rappel (the damaged side becomes the pull rope).

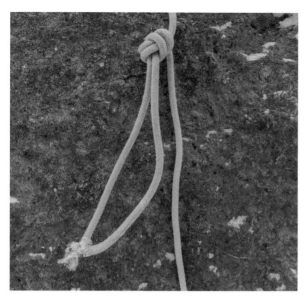

Ropes can be damaged from ice fall, rock fall, sharp edges, ice tool picks, and crampon points. Isolate the damaged section with a long overhand on a bight and use the jammed-knot method for single-strand rappelling on the good side of the rope using the damaged side as a pull line.

Stuck Rappel Ropes

Rappel ropes can sometimes become stuck due to friction over rock or freezing into wet ice. Try to anticipate this and mitigate it by relocating or extending rappel anchors if need be. If you complete a rappel and the ropes will not pull, try pulling with the combined force of all members, being conscious of crampon and ice tool points. If the issue appears to be just too much friction, then set up a 3:1 or even a 5:1 hauling system to use mechanical advantage to assist the pulling.

If this does not work, the final option is to ascend the ropes (using two prusiks around both strands of ropes) all the way back up to the anchor to readjust. This can be an intimidating and time-consuming process. Never ascend just one of the rappel rope strands.

Dropped Ice Tools

It is not uncommon for a novice ice climber to drop an ice tool while seconding. Two options exist depending on where they are on the pitch. If they are halfway up, lower them back down to retrieve their dropped tool. If the ice climbing leader is using an auto-braking device, they will have to use either the Load Strand Direct method to lower (if the second is able to unweight the rope) or a full load transfer to a dedicated lowering system (if the rope cannot be unweighted). If the climber drops their tool near the top of a pitch, it may be possible to lower a replacement tool with the extra rope at the belay.

Slipped Off Ice Tools

If a second begins to fatigue, they might get too pumped to hang on to their ice tools and may slip off them. With rope stretch on steeper routes, it may be difficult for them to reach and regain their tools above their head. The best mitigation for this situation is always keeping seconds tight on the rope. However, if this situation does occur, set up a simple 3:1 raising system to help winch them back up to their tools.

CHAPTER 8

Mixed Climbing

Yvon Chouinard described mixed climbing in his 1978 book *Climbing Ice* as "climbing on both ice and rock, either in quick succession or actually at the same time." Mixed climbing has come a long way since those words were written more than forty years ago, but it is essentially still the same game. As the name implies, it is a mix of ice climbing, rock climbing, and even aid climbing, combining existing skills to travel over complex mixed terrain.

Whether you are climbing ice with the odd rock move or climbing rock with the odd ice move, it is all mixed climbing. Drytooling has been taken to its illogical conclusion—climbing rock with ice tools for its own sake with no ice in sight. Modern mixed climbing with bolt protection can be thought of as winter sport climbing. For those who must endure a long winter due to their geographic location, drytooling offers something different than the same old swing, kick, kick of pure ice climbing. The mixed movement is more like rock climbing. It can be thought of as free aid climbing

The skills learned in the relatively sterile setting of the bolted mixed crag have also helped advance mixed climbing in the alpine arena, where long sections of cold, snowy rock are drytooled. Mixed climbing can be subdivided into three categories: sport mixed with bolted rock sections, trad mixed where traditional protection (nuts, cams, and pitons) is used, and pure drytooling where there is no ice and which can even be done in non-winter months.

Mixed Climbing Equipment

The same equipment can be used for mixed climbing as for ice climbing, except that mono-point crampons are infinitely easier to use on rock than dual points. Also, ice tools with an upper grip position facilitate matching and swapping tools. It might seem like drytooling would dull picks, but not necessarily. Simply hooking rock holds, especially soft rock like limestone, does no damage to the picks since the rock is softer than the metal. However, granite and other hard rock can be more wearing on picks. Picks more likely get dulled by misjudging the thickness of thin ice and swinging too hard, hitting the rock beneath. Torquing picks in cracks can put a lot of strain on the pick and the tool itself, but most modern tools are designed and tested to withstand these forces.

Another equipment progression in mixed is comp boots. These specialized, lightweight boots have crampon points bolted directly to the sole. As the name implies, comp boots were developed for competition climbing, but they are also used at mixed crags on difficult routes. A mixed climber would approach in their normal ice boots then switch to comp boots just for climbing the route, like a rock climber would switch to rock shoes for a pitch of

Aaron Mulkey cuts loose on Devil's Doorbell (M9, 30 m) behind Ramshorn in Pilot Creek, Wyoming, USA.

171

sport climbing. These boots often do not have points under the heel but instead have a rubberized heel like a rock shoe to help facilitate heel hooking.

Mixed gloves are often thinner and offer more dexterity than regular ice gloves, allowing for easier clipping of draws and better contact with the grip of the ice tool. A good mixed glove will be snug fitting and have a tacky palm material for better grip on ice tools. They usually lack much in the way of insulation so are not very warm.

Mixed Climbing Hazards

Mixed climbing is subject to the same hazards as ice climbing (as described in detail in Chapter 3), but those same hazards are often exacerbated due to not only the more dynamic nature of mixed movement but also the environment in which it is practiced.

Falling

While "no falling" is a steadfast rule for pure ice climbing, it may sometimes be okay to fall off in certain specific mixed situations—overhanging, not ledgey, and well protected. However, sharp ice tool picks and crampon points are still a hazard even in controlled falls: Crampon points can catch on rock or ice features, resulting in sprains or fractures, and ice tool picks can stab legs or abdomens. The fact that ice tools can pop suddenly and unexpectedly usually results in flipping upside down and falling headfirst, which is definitely not ideal.

It is common to see the mistake of belaying a mixed leader while standing directly below the first bolt as in summer sport climbing. This is a major hazard in itself because the belayer is exposed to the crampons of a falling leader, dropped ice tools, loose rock, and ice fall. An all-too-common scenario for unaware sport mixed lead climbers is that the belayer initially stands close under the first bolt, then as the leader moves higher or onto the ice, the aforementioned hazards become more obvious. Their "mitigation" is to move back out of

A ground anchor makes good sense when belaying mixed routes in order to help the belayer maintain their position away from ice fall, rock fall, falling tools, and crampon points.

the fall line of the newly recognized overhead hazards (crampon points, ice fall, dropped tools, etc.). However, by moving back far enough to avoid the overhead hazard, the belayer creates a new, equally significant fundamental hazard—a poor belay. The sharp angle that the rope would now be running to the first bolt increases the vector force. No matter how solidly the belayer is braced, if the leader falls, the belayer will be forcibly yanked toward the wall, causing a larger fall force. All of this equates to a longer fall as well as the belayer possibly getting hit by the falling leader and their crampons. Anticipation is the key risk management principle in this situation, so recognize the hazard and secure the belayer with a ground anchor out of the way.

Getting to the first bolt on sport mixed routes can be risky. Unlike rock climbing where a leader can be spotted by the belayer until they clip the first bolt, this is not an option for the obvious reason that they have crampons on. It is also not a good idea to boulder the first moves because even short ground falls with crampons on can result in twisted or broken ankles and even lower leg fractures. It is therefore prudent to have a stick clip and use it to pre-clip the first bolt (or even first two bolts) to protect not only the leader but also the belayer. Even with a pre-clipped high bolt, a lead climber could still fall off and swing into the belayer with their crampons, so again, a ground anchor should be used to keep the belayer safely out of the way.

An all-to-common scenario is to start belaying under the leader . . .

Then realize the obvious hazard of crampons overhead so move back out of the way . . .

Then if/when the leader falls, the belayer is violently yanked (vector force due to the low first bolt) into the plummeting crampons of the leader.

A stick clip is necessary for sport mixed climbing since it is impossible to spot a leader due to the hazard of their crampons.

Loose Rock

Loose rock becomes more of a hazard with mixed climbing compared to pure ice climbing. Winter rock is susceptible to the effects of freeze-thaw cycles, which can loosen seemingly solid rock. The tools themselves act as crowbars and can lever off holds and blocks. As with climber-generated falling ice, mixed climbers must be aware of falling rock. Of course, a helmet is standard equipment and should always be worn, but more importantly, the belayer should be situated so they are not exposed to potential rock fall. This might mean using a ground anchor to help the belayer maintain their stance far enough back and away from the leader. If the leader pulls or kicks off loose rock, be sure to shout "Rock!" to make climbers below aware of the immediate hazard.

Equipment Hazards

The wrong equipment can be a hazard when mixed climbing. Ice tools that have adzes instead of hammers (or better yet, nothing) on the back of the head are never to be used. If the tool pops off a hold unexpectedly, the adze could inflict serious injury to the climber's face. Also, leashes (which are pretty much nonexistent now anyway) should not be used when drytooling and mixed climbing since they can cause shoulder injuries if feet suddenly pop and can also leave a climber stranded hanging from their wrist on steep routes if too pumped to hold the grip.

Dropped ice tools tomahawking through the air are indeed a hazard at mixed crags. Despite the temptation to use umbilical leashes to prevent falling tools, it is not a good idea. The bungee umbilical leashes will only increase the hazard since they will fling the tools at the climber they are attached to. The best mitigation for falling ice tools is situational awareness of what is happening above you and not belaying or standing under someone climbing.

Bolts

The bolts on mixed routes are often exposed to a fair amount of moisture during the non-winter months. In fact, some mixed routes are in actual waterfalls during the summer. This presence of water can lead to bolts corroding, especially if any of the components are not stainless steel. Any rusted bolts or hangers should be treated as suspect. Also, the freeze-thaw of seasonal temperature fluctuations can affect both bolts and the rock surrounding the bolts in a negative way by loosening them. Often the rock on winter mixed and drytool routes is not of the highest quality. Bolts could be placed in sections of stone that at one time seemed solid but through the effects of melt-freeze cycles became loose. The expanding and contracting influences of temperature can also loosen the nuts on bolts, causing hangers to not only spin but fall off. Some belay devices are designed so that the rope slots can be used to tighten bolt nuts, but it is not a bad idea to carry a small adjustable wrench in your pack.

Free-Hanging Ice

Unformed free-hanging pillars and curtains as well as fully "formed" yet skinny or fragile-looking pillars are abundant when mixed climbing. A mixed climber must assess these features and decide whether they should be climbed or not by taking into account the size of the ice feature, temperature, softness of the ice, and if the ice already has hook placements. Some considerations to minimize the risk of free-hanging features include:

- **Avoidance:** If the ice feature is too big or too fragile or too cold, then simply avoid it. It does not have to be climbed. Also, avoid standing or walking beneath these features. It is important to reiterate that if the overnight temperature has swung very low, definitely avoid all free-hanging icicles, hollow curtains, and skinny pillars—even larger, fully formed pillars should be avoided during cold temperatures.

Free-hanging daggers of suspended ice are an obvious hazard on mixed routes.

- **Toprope:** Obviously, toproping the feature is less hazardous than leading it, so reduce risk by setting up a toprope from above instead of exposing yourself to the increased danger of leading. The top may be accessed by walking around, rappelling in from above, or leading an easier route to the side. Having said that, there can still be significant hazard for both the climber and belayer, even on toprope, if a big dagger snaps.

- **Directionals:** Clipping certain directional protection points like bolts might help keep the toprope climber from swinging out (if they fall) and hitting icicles. Any directional ice screws must be well above potential fracture lines. This is extremely important, because if the ice breaks with the screw in, it will slide down the rope, striking the toproped climber and potentially flossing them off the end of the rope.

- **Cleaning ice:** If setting up a toprope from above, prepare the ice by knocking off fragile icicles, mushrooms, and bulges that could possibly break off and injure a climber. Be sure that the belayer is anchored far off out of the way and that any other climbers are clear. If rappelling, either pull up and coil the rope hanging below or have someone hold the ropes out to the side so any falling ice chunks do not damage the rope. Be sure that your body is well above any potential fracture lines if kicking at fragile ice features.

- **Preparing ice:** If the ice at the crux is steep/overhanging and is not hooked out, use your ice tool to chip hooks in the ice so that you can simply hook. This will also decrease the chance of knocking ice on your face.

Drytooling

Drytooling is the use of ice tools and crampons on rock. Once learned, drytooling is easier, more comfortable, and more efficient than trying to use

Drytooling can be hard on the rock, scarring it with scratches and worn-out holds.

gloved or bare hands to climb winter rock. Never drytool on established summer rock climbs since it can break holds and scratch the rock.

Drytool holds generally fall into a handful of specific categories. With all of these, you must learn to use the shaft of your tools as an extension of your arms and your picks as fingers. When rock climbing in summer, you can reach up to a hold and, regardless of whether you can see it or it is blind, feel the best way to grab the hold. This becomes harder with drytooling, and you must learn how to "feel" with your picks to find the most positive part of the hold—the "sweet spot." This could be a pin-sized divot on a big sloping ledge, creating the feeling of searching for the metaphorical needle in the haystack.

The best technique for finding sweet spots or feeling if a hold is positive is to reach up and place the pick on the front of the hold and slowly slide it back until you feel it drop down onto something positive. Alternatively, you can reach to the back of the feature and drag the pick forward to see if it grabs or just slides off. Regardless, if you think you have something that will stay put, test it by yanking sharply downward on the tool. If it doesn't pop off, you should be able to commit your full weight to it.

On more popular mixed routes there will most likely be scratch marks on and around the holds. The scratches are comparable to chalk on summer rock climbs. Just connect the dots from scratched hold to scratched hold. Of course, this highlights an ethical quandary about the impacts of drytooling. Like chalk for rock climbing, scratch marks are an accepted evil of mixed climbing that should be minimized as much as possible. Good technique with tools and crampons will help decrease rock scarring.

Edges

The most common type of hold you will encounter is the edge. They can range from the thickness of a dime to a large ledge; they can be incut and very positive, or flat and even sloping outward. Regardless, they represent the most basic form of drytool placement in that they are simply hooked. No matter how shallow or small an edge may be, it can almost always be matched on. If a hold seems positive for one pick, then place the other pick right beside it. This saves looking for another hold.

Pockets

Pockets are holes in the rock. Like edges, they can range from tiny pinholes to large huecos and can still often be matched; however, unlike edges, the sweet spot maybe not be pulling straight down. They may be more positive as sidepulls or underclings. Pockets can often be stein pulled as well.

Pockets are holes in the rock.

Slots

Slots are vertical seams or cracks, often found in corner features. Slots can be shallow, just allowing the tip of the pick, or deep, swallowing the entire length. These holds can feel very stable due to the narrow sides that keep the pick from wobbling. Slots are tricky to match picks in, but one pick can be placed directly on top of the other.

Stein Pull

Stein pulls are tool placements where the tip of the pick and the top of the pick (where it attaches to the head of the tool) are cammed in opposition. By applying the physics of levers to ice tools, you can find stein pulls on almost any mixed climb. They are often located under overlaps or roofs at the convergence of the vertical and horizontal axis, but any three-dimensional feature in the rock can work as long as there is something for the top of the tool to brace against. In the case of an overlap, place the pick on a hold a few inches below the roof, then pull back on the grip so the head cams against the roof, wedging the axe in place.

Stein pulls are more stable than conventional placements like edges because the tool is firmly wedged. This allows you to reach farther because you can pull out on the tool as well as up on it. Just

Stein pull with the head of the tool cammed against the roof.

Inverted stein pulls are very satisfying drytool moves that can provide long reaches.

be sure that the hold is solid enough to withstand the prying forces involved, as the mechanics are similar to that of a crowbar.

Inverted stein pulls are achieved by re-grabbing the grip of the tool upside down, thumb toward the pommel, and inserting the pick up into a hold, be it a crack or overlap. Pulling down on the grip cams the head firmly against the wall, creating a stable bar to match and monkey around on.

When stein pulling, you must find sweet spots not only for the pick but also for the head of the tool to cam against. Moving the head slightly one way or another may provide a better camming action. A good trick is to look for stein-pull scratch marks, which are the marks where the head of the tool previously scraped the rock.

Cracks

Cracks, which are varying size fractures in the rock's surface, are common drytooling features. The technique used will depend on the width of the crack. Seams are the thinnest cracks, which are narrower than the width of a pick. Look for slots where the seam opens up enough to accept the pick.

If the seam is filled with ice or dirt, it is possible to swing at the crack to set the pick. This takes precision and control; if you miss the crack and hit the rock on either side by accident, it will blunt the tip of the pick. To increase accuracy, place your thumb on the back of the grip. This chokes the swing but adds control. Small taps at the ice or dirt in the crack work best to chip a hole that can be hooked. Another effective trick is to use the hammer of the other tool to tap the pick deeper, similar to pounding in a piton. These types of placements can be very secure.

Anything wider than a slot will have to be torqued because the pick will slide out if simply pulled straight down. Torquing is done by inserting the pick as deep into the crack as possible then pulling sideways on the shaft, thus applying a twisting force to the pick to gain purchase. Torques are very technical and strenuous because constant body

Picks can be tapped by the other tool into thin cracks like pitons.

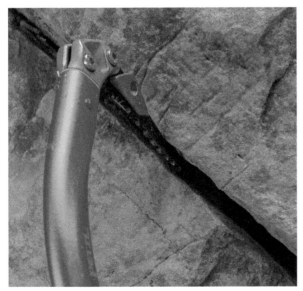

Torquing requires twisting the pick in a wide crack and maintaining steady sideways pressure.

tension is required to keep the pick from slipping. Always look for chockstones wedged in the crack. These can range from small pebbles to big boulders. They will feel very secure to hook and will be less tenuous than trying to torque the crack itself.

Torquing is stressful on picks, especially if it is a shallow crack that only accepts the first few centimeters of the pick. This situation could bend or even snap the tip of the pick off. If the pick is inserted all the way to the head of the tool, it should be able to hold full body weight without deforming.

Sometimes cracks can be easier to deal with by holstering your tools and jamming with gloved hands. Wearing gloves turns cupped-hand cracks and even fist cracks into bomber hand jams. Likewise, loose finger cracks become good locks with the thickness of gloves.

Shaft Placements

The shaft of the tool itself can be cammed into deep cracks. Either end—the head or the grip—can be used for this. The whole head of an ice tool can

Sometimes the entire head and shaft of the tool can be jammed in a horizontal crack.

be inserted sideways into a horizontal crack. Pulling down on the grip should wedge it solidly. Although sometimes tempting, never place the hammer of an ice tool in a crack for the very obvious reason that the pick will be pointing straight at your head and face.

Geology

The type of rock you are climbing can often dictate the drytooling technique you will be using. Each type of rock has its own personality. Whether it is soft rock like limestone, sandstone, or shale or hard rock like granite, quartzite, or basalt or even a combination like conglomerate, each rock offers a different style of holds requiring a different style of technique. Knowing the characteristics of each rock type makes reading the holds and moves easier. Of course, the following guidelines are only generalizations. For example, splitter cracks typically associated with granite can be found in limestone, and pockets normally found in limestone are not unheard of in granite.

Soft Rock

Soft rock is almost always a form of sedimentary rock, which is made from layers of sediment that are buried and subjected to increasing pressure and so over time become consolidated into rock through compaction, cementation, and recrystallization. These could be deposits of shells and other remains of marine organisms, which form limestone, or sand that is compressed into sandstone.

Limestone seems to be the most common rock for sport mixed climbing. Like summer sport climbing on limestone, the angle tends to be steeper and the movement more gymnastic. Water flows though the bedding planes in sedimentary sequences, resulting in seeps, smears, drips, and other ice formations that mixed climbers seek. For the advanced sport mixed climber, it also offers interesting cave formations. Limestone can be quite soft, which is both a good and bad characteristic. The advantage is that sharp picks can bite into the surface to feel less skatey. However, it is susceptible to damage via unsightly scratching and inopportune breaking. Limestone offers an unlimited collection of unique and varied holds. Pockets, edges, cracks, seams, slopers, sidepulls, and blocky jugs are just some of the holds that your picks will encounter.

Other common types of soft rock found at mixed climbing venues include sandstone and shale. Sandstone tends to be very friable and shale very loose, but both can offer a magnitude of seeps and drips due to their porous nature. Shale can be decomposed as well as loose. This makes it feel steeper than it actually is because you have to pull straight down on holds. Pulling out to keep your body away from the rock often results in the pick shearing through the loose layers. Shale can be so chossy and soft that you can swing at the holds to set the pick.

Hard Rock

There are essentially two types of hard rocks: igneous and metamorphic. Igneous stone is formed from magma, molten rock below the earth's crust, or lava, molten rock above the earth's crust. Intrusive igneous rock is cooled slowly belowground, forming coarse-grained rock with obvious crystal structure (granite). Conversely, extrusive igneous rock (volcanic rock) is formed by rapid cooling aboveground, producing smooth, fine-grained rock (basalt). Metamorphic rock occurs when either sedimentary or igneous rock is exposed to extreme heat and pressure, thus altering its geologic composition into an even denser, harder stone. Examples include limestone turned to marble, sandstone turned to quartzite, granite turned to gneiss, and shale turned to slate.

Igneous rock tends to offer crack systems separated by featureless faces. Crack techniques like pick torquing, shaft jamming, and gloved hand jamming are often required. Alpine granite is usually more shattered but when frozen solid can offer a plethora of flakes, blocks, and horns to hook. Likewise, basalt can be quite featured with edges and small pick-accepting divots. Quartzite is very hard and commonly horizontally stratified like most metamorphic rock. Quartzite can be so hard that pick and crampon placements feel skatey. No matter how sharp your points are, they do not bite into the rock like they do with softer rock.

All these types of hard rock are merciless on misguided swings. Both picks and front points will mash and flatten and need extensive retuning or even replacement after only a couple days of mixed climbing.

Conglomerate is made up of hard rock cobbles embedded in a matrix of a softer material. The cobbles, due to their rounded nature, make for difficult drytooling. An option is to hook the matrix material between the cobbles. This "mortar" can be soft enough that it can be pecked at to produce a small divot to hook.

The thumb catch.

Letting Go

An important skill to fluidly master is being able to let go of a tool to shake out, clip bolts, and place gear. On ice you can simply plant the tool and let go. Some drytool holds will allow this (cracks and corner placements), but on most drytool holds you will risk the tool falling when you let go of it. Of course, you could clip it to a racking clip on your harness if you need to let go of a tool for extended periods of time, like when climbing using hands. However, this is not practical or efficient for simple tasks like clipping or resting. There are three main "holstering" positions on your body that can be used.

Thumb Catch

The thumb catch is executed by slotting the pick of the tool into the crook of the thumb of the gripping hand. This is the recommended technique since it is easily accessible (thumb is directly in front of you) and secure (thumb is gripping the tool by the pick). The thumb hook is ideal for clipping bolts, unclipping directionals, placing protection, and quick shake outs.

Shoulder Hook

The shoulder hook works well for extended shake outs when trying to recover by constantly alternating hands and shaking. Despite being a popular method of letting go of an ice tool, there is always the risk of it slipping off your shoulder. It should only be used on well-protected, single-pitch mixed routes. It is not appropriate for pure ice climbing (unless umbilical leashes are being used) since the consequences of dropping an ice axe is major.

The shoulder hook.

The mouth bite.

Mouth Bite

Some mixed climbers choose to place the shaft of the ice tool in their mouth. This frees up hands while still maintaining a "grip" on the tool. Rubber tape wrapped around the midpoint or balance point of the shaft makes this more comfortable on the teeth and mouth. Climbers with smaller mouths may find this technique awkward or even impossible.

Ice Tool Handling

The movement of mixed climbing is similar to that of rock climbing. The main difference is that instead of using hands and feet you have ice tools and crampons. A proficient climber at both ice climbing and rock climbing should adapt quickly to the intricacies of moving over mixed ground.

Control and Tool Stability

Picks do not grab like fingers—they hook. This means how you pull on the tool is crucial. Whether it is a normal edge, a sidepull, or an undercling, maintain the same direction of pull throughout the move. This is accomplished with footwork and body positioning. A common mistake with novice drytoolers is that once the new hold is hooked, the lower pick pops off. This is because they forget to keep tension on the lower tool. The same holds true when torquing off-size cracks (anything wider than the thickness of a pick). Tension must be constantly applied to the pick to keep it from sliding out as you move your feet up and gain the next placement.

Using Hands

When first learning mixed climbing, climbers coming from a strong rock-climbing background will feel the urge to use their hands. This will be short lived, though, as they figure out that metal and carbon fiber do not get tired, unlike muscles and tendons. In addition, you can hook tiny dimples many

Sometimes it may be easier to grab holds with hands.

times smaller than you'd ever be able to grab with your hands. Think of ice tools as extensions of your arms in that you have an extra 50 centimeters (20 inches) of reach and sharp fingertips of steel.

Having said that, some situations call for using hands. On low-angled terrain, try holstering your tools and using your hands for balance while your feet do most of the work. Palming and mantling are also moves better suited for hands. Pushing to the side with your hand to move a foot higher makes for more fluid movement than just hanging onto both tools and thrutching your foot up.

Short Tooling

Short tooling is choking up on the tool by grabbing the upper grip. This can increase your reach by up to 10 to 15 centimeters (4 to 6 inches), which can make a difference for seemingly out-of-reach holds. Do not grab the shaft any higher than the upper hand grip. The higher you grab the shaft, the more outward pull there is on the pick. If you grab

Choking up on the tool for more reach.

too high, the pick can suddenly pop off the hold and possibly hit you in the face.

Swapping

The ability to swap tools makes the idea of sequences almost obsolete because there is usually no such thing as getting a hold with the wrong tool. If you hook a hold with your left tool but you'd rather have your right tool in it, simply change hands. First, stash your free tool on your body with either a thumb hook, shoulder hook, or mouth bite. Then grab the upper grip of the left

tool with your free right hand and release your left hand off the bottom grip. Now you have the hold with your right tool, and you can grab the holstered tool with your newly freed left hand to make the next move.

For those who prefer the thumb hook method of holstering, hook the pick into the thumb of the tool you wish to change hands on. Grab the upper grip position with the newly freed hand. Let go of

Swapping tools (A).

Swapping tools (B).

Swapping tools (C).

Swapping tools (D).

Swapping tools (E).

Swapping tools (F).

the lower grip position, keeping the pick cradled over the thumb, and over the thumb of the higher placed hand.

Crampon Footwork

Footwork on mixed terrain is similar to that of normal rock climbing except you must adapt your technique slightly to compensate for the fact that you have metal points instead of sticky rubber on your feet. Look at your feet as you place your points on holds. Looking down is as important as looking up. The same basic principles of precision and accuracy still hold true. Placing crampons exactly where you want them takes practice since you are dealing with a tiny point instead of a whole foot. The friction between metal and rock is almost nil, so maintain tight core tension to prevent feet from skating off. Sloppy footwork inevitably means you'll tire prematurely.

Front Pointing

Front pointing on rock is the same as in ice climbing. It is similar to toeing-in with rock shoes on, except you have a single pointy metal toe sticking out the front of your boot that doesn't bend. Mono-points are best for mixed climbing because

they can fit into seams, tight corners, and tiny edges where dual points would just get in the way of each other. Mono-points also allow for advanced footwork maneuvers like pivoting into a drop knee.

Edging

Crampons can edge like rock shoes by using the secondary or tertiary points. Experiment with both your inside and outside edges. Edge with the inside points for high-stepping; use the outside points for backstepping. Both inside and outside edging will help keep your hips closer to the rock, placing the weight over your feet. It also relieves flaming calf muscles from front pointing all the time.

Raking

Raking is a term used to describe "grabbing" footholds with the backswept third or fourth points that are standard on most modern technical crampons. These aggressive backswept points allow you to pull with your hamstrings on edges that may be at waist level. Raking can help pull you into balance on high holds.

Mono-points are crucial for mixed climbing.

Raking uses the backswept points under the middle of the foot.

Heel Hooking

Heel hooking on mixed routes is executed in a similar fashion to rock climbing. On steep routes, kicking your foot up and hooking the heel of your boot on ledges or other rock features can help take weight off your arms and assist in making moves. Crampons' heel levers obviously get in the way and make heel hooking a bit awkward, but it can still be an effective technique. Mixed heel hooking truly comes into its own when using comp boots, since they do not have crampon attachments on the heel—just sticky rubber like a rock shoe.

For a short time in the early 2000s, mixed climbers experimented with using heel spurs—a backward-facing point/pick jutting out from the heel of comp boots. After a couple years of use, they were deemed to be cheating since they made climbing out cave-style mixed routes too easy because it was possible to hang almost anywhere by only feet.

Drytool Movement

Efficient movement or lack thereof will make or break a mixed ascent. Avoid jerky body movements. Concentrate on deliberately placing points and picks and moving fluidly from hold to hold. Shake out and evaluate upcoming moves from straight arms. Bent arms means your muscles are flexed, thus slowly draining their reserves. Try not to chicken wing (elbows splayed out to the side) by focusing on keeping elbows tight to your sides and pulling down. Even when the climbing is overhanging, proper footwork and body awareness can help take much weight off tiring arms.

Matching

Matching, whether with both picks on the same hold or both hands on the same tool, can be incorporated into the movement of drytooling. With both picks matched side by side on the same hold, hang straight arm and locate the next hold. When ready to move up, both arms can be involved in the pulling before locking off. Be sure to add a bit of a twist lock to keep your hips in. Once the new hold is latched, re-match picks and repeat the process.

Heel hooking with boots and crampons.

Picks can be matched side by side on the tiniest of holds.

Stemming

Stemming is often the epitome of mixed climbing: one foot and one hand on ice, the other foot and other hand on rock—climbing both mediums at the same time. The technique is the same as stemming on rock except more variations exist. Stems can occur in ice grooves, in rock dihedrals, or between rock and ice. Think three-dimensional and always be looking around and even behind you for something to stretch a foot out to. The idea is to help take weight off your arms and maintain a balanced body position.

Stemming between a free-hanging ice dagger and the rock behind it can offer an almost complete rest. Throwing a foot behind you to a far-off drip can provide enough balance to move tools higher. Stemming also helps with upward progress when holds are few and far between by palming and pushing between features. In this situation, holds are not as important since you are using the opposing pressure of the feet to maintain contact.

Twist Locking

Twist locking (I-frame, as opposed to the triangular A-frame) is the most important movement principle to master for drytooling. Basically it is pulling and pushing with the opposite arm and leg. This creates an axis down the centerline of the body to rotate around, allowing hips to move inward. It also incorporates the entire width of the shoulders to increase reach.

Climbing with a straight-on body position forces the body's center of mass outward. This is fine for slabs because you want the weight out over the feet. However, hips sticking out on vertical and overhanging rock will only result in strenuous locked-off arms. If the holds are not too far apart, you can climb with almost straight arms (not bending your elbows). By twisting your torso and rotating the leading hip into the rock, you can use the breadth of your shoulders to make the reach instead of your arms.

Twist locking is an efficient movement principle that gets the hips close to the rock and increases reach.

Step-by-step twist lock description:

1. Hang straight arm off the higher tool (left) with body square to the rock.
2. Place opposite front point (right) on a hold directly under (plumb line) of the higher tool at about knee to waist level.
3. Turn knee (right) slightly to the inside (leftward) by pivoting on the front point.
4. Place free foot (left) out far to the side, either on a hold or flagging against the rock.
5. Push up with the leg (right) and twist the hip inward (leftward).
6. Rotate chest inward (left) as well.
7. If the reach to the next hold cannot be made with straight arms, continue following through

with the twist by pulling the fist (left) tight to opposite side of chest (right).

8. If executed properly, you should be able to gain almost two tool lengths of reach.

9. Key is to find high holds for pushing leg so body does not get too stretched out (thus losing pressure on front point).

Scumming

Scumming is when any body part is braced, or "scummed," against rock or ice. More surface area equals better scum-holding power. The most frequently used scums include knees, hips, shoulders, and back. Knee scums (aka the alpine knee) work well on ledge features instead of awkwardly trying to high-step with crampons. Knee bars—between rock features or even between rock and hanging ice curtains—can sometimes offer no-hands rest. Scum a shoulder or hip into a shallow corner to rest or gain purchase. A back scum is essentially the old tried-and-true technique of chimneying. There are often rock and/or ice features to brace your back against for a rest or to assist in moving up feet.

The alpine knee. A knee scum often works better than trying to high-step with crampons.

Figure-4

The Figure-4 was first used for rock climbing by American Darius Azin in 1988 on Chouca, a hard sport climb at Boux in southern France. The next year, Tony Yaniro was featured in a French climbing magazine using the same move on the same route. This is why the Europeans call this technique a "Yaniro." It never really caught on for rock climbing and was long forgotten. But with ice and mixed climbing gaining momentum in the 1990s, this obscure technique was revitalized. Magazine photos of Jeff Lowe's first ascent of Octopussy (M8) in Vail, Colorado, in 1994 showed him contorting into a series of Figure-4s on a free-hanging icicle.

It is surprisingly effective in roofs where it is hard to keep crampons pasted to rock. Figure-4s will extend your reach—without having to perform a strenuous one-arm lock-off—when the only other option for your feet is dangling in space. The move is accomplished by hooking a leg over the opposite arm and rocking up onto it to gain your next tool placement. Basically, the crook of the knee is hooked over the crook of the opposite elbow. The other leg is flagged or braced against the wall for stability. To gain more height from a Figure-4, try to hook your knee around your hand by squeezing it with your bent leg. The unused leg can also help by pushing off any available holds to further extend your reach.

At first this sounds like a contortionist's trick that only years of yoga would give you the flexibility to perform, but with a bit of practice you will be moving in and out of Figure-4s like a pro. Needless to say, dangling from one tool on a free-hanging icicle is not the place to learn any new technique. Familiarize yourself with the intricacies of the movement while hanging from your tools on a pull-up bar or in a climbing gym.

Figure-4s are usually not required on vertical or even moderately overhanging routes because you can easily keep your feet on the rock. Plus it is awkward to get into a Figure-4 position with the

The Figure-4 is effective for pulling roofs.

rock wall in front of you. Figure-4s become useful once the angle of the rock tilts to 45 degrees and beyond. Pulling the lip of roofs—rock or ice—is a prime situation that might call for a Figure-4. Dry-tooling across huge horizontal roofs is also Figure-4 territory.

When entering a Figure-4, make sure your tools are at least a foot apart to ensure enough space between them to get your leg through. It is possible to enter it with both picks matched on the same hold but is more awkward since there is limited space to work your leg between. Once the desired hold is latched from a Figure-4 and weighted, disentangle by lifting your hooked leg off your arm. Another way of exiting from the position is to simply let go, allowing your leg to drop free. For this to work though, the hold must be positive enough that the tool does not fall before you have a chance to re-grab it.

Always be wary of crampon points that can easily cut or puncture skin. As with all ice and mixed climbing, it is a good idea to always wear gloves as standard hand protection.

A Figure-9 is a variation of a Figure-4, using the same leg over the same arm. It is a move that can be done on its own, but it is more effective when used in conjunction with Figure-4s to negotiate large horizontal roofs or footless traverses. From a Figure-4 grab the next hold, then instead of completely exiting the Figure-4, simply move your leg from one arm to the other. This saves your abdominal muscles and hip flexors from having to drop your legs down completely then lift them back up into another Figure-4. From the Figure-9 you can match picks on the hold and move the leg back over into a Figure-4 position. Repeat this series of Figure-4s and Figure-9s to traverse from hold to hold out the roof.

Free-Hanging Ice

Mixed climbing is synonymous with free-hanging ice features ranging from skinny icicles to massive daggers. All of these take special techniques to climb and have their own unique hazards to manage. All free-hanging ice should be treated with respect and caution. Evaluating these features is an advanced skill, so if in doubt the best mitigation is avoidance. Slight temperature changes are enough to cause catastrophic collapse.

The following are a few guidelines that will reduce some risks when dealing with free-hanging ice:

- Stay away from free-hanging ice after an intense period of cold weather or major temperature fluctuations. During these cold snaps, even thick, fully formed pillars can spontaneously collapse without warning since the ice is under great tension. The added stress of a climber swinging ice tools will almost surely cause the ice to fracture. Wait for optimal conditions—temperatures just below freezing with well-bonded, plastic ice.

- Warm weather and direct sun can cause the hanging ice to detach and delaminate from the

Be sure to cimb high enough on the ice before placing an ice screw to be certain that it is above the potential fracture line.

Stemming between rock and a dagger helps to keep weight on the feet and off the arms while transitioning to the ice.

rock behind its attachment point, making it unpredictable and weak.

- Protect your belayer by making sure they are sheltered and anchored so they cannot be hit or pulled into the falling debris if the ice breaks or if catching a fall.

- Once fully committed to the icicle, tread lightly. Heavy-handed tactics will surely break it. Swing gently with controlled, deft blows. If the ice feels brittle or fragile, use small taps to chip a hole for hooking.

- Never place ice screws in free-hanging ice features. Once committed to an icicle, run it out until you are above the potential fracture line. This is usually where the ice securely attaches to the rock behind. The ice can break much higher though, particularly if it has melted away from the rock.

Some of the most memorable moves in mixed climbing are when committing to the ice from the rock. After a section of pumpy drytooling, always

Chimneying between the ice and rock can often provide a no-hands rest before committing to the ice.

be looking behind, ready to stem wide to the ice—anything to help get weight off your flaming forearms. The earlier you can stem, the sooner you can rest. Continue stemming the gap between rock and ice for as long as possible before fully committing to the ice. Drytooling is all hooking, but ice climbing usually requires swinging, even if it is picked out. It is challenging to swing ice tools with any precision or force if your arms are pumped. Nothing is worse than finally reaching the ice with useless arms (known unflatteringly as "dumbing arm"), so it is a critical tactic to try to cop a rest any way you can between the rock and ice. The best recovering position is when you can place your back against the ice while your feet are still on rock for a full no-hands chimney rest.

Traditional Mixed Climbing

Traditional mixed climbing refers to the style of mixed climbing practiced before bolted drytooling routes became common. It means climbing ground-up, placing removable protection as you climb—similar to what traditional rock climbing is to sport rock climbing. Traditional mixed climbing is as old as mountain climbing. It has been occurring on alpine routes since climbers first began using ice axes and crampons. In some areas, like Scottish winter mountaineering, traditional mixed climbing is the only type of mixed climbing, since Scotland adheres to a strict no-bolt ethic on winter routes. Classic traditionally protected mixed climbing is as much a mental challenge as it is a physical challenge, especially when it comes to solving the riddle of quality protection.

Ice Runnels

Ice runnels are aesthetic features often associated with alpine mixed climbing. Narrow veins of thin ice weaving up corners, chimneys, and gullies are the features that mixed enthusiasts dream about. They can range in width from many meters (bordering on becoming a couloir) to a

Trad mixed climbing is a completely different game to bolt-protected sport mixed climbing. It takes skill and experience to sniff out solid protection in snowy and sometimes loose rock.

few centimeters. The former demands pure ice climbing technique, but once runnels narrow to a body width or less, it becomes the realm of mixed climbing.

Common in the French Alps of Chamonix, these *goulottes* form from the melt-freeze cycles that allow snow to turn to water, which flows down the rock freezing into strips of ephemeral ice. This melt-freeze ice is often soft and plastic, easily accepting picks with one swing. Runnels can also be old, permanent glacial ice, which never melts but is present year-round in cold, sunless recesses

Runnels are very aesthetic ice features that usually require some mixed moves and rock protection.

of mountains. This old ice tends to be very brittle, shattering into plates of ice when struck with picks and crampons or when ice screws are twisted into it.

These icy veins can also form from spindrift avalanches constantly sliding down a narrow rock enclosure. The spindrift slowly accumulates against the rock's surface, hardening enough to support itself. This sn'ice is typically the consistency of whipped cream, making for insecure pick placements that can easily shear through. In addition, ice screws are useless in this medium, so protection must be found in the rock on either side.

Since runnels usually form in corners or gullies, stemming between the walls with tools in the ice usually works best. Runnels can also be deep in a chimney, requiring chimney techniques to climb. In this case, wedge yourself into the gash with your back on one wall and feet on the other. If the chimney is really tight, it is going to be awkward for swinging, and probably only one tool (the inside one) will be usable.

Snow-Covered Rock

Finding tool placements on snow-covered rock can be tedious, time consuming, and frightening. Snow buildup usually occurs on slabs and low-angled rock. Rime, found in maritime ranges like Patagonia and Scotland, can stick to vertical and even overhanging stone. Two basic approaches are possible. In the first, sweep the terrain clear with your gloved hand or ice tool to locate holds and/or ice. Try to avoid doing this on every move as it is slow. Alternately, troll your pick through the snow until you feel it hook on something beneath the surface. Trusting holds you can't see feels sketchy, so test each placement by yanking on it (like bounce testing in aid climbing) before committing. If the rock is less than vertical, most of your weight should be on your feet and the tools are mainly for balance.

Chockstones

Chockstones are common on alpine mixed routes, which often follow gullies or chimneys. These wedged boulders typically create overhangs, allowing you to capitalize on sport mixed climbing techniques and fitness. When attacking these obstacles, think three-dimensionally. Use chimney techniques to wedge and stem between the walls or between the wall and chockstone. The constriction where the stone touches the wall typically forms a useful hold, often a jug. Pulling over the chockstone can be cruxy, requiring some grunting and ungraceful body English. Liberal use of knee, hip, and even stomach scums (belly flop) is usually required.

Turf

Turf is moss, grass, roots, dirt, bushes, and any other frozen flora and can be swung at. Moss and grass when well frozen can provide secure pick placements. Hard, frozen dirt can also offer good sticks. Be aware of pick-dulling rocks that might be embedded in the dirt. Sometimes you have to dig pick placements out of the dirt. By repeatedly swinging at the same spot, a small hole will form to hook. Trees and bushes make for good hooks. Many lower-elevation mixed climbs terminate with

an ungraceful grovel into the forest. Liberal use of exposed roots, branches, and shrubs is fair game. With all forms of turf, be sure that it is well frozen and attached. Moss can suddenly fall off, and apparently solid bushes can rip out. Do not swing at live trees; instead hook branches or roots rather than harm the tree.

Protection

Protecting traditional mixed routes takes more know-how and experience than simply clipping bolts on sport mixed routes. It can take the nose of a bloodhound to sniff out placements, especially if the rock is compact or covered in snow and verglas. The name of the game is patience. An impatient trad mixed climber will invariably miss key protection opportunities, which could result in long runouts and overall increased sketch factor. Mixed protection is the same as rock protection, but some special considerations are often required due to the icy and snowy nature of the rock.

The lightest and simplest rock protection is wired nuts. The pick of your ice axe can be used

Turf placements in frozen moss, grass, or dirt can be as solid as ice.

Stopper heading to set a nut in a crack.

Hexes are important protection for trad mixed routes if the cracks are icy because camming devices will slip.

to tap nuts into cracks. Stopper heading (called this because it is similar to copper heading in aid climbing) helps you set tricky placements but thrashes the nut. Be careful, though, not to fray the wires. Hexcentrics, more commonly called hexes and taunted as cowbells, get a bad rep but are key mixed protection, especially in icy cracks. A standard Scottish mixed rack may even include a double set of hexes. Hexes can also be hammered to help set them into awkward cracks.

Spring-loaded camming devices—or cams for short—are heavier but fit parallel-sided cracks, and often are quicker and easier to place than nuts or hexes. If the crack is glazed with verglas, the cams will slip out when weighted, so it must be scraped clean with your pick. This is a tedious process but is the only way to get the cams to hold. A strong tug should help you decide whether a cam can be trusted. Tricams work better in icy cracks than cams because the pointed beak protruding from one side bites into the verglas. They are also well suited for

pockets, common in limestone and other porous rock. Unfortunately, they are tricky to place and even trickier to remove, especially if they have been weighted.

Pitons are especially useful for protecting mixed routes. They often are the only source of gear for compact and/or loose rock. Protecting loose rock is often more of a challenge than climbing it. Finding quality gear placements is usually difficult at best, so try to place lots of it, hopefully increasing the likelihood that something will hold if a fall were to happen. Long, thin Knifeblades are the gear of choice on many Canadian Rockies limestone routes. Learning to properly place pitons is a difficult art to learn. Clean climbing—only using non-damaging, removable protection—is less destructive to the rock, therefore more popular these days. The continued hammering and removing of pitons scars the rock.

Climb with an array of Knifeblades (both short and long), Lost Arrows (long and thin are better), and angles (the two smallest sizes). Hold the piton with one hand and hammer with the other. Things get tricky if you cannot free both hands as in most technical climbing situations. In these cases, make do by slotting the piton as best as possible by hand so it stays put. This may involve jabbing it at the crack and hitting it with the palm of your hand. Once seated, a few accurate taps with your hammer should get it started. Most modern ice tools are awkward to hammer with, so it is recommended to carry a small, lightweight piton hammer for mixed routes that may require a lot of piton hammering.

Ice hooks were originally designed as thin ice protection but have proven more useful for icy cracks and turf. They can be hammered into thin cracks like an oversized bird beak. They tend to go into ice- and dirt-choked cracks better than regular pitons because of their aggressive pick-like point. They can even be pounded into clumps of hard, well-frozen moss when no other opportunities for protection exist. An ice hook can often be placed wherever you have a good pick placement in a crack.

Styles of Ascent

There are basically four different styles of ascent for completing a route all free: on-sight, flash, redpoint, and free solo. It can hardly be recommended to free solo mixed routes. The leverage that ice tools place on holds can cause seemingly solid placements to break without warning. The other three styles of roped ascent all involve climbing a pitch free—meaning no falling, hanging, or pulling on gear—from bottom to top. In all these facets, visualization is an important strategy. Like warming up physically to loosen muscles, the mind must also be warmed up. Go over the moves in your head. If you have never been on the route, imagine yourself climbing calmly and smoothly. Picture yourself succeeding and topping out. The mind is a powerful tool that can push your body to its physical limits and beyond.

On-sight

On-sighting is climbing a route without any previous knowledge or information about the details of the climb. This means no watching another climber and no hints about where a hidden hold might be located. On-sighting is considered the purest form of roped ascent because you simply walk up to a pitch you have never climbed and send it without falling.

When stepping up to a potential on-sight, scope the entire line well from the ground or any other good vantage points. Use your best judgment on what kind of scoping is acceptable—rappelling down the route is probably pushing things too far. Locate all the holds (or all the holds you can possibly see) and make a mental map of the route and how it will climb. On popular routes, the rock holds will most likely be scratched up, helping you identify them. Look for stein-pull marks above possible holds. These are scratch marks from the top teeth of the pick where the stein pull lodges. Try to figure out where the crux will be and come up with a plan for how to deal with it. Strategize a few possible sequences but keep an open mind in case these do not work once engaged in the crux.

Routes always look different from the ground than when you are actually on them. Locking off on one arm to search with the other tool for out-of-sight holds is extremely pumpy and can be demoralizing. Learn to find rests and recover. While resting and shaking out, examine the stone ahead of you for the next holds and potential rests. Techniques such as stemming, chimneying, and knee barring behind hanging curtains, or sneaking arm or leg hooks around bomber stein pulls, are especially useful.

On traditional routes try to suss out the protection possibilities and carry a rack you deem appropriate. As long as the protection is good and the fall is clean, do not be afraid to go for it. Note that this may result in an irreversible stretch of climbing. Try to anticipate such situations and decide beforehand, while you are still in control, whether to commit to the climbing ahead or call it a day.

Regardless of how strong you are or how good your technique is, the mind is the key to on-sighting. Stay relaxed (easier said than done) and always look ahead. Maintain composure and do not let small mistakes like tools popping or feet swinging off rattle you. Stay focused and calm, handling each move and sequence as they present themselves.

Flash

A flash is similar to an on-sight in that a climber sends the route on the first try without falling or weighting the rope. However, the difference between an on-sight and a flash is that the climber has beta. Beta is any information garnered about how to climb the route. This could minor, like a hint as to where a hidden hold might be located, or major, like watching someone climb a route many times then receive a full running, move-by-move commentary while climbing. Both constitute a flash; however, the latter is often referred to as a beta flash.

The difference in effort between on-sighting and flashing is much greater in mixed climbing than regular summer rock climbing. Finding the holds can be the most difficult part of the route since you are often searching for minuscule divots so having a bit of beta can make all the difference. Most climbers can often flash much harder routes than they can on-sight with good beta.

Redpoint

So you tried to on-sight or flash a mixed route but fell off. You either proceeded to the anchors or lowered off and pulled your rope, then tried again and climbed the pitch to the top without falling. This would be considered a redpoint. Redpointing usually entails working on the route and figuring out the moves until you are confident that they can be linked together for a clean ascent. The term originates from Germany where in the 1970s local climbers would paint a red dot at the base of old aid routes that were eventually led free without aid or falling. Hard redpointing is like a well-rehearsed gymnastic routine. The focus is athletic performance—executing moves and sequences perfectly. A pinkpoint is similar but means that the gear or quickdraws are pre-placed. This term has all but fallen by the wayside in sport climbing circles, as movement and technical difficulty are the goals, not whether you put the quickdraws on yourself or not. However, placing the protection on traditionally protected mixed routes is half the battle. If a route requiring natural protection is done with the gear already in place, then it qualifies for pinkpoint status or simply stating "sent with pre-placed gear."

Redpointing technically difficult drytool routes can be very rewarding.

While on-sighting may be considered purer, redpointing is extremely satisfying. Figuring out moves and sequences that at first may feel impossible, then after practice become second nature, is a rewarding process. There is something to be said for a hard-won on-sight battle, but the same can be said for effortlessly floating a route that is well above your on-sight ability.

Like on-sighting and flashing, redpointing has some tricks of its own. With the advent of leashless climbing, learning sequences have become a moot point since tools can usually always be swapped and hands matched. Therefore, when working on a new project, the first task is to find all the holds. Once holds are located, start to figure out the moves from hold to hold. If you have trouble remembering all the holds, draw yourself a topo map detailing all the holds (highlighting clipping holds), moves, and sequences.

A route will always have two cruxes: a technical crux and a redpoint crux. The technical crux is the hardest single move or series of moves on the pitch. The redpoint crux differs in that it is the spot on the route, usually near the end, where you are most likely to fall. The technical crux could be near the start of the pitch, while the redpoint crux could be technically easier moves that provide a stumbling block due to accumulative pump. Conversely, the technical crux could be the last moves, making it and the redpoint crux the same.

A common mistake when working routes is to dial the technical crux but ignore the easier finishing moves. Nothing is more disappointing than to fire the crux then fall off easy moves just before the top because you did not give enough attention to that section while working the route. I always make sure I have the end of a route dialed, so no matter how pumped I am, the finishing moves are automatic and can be executed without hesitation.

In addition, do not just work the rock and forget about the ice. After a length of hard drytooling, normally straightforward ice can feel like the crux if you are too pumped to swing. Before your redpoint burns, be sure to climb the ice at least once. If necessary, pre-place screws, chip hooks in the ice, and kick out generous crampon holds. This practice of "preparing the ice" may sound ethically dubious, but do not kid yourself. Hard sport mixed climbing is no different than hard summer sport climbing. Making your own holds in the ice is the only time when chipping is condoned.

Gord McArthur climbing Piltdown Man (M12) at the Upper Haffner Cave in Kootenay National Park, British Columbia, Canada.

CHAPTER 9

Training, by Steve House

Calves burning, hips locked in hard against the ice, one arm locked off low as I swing an ice tool high overhead. I've trained for ice and mixed climbing since the first season I discovered it way back in 1988. And today, when I close my eyes and remember all the spectacular places ice and mixed climbing have opened to me, there is no doubt that my training has taken me into some of the wildest places on the planet. Ice and mixed climbing are both core skills to alpine climbing, and fun in their own right.

To know how to train for climbing ice and mixed terrain, you need to know what is involved physically.

The quintessential ice climbing movement taxes in particular the calf muscles, the shoulder girdle muscles, the triceps, and the forearms. The rest of the movement is also physically demanding. Your core must be strong in extension and in convex and concave positions. You have to be able to pull your knees up—sometimes close to your chest—while wearing heavy boots and crampons. You have to be able to stem out laterally with your feet. And last but not least, vertical ice demands you pull yourself up with your arms over and over again.

Mixed climbing terrain—climbing rock interspersed with ice—is especially common in alpine climbing and attracts a small subset of recreational and professional mixed climbers (yes, there is a world cup series for ice/mixed climbers!). This terrain, especially at the crag, can become very steep, and the physical demands are akin to steep sport (rock) climbing. Long reaches, low one-armed lock-offs, and extended toes, as well as more unusual techniques such as dropped knees and Figure-4s and Figure-9s, make hard mixed climbing one of the most strength-intensive subspecialties of climbing as a sport.

What is the best way to prepare? It all sounds complicated, and movement-wise there are many ways in which we can use our bodies to ascend steep ice and mixed terrain. But underlying it all is a certain basic level of strength. For this reason, ice and mixed climbing training is largely done in the weight room and climbing gym. There just isn't much aerobic demand in this sport. The notable exception will be for people who would like to lose weight in order to optimize their climbing. If that is you, I recommend adding two to three aerobic workouts per week to increase your overall health and help you shed the weight.

How long does it take to prepare? The answer to this depends on how high you set your expectations. If you wish to be the very best you can be, the timeline will be many years, probably more than a decade, of purposeful, smart training. This is how the world's best become the world's best. Training trumps talent every time.

Jeff Mercier on the first ascent of Snowstorm (M9 WI6, 35 m) in Pont-Rouge, Quebec, Canada.

I recommend that people train for at least eight weeks. A two- or four-week plan is good if that is what you can wrap your head around, but most people won't see much progress in that time frame. So, if we establish that eight weeks is a good minimum time frame for producing meaningful results, then the more time you can dedicate to progressing, the more significant and bigger the gains you will see. Sixteen weeks is a time frame I often ask people to adopt, and if they can do it, twenty-four weeks is even better.

The reasons behind these time frames lie in our human physiology and how we adapt to exercise and training stress. Training itself is described by a simple recipe: Apply a training stress followed by rest, then repeat, applying a slightly higher training stress, over and over and over again. Because of our physiologies, we're locked into this longer-is-better method, and it takes a long time to go through enough of these training stress, rest, repeat cycles to make gains.

The Principles: Continuity, Gradualness, Modulation

Continuity means to train without break. This is not to say that we should train constantly, or even daily. No, that would surely lead to injury. Continuity means to time each subsequent training session so that it corresponds to the period when you are fully recovered—supercompensated, to use the coach's term.

Gradualness means that you need to gradually increase the training stress from workout to workout or week to week. Failure to increase the training stress will result in a plateau. Ramping up the training stress too fast will result first in stagnation, then in regression.

Modulation means varying the training stress from hard to easy. This will be on both a day-to-day cycle and a week-to-week cycle. Correct modulation gives your body a chance to absorb the previous stress.

It is the careful combination of these three elements that best enables long-term gains.

Many people will think, as I originally did, that ice climbing training simply consists of doing a lot of pull-ups. That's a good start, and if you're young and motivated and have strong elbow and shoulder joints, this might work. The reality is that there are at least three important components to ice climbing training.

Core strength is, if you think about climbing movements, incredibly important. But oversimplified Fitness Blender–style workouts are rarely useful for more than helping you do something, where anything is better than nothing. P90X, for example, is muscular endurance training misunderstood and misused. Core training, like all training, needs to follow the principles of continuity between workouts, a gradual increase in challenge, and modulation.

Upper-body strength—pulling yourself up and holding yourself up—is the most obviously important aspect of ice climbing fitness. Besides the required continuity between workouts, gradual increase in challenge, and stress modulation, you need to do two things: first, develop a high level of maximal strength in your arms and shoulders; and second, develop endurance in a strength sense of the word. I call this "muscular endurance," but other authors and coaches may use a variety of other terms, including "strength endurance."

Developing both of these attributes isn't that hard, but it requires tackling the process in the correct order. Too many people, including a younger me, started with muscular endurance. I used to simply do loads and loads of pull-ups, as many as I could do in a day, then I'd repeat that again in a few days when the soreness started to wear off. This common approach is backwards. Instead, you need to approach strength development in three phases:

1. **Conditioning:** This is a crucial stage and one of the hardest. The workouts are fairly long, containing a lot of sets and reps, and it can be

difficult to stay motivated for the necessary four to eight weeks of this training because the gains are not obvious. Gains come fast and furious in the next two stages, but if you skip step one you stand a good chance of getting injured and derailing the whole process, sending yourself back to square one.

2. **Maximum strength development:** These workouts are fun and quick to do, and you see clear gains from week to week. Everyone loves this stage. The basic principle behind max strength sessions is to teach your nervous system how to fire more muscle fibers together, in concert, to produce more power. Or to put it another way, this is training your muscles to "wire together to fire together."

3. **Muscular endurance training:** This is what many of the current fitness fad workouts consist of because this training feels hard and fun, and the gains are fast and noticeable—until you reach the limit of your physical potential, which, by no coincidence, is either what you show up with or what you built in phases 1 and 2.

If you go through phases 1 and 2, your physical limits will progress much further than if you skip straight to the muscular endurance workouts.

The good news is that you can cycle back and forth between phases 2 and 3 many times, at least two or three times, before needing to go back and address the fundamental conditioning of phase 1. That means that you can cycle max strength periods and muscular endurance periods for thirty-two to forty weeks. After that you'll have to taper and enter a performance phase.

I like to say that climbing injuries aren't caused by overuse, they're caused primarily by ignorance (and secondarily by hubris). Every athlete needs to return to fundamental conditioning work at least once a year. The highest-level professionals do this, and you should too. Failing to recognize this fact results in injuries. To put it another way, there is no such thing as overtraining, only under-recovering.

Big Enough to Be Strong Enough

There is one important caveat: Some people, most commonly teenagers and older athletes who have become de-trained, need to put on muscle mass. They simply don't carry enough muscle mass to be strong enough for their activity, and no matter how much strength the muscle fibers develop, there aren't enough fibers. In this case, a muscle-mass-building cycle, also known as hypertrophy, is in order. These are simple to plan and execute, as they involve lifting or pulling heavy weights for enough reps to reach muscular failure (usually eight to twelve). This is so simple, in fact, that it's why a lot of people who don't understand the concept of

Takeshi Tani flags out a roof on Pilsner Pillar (WI6, 40 m) in Field, British Columbia, Canada.

hypertrophy inadvertently get bigger than is optimal for their sport. Climbers have to carry all those heavy muscle fibers around, so we want to keep them to a minimum.

Let's walk through it now and get down to specifics, because I know you want a workout to do. Here I detail the three crucial workout phases and how you should progress through them to maximize your ice and mixed climbing fitness.

Phase 1: Ice/Mixed Climbing Conditioning or Transition Period

This first phase, the conditioning or transition period, encompasses core work, general strength training, and climbing. It should constitute the first eight weeks of your training, no matter how many weeks you have until you want to peak.

Core Training for Ice Climbing

Do the ten Killer Core exercises as described in *Training for the New Alpinism*. Start with 1 time through. Each week add a lap and drop any exercises that become easy and/or add resistance to keep them challenging. Do each core movement 10 times or 5 times per side.

Go to this link to download a PDF of these exercises: www.uphillathlete.com/scotts-killer-core-routine-pdf/.

Go to this link to watch the video and follow along: www.uphillathlete.com/how-to-do-core/.

General Strength

Start with 1 lap of the following circuit, doing the exercises as ordered, 10 reps of each exercise.

- Do this workout 2 times per week with at least two days in between.
- Every second week, add a lap to the circuit.
- In weeks 4, 6, and 8, increase weight and drop reps by 2 for each exercise.

1. Turkish get-ups.

2. Pull-ups.

3. Split squats.

4. Incline pull-ups.

5. Toe raises. Wear boots and stand on a step or block. Most people will need to add weight to make this effective. The ideal weight would allow you to do 20 to 25 reps before failure; you're only doing 10 to 12. Reps are per leg.

6. Hanging leg raises.

7. Dips. Bench or bar dips, depending on your strength level.

8. Ice axe hangs. These are two-tool, 10-second hangs. Simply hook your ice tools on something and hang there. Once you can easily hang for 20 seconds, add weight with a weight vest or by hanging weight off a climbing harness. Use enough weight that you can only hang a max of 12 to 15 seconds. Keep your shoulders activated and tense throughout the hang—never hang totally relaxed on your shoulder joints when training. (Note: Either wear gloves or pull a sock over the shaft of each ice tool and tape it at the top. This is much more comfortable on the hands.)

Climbing

On top of this, I recommend climbing, ideally outside, but a climbing gym may be substituted.

If you're under 25 years old, do the above gym-based strength workout on Tuesdays and Thursdays and rock climb both Saturday and Sunday. You can reorganize that schedule to climb on weekdays as well, just respect the minimum one day off (nothing resembling strength training, including manual labor) in between those two workouts and two climbing days.

If you're over 25, you probably can't recover quickly enough to fit in four strength workouts per week. The only likely exceptions are that you're essentially climbing full-time or you're coming off some other longer-term athletic career. For most people this means two gym-based strength training days plus one climbing day per week. If you need or want to train or exercise more often than that, add aerobic workouts, 90 percent at low intensity, on the other days of the week. Everyone needs at least one full rest day per week. Keep in mind that manual labor, and I would include most forms of climbing guiding in this category, is not restful and does not count as rest.

During this period your rock-climbing days should be focused on volume. And for the best results, don't randomly approach this as "just going climbing." Here are some ways in which an intelligent athlete can structure climbing days:

- Increase the volume of climbing, easily measured by pitches or vertical feet/meters, by 5 to 10 percent (maximum) each week.

- Focus on volume of pitches, not difficulty of pitches. Do not get tempted onto harder lines. The climbing days are suggested to be back-to-back for this reason.

- Search out a style of rock climbing that mimics the style of ice/mixed climbing that you're training for. If you're training for Polar Circus, the Canadian mega-classic, most of your climbing needs to be on less-than-vertical rock. If you want to crack the podium on the ice climbing world cup, then you need to focus on overhanging rock climbing.

- Don't take this specificity idea too far just yet. The ice climbing world cup aspirant should not (yet) worry about what style of overhanging climbing they seek out; they need it all: dynamic one-move cruxes, multi-move endurance, and power-endurance.

Here you can read about why training power/strength in the same session is (usually) a bad idea: www.uphillathlete.com/endurance-and-power-dont-mix-in-the-same-workout/.

Here is a sample of how to build volume, based on pitches, over an eight-week period:

Week 1: 5 pitches
Week 2: 6–7 pitches
Week 3: 7–8 pitches
Week 4: 5 pitches (this is a planned easy week)
Week 5: 7–8 pitches
Week 6: 8–9 pitches
Week 7: 10–11 pitches
Week 8: 12–13 pitches

If you are under 25, here is your training schedule:

Sunday	Monday	Tuesday	Wednesday	Thursday	Friday	Saturday
Climb	Off	Core and General Strength	Off	Core and General Strength	Off	Climb

If you are over 25, here is your training schedule:

Sunday	Monday	Tuesday	Wednesday	Thursday	Friday	Saturday
Off	Off	Core and General Strength	Off	Core and General Strength	Off	Climb

Lindsay Fixmer climbs Chalice and the Blade (WI5, 70 m) in Ranger Creek, Kananaskis, Alberta, Canada.

Respect the rest: It is important to respect the rest intervals between the workouts. You can move the training days around on the weekly calendar, but space the workouts as I have laid them out above.

Trust the process: Remember what I said about motivation at the beginning of this article? For at least the first month, it won't feel like you are doing that much training. But it adds up over time and you'll begin to carry some fatigue.

Phase 2: Ice/Mixed Climbing Base Period

This period lasts as long as you have time for: It could be as short as four weeks, or as long as thirty-two weeks. To get started, here's a good first max strength protocol in four parts:

1. Do a light warm-up of 10 to 15 minutes of aerobic exercise. If you want, you can invent a little circuit of aerobic work, including some floor exercises such as burpees, some easy climbing, or whatever else you can imagine. It doesn't matter as long as it is at a moderate pace and leaves you feeling bouncy and warm, typically with a light sweat.

2. Pick your four hardest core exercises from those exercises you've been doing. Do each of them for 10 seconds or to 4 reps, with a max of 6 reps (3 per side where applicable). Add resistance as needed to limit reps or limit your hold time. For example, if the hanging leg raise is one of your hardest core exercises (it's one of the best for ice climbers), then use it as one of the four. If you can do 12 reps without weight, then hold a weight between your feet or wear boots while doing the exercise to limit yourself to 4 reps (ideal), but no more than 6 reps. To summarize: Do four core exercises of your choice, 1 set of 4 reps of each exercise.

3. Follow the Ice Climbing Max Strength Workout as detailed below:

Ice Climbing Max Strength Workout

First, a note on weight: The typical weight for max strength protocol is 85 to 90 percent of your 1-rep max (1RM). You can estimate your 1RM by doing a given exercise to failure with a weight you think you can handle for 4 to 12 reps. Then use a 1RM calculator. In that calculator you will enter the weight lifted and the number of repetitions done, and it will calculate your 1RM. Start with about 85 to 90 percent of that number for each of the exercises listed below.

This weight should allow you to do the exercises without reaching muscular failure or exhaustion. In fact, these workouts should leave you feeling somewhat exhilarated and should have a restorative effect. If you find any given week's max strength workout to be draining, I recommend that you go back and repeat the previous week.

You will do the exercises as couplets: a pair of two exercises. I recommend you do one upper-body exercise and one for core. For example, do the pull-ups, then switch to max tool hangs, then rest 3 minutes. Then go back to the pull-ups and repeat as a couplet circuit until you're done with all the prescribed reps. Then move to the second couplet, in this case incline pull-ups and weighted hanging leg raises.

COUPLET #1

1. Pull-ups
2. Max ice axe hangs

6 sets of 4 reps (6x4)

COUPLET #2

1. Incline pull-ups
2. Weighted hanging leg raises or, for the advanced, a Figure-4 couplet

6 sets of 4 reps (6x4)

COUPLET #3

1. Weighted lock-offs. One arm at a time with a weight you can hold for 10 seconds, but hold only 6 seconds.

2. Weighted toe raises

6 sets of 4 reps (6x4)

Here are descriptions of the exercises for this phase:

- **Pull-ups:** Do them on your ice tools if possible.
- **Incline pull-ups:** These are best done on gymnastic rings. I have also used a squat cage with the big bar set across the cage and my ice tool hooked over the bar. You can vary the difficulty of incline pull-ups by varying where you put your feet, the starting angle of your torso, and what you put your feet on (try a large ball for an additional challenge).
- **Ice axe hangs:** Do 4 sets of one-armed, 10-second hangs. Use enough weight that you can only hang a max of 12 to 15 seconds. Rest 1 minute between hangs. Keep your shoulder activated and tense throughout the hang. Don't hang totally relaxed on your shoulder joints with this much load.
- **Weighted hanging leg raises:** Hang from your tools or the bar. Hook your toes into a kettle bell and lift your knees as high and tight to your chest as you can. You can also use ankle weights or wear boots.
- **Figure-4 couplet:** You can learn how to adapt this climbing movement to be a training exercise here: www.uphillathlete.com/ice-climbing -figure-4/. To add weight, if needed, simply hold a dumbbell in your free hand.
- **Weighted lock-offs:** Lock off on one tool and hang there, holding a dumbbell in your free hand.
- **Weighted toe raises:** Put your climbing boots on (it is important to do this with a rigid-sole boot) and do this one leg at a time. It's common for one side to be significantly stronger than the other.

For more details on how to correctly progress through a max strength training plan, consult Steve's training book: *Training for the New Alpinism* or Uphill Athlete's "Ice and Mixed Climbing Training Plans."

Patrick Lindsay climbs Iron Curtain (WI5, 85 m) in Yoho National Park, British Columbia, Canada.

Phase 3: Ice/Mixed Climbing Muscular Endurance Period

For another eight weeks, add this workout to your program once every ten days. This is a difficult, and also very powerful, workout. Do not overuse this, as you'll end up sick and/or injured without sufficient rest. Note that you should not cycle through more than two muscular endurance periods in a season. During a muscular endurance period, I recommend the following schedule:

Sunday	Monday	Tuesday	Wednesday	Thursday	Friday	Saturday
Climb	Rest	Rest	Ice-Beast Workout	Rest	Rest	Climb

Ice-Beast Muscular Endurance Workout

WARM-UP #1

Ten-minute warm-up run followed by 5 minutes of dynamic stretches of your creation. Dynamic stretches simply mean moving your joints and limbs through their full range of motion. Be creative.

WARM-UP #2

Twice through the following exercises at a steady pace with about 30 seconds rest between exercises.

- 6–10 pull-ups
- 10 burpees
- 10 TGUs (Turkish Get-Ups) per side with 10 kg/22 lb, or an appropriate weight that still allows good form
- 6–10 pull-ups

Rest 3 minutes before starting the workout.

WORKOUT

Sixty seconds on followed by 30 seconds recovery. Pace yourself. The idea is not to do this as fast as you can but to maintain quality and form throughout each movement. The training effect comes from the volume of work done, so if you blow up halfway through by going too hard, you will not get the desired endurance effect.

- Hanging leg raises x 60 seconds. As many as you can do in 1 minute. (30 seconds recovery.)
- Static lock-off x 60 seconds. Hang on your ice tools with your chin as high as you can manage for 60 seconds. Two-armed for most or one-armed for the advanced. (30 seconds recovery.)
- Hanging windshield wiper x 5 each side. If this is too hard, then do a weighted windshield wiper (wear boots or grip a soft weight, like a small medicine ball, between your feet). (30 seconds recovery.)

- Pull-ups x 20. Drop off as needed to complete 20. (30 seconds recovery.)
- Grip strength x 60 seconds. Grip only the shafts of your ice tools, without support from the handle. Hook the weight(s) with your ice tools (kettle bells work best) and hold that weight for 1 minute. Use good lifting posture: back straight, shoulders shrugged up toward the ears, and arms active, with the weighted tools hanging to your sides. The weight should be heavy enough that you could hold it for about 90 seconds. To decrease the difficulty, use the grips of the ice tools. (30 seconds recovery.)
- Incline pull-ups x 60 seconds. As many as you can do in 1 minute. (30 seconds recovery.)

Rest 3 minutes. Repeat each exercise one more time for a total of 2 rounds with a 3-minute rest between each round.

Do your reps at roughly a 1- to 2-second tempo, except for the pull-ups, which are slower. Set a pace that allows you to make it all the way through.

To progress the Ice-Beast Workout, add rounds per the following schedule:

Weeks 1 and 2: 2 rounds
Weeks 3 and 4: 3 rounds
Weeks 5 and 6: 4 rounds
Weeks 7 and 8: 5 rounds

Climbing during the Muscular Endurance Period

Now is the time to try hard. You won't be at your peak, actually far from it. You won't feel exceptionally strong due to the carried fatigue from the difficult Ice-Beast. But I'm willing to wager that you'll be stronger than ever, and you need the increased difficulty to keep up enough challenge to progress. Structure your climbing day so you do a warm-up of at least two or three pitches, then ramp up the difficulty until you're close to your limit for that

day. If you're toproping or sport climbing, you can push your limit to the point of falling. This is a fun time as you'll be discovering new strength, and if this is a new level for you, your technique will probably not be on par with your strength.

Max Strength Maintenance

Every other week you'll want to add the following max strength maintenance workout to, well, maintain your maximum capacity for strength:

- 15-minute warm-up run or steep hike: 10 minutes easy plus 5 minutes alternating between 1 minute fun-fast and 1 minute easy.
- 20 burpees
- 20 pull-ups

Once you are warmed up, complete your last full core/max strength workout, but cut the number of sets in half from the regular workout. For most people, this will be 2 sets of 4 reps with heavy weights.

Summary

Training is not randomized exercise, nor will "just going climbing" allow you to improve unless your technique is the primary limitation in your climbing. Training is a strategic process, and it absolutely works! This outline, and the workouts set forth, will put you on your way to your strongest ice and mixed climbing season yet.

The workouts I share here are workouts I've been developing, primarily on myself, but also with all our ice and alpine climbing Uphill Athletes over many years. They work like a puzzle; each workout is just one piece of the big picture of the best shape of your life.

Go simply, climb well.

If you want this puzzle worked out for you, consider our ice and mixed climbing training plans at www.UphillAthlete.com.

Brette Harrington climbing Hydrophobia (WI5+, 150 m) in the North Ghost, Alberta, Canada.

CHAPTER 10

Destinations

Climbing trips are rituals of the climbing lifestyle. Experiencing new locations and the different routes they offer helps us grow and improve as climbers. Successful climbing trips will allow you an opportunity to connect with friends on a deeper level, make new friends along the way, and experience new places. Going to different climbing destinations will make you a more well-rounded climber since new locations typically call for different styles than you are used to at your local crag. If you visit the Canadian Rockies from Michigan, you'll get a great tutorial in multi-pitch climbing. Take advantage of an opportunity to go on a climbing trip and escape the stress of day-to-day life.

If you crave exploring a new area to climb, this chapter will help you dream up your next trip. Every location mentioned below is worthy of visiting for at least a couple of weeks. Some spots are easier to get to than others, and most areas have a guidebook worth buying. Use the suggestions below to search out new areas and design your own adventure using guidebooks and online resources.

Planning Your Trip

A majority of climbing trips are road trips where you get the opportunity to see different parts of your own country and potentially others. Sit and watch the landscape go by and be ready to create lasting memories that are hard to make at home. Most climbers are perpetually planning their next road trip. There are numerous advantages to climbing in a different location than you are used to. Often, the climbing requires a different skill set, routes can be longer, the rock can be different, and traveling to an alpine destination requires increased knowledge and skills to stay safe in avalanche terrain.

One of the best parts about a road trip is meeting new people and connecting with locals. A key component to a successful climbing trip is making friends with a local who can share route and conditions beta with you. Make sure to return the favor to others when they visit your locale.

A well-planned climbing trip is an opportunity to connect with the outdoors and get away from your habitual schedule. Climbing road trips are an essential part of what it means to be a climber. Before you head out or begin your Google search, here are some things to consider that will help make sure your trip is as fruitful as possible.

Local Conditions

Ice climbs change and vary every year; some years they form and some years they don't. This has made online ice climbing conditions pages useful to the climbing community. Previously the best sources to get information were local guides or gear stores, but

Stas Beskin attempts the first pure-ice ascent of the mixed route ***The Real Big Drip (WI6+, 200 m) in the Ghost River Wilderness Area, Alberta, Canada.***

you didn't know what was "in" until you arrived. Finding out conditions beforehand helps avoid weekends where you drive for five hours, hike an approach for another hour, and then find out that the route hasn't formed. Some say that knowing an ice route is formed before you go to climb it removes a bit of the adventure from ice climbing, but to others, conditions pages are extremely valuable.

If you are looking for conditions info, here are a couple of great places to start for the more popular ice climbing destinations:

- New England—www.neice.com
- Cody Wyoming—www.coldfear.com/conditions
- Canadian Rockies—www.gravsportsice.com/ icethreads
- Quebec—www.escaladequebec.com/forums/ forum/conditions-de-glace/

Social media sites have also become a great resource for up-to-date ice climbing information. The ease with which you can post and upload photos has led to people using these sites as a resource to gather conditions info. Many climbing areas have a Facebook group for their ice climbing community. In the Canadian Rockies it's Canadian Rockies Ice Climbing, in Colorado it's Colorado Ice Conditions, in Quebec it's Escalade de glace au Quebec, and for British Columbia and the Pacific Northwest it's West Coast Ice. If you don't know the local group for your area, a quick search online should help you out, or ask around at the local gear shop.

If you are looking for route information but not necessarily conditions info, both Mountain Project (www.mountainproject.com) and SummitPost (www.summitpost.org) have many of the Northern American ice classics listed.

Also, in the Canadian Rockies, check out Will Gadd's app called Ice and Mixed. It combines route information along with the ability to navigate during the approach to the climbing. You can also submit conditions info and work offline. The app is becoming the go-to resource for locals and is perfect for visitors who don't want to get lost looking for a climb.

North America Ice Climbing Destinations

North America has some of the best ice climbing locations in the world. The Canadian Rockies are always in condition during the winter months, and locations such as Lake Willoughby in Vermont offer what is probably the highest concentration of ice on the planet. British Columbia has the hardest, highest-graded ice route in the world, while Ouray in Colorado has a large man-made ice park. Out west, one is never too far away from an ice climb, and at the right time of the year in the East, when conditions are good, Quebec and New England offer world-class destinations for ice and especially steep, traditional mixed climbing.

Canadian Rockies

The Canadian Rockies are the mecca of ice climbing for North America. At some point, everyone who ice climbs should visit. Whether you are a beginner or the best in the world, the Canadian Rockies has something for everyone. Every winter, usually around mid-October, it is possible to start ice climbing in Canada. If you are willing to seek it out and take your tools for a walk, there is normally something to climb on the high and north-facing areas. Avalanche hazard is a serious concern in the Canadian Rockies; be sure to check out www.avalanche.ca to get more info on avalanche conditions.

There is a lifetime of quality ice and mixed climbing in the Rockies, and a quick Google search will bring up an unlimited tick-list of "must-do" routes during a visit.

Most people stay in Canmore, Banff, Lake Louise, Field, or Jasper when visiting the Rockies, but two other locations that should be explored more

Etienne Rancourt climbs Piller Crystal (WI4+, 110 m) at Chutes Montmorency in Quebec City, Quebec, Canada.

regularly are Waterton Lakes National Park and the David Thompson Highway, west of Nordegg. Every one of these areas has a large selection of ice and mixed routes that would make it a classic destination location.

The Icefields Parkway, one of the most scenic drives in North America, is home to all-time classic routes like Polar Circus (WI5), Weeping Wall (WI4-6), and Curtain Call (WI6). There are hostels located along the Parkway where you can stay instead of commuting back to the towns but be warned there are no services and no cell phone service; shortly after turning onto the Parkway you are disconnected from the world of text messages and social media.

In Banff, you'll find classics like Cascade Falls (WI3), Professor Falls (WI4), and, if you are lucky, the Trophy Wall (WI6). There is an unlimited supply of ice in the Canadian Rockies worth seeing for yourself.

Northern Ontario/Thunder Bay (by Brandon Pullan)

Ice climbing in northern Ontario stretches from Sault Ste. Marie on the eastern shore of Lake Superior all the way to Thunder Bay on the western shore, some 700 kilometers (435 miles) away. Along the Trans-Canada Highway, you pass dozens of world-class areas. Agawa Canyon, which is accessed by train, offers 60-meter (197-foot) routes from WI3 to WI5 and is where some of Ontario's most remote classics abound. Farther north near Nipigon is Kama Bay, with tall routes like the stout Icebreakers Arete, a 60-meter (197-foot) WI6. North of the town of Nipigon is the well-known Orient Bay, with nearly one hundred pitches of outstanding non-avalanche-threatened routes, such as Reflection Wall (WI5), Obsession (WI4), and Starquake (WI6).

As you move closer to the city of Thunder Bay, you pass dozens of isolated routes that form from summer flows down an old mountainous area called the Nor'Westers. Around the city are many classic climbs, such as the 40-meter (131-foot) White Lightening (WI3+) and the chimney ice of the 30-meter (98-foot) Lost Falls. On the mighty Mount McRae are the epic Child's Play and Nanabijou, both WI6+R testpieces. With hundreds of pitches of ice, some close to the road and some far, along the shore of Lake Superior, you'll require many trips just to climb the absolute best.

Quebec (by Jas Fauteux)

Quebec boasts some of the best ice climbing in North America and is definitely one of the best-kept secrets in Canada. You can expect beautiful, untraveled ice that is often easily accessible from the road. The Quebec City area and the whole North Coast of the St. Lawrence River from Charlevoix to Sept-Îles, including the Saguenay area, have a lifetime's worth of climbing. Not to be missed are La Pomme d'Or (WI5+), Le Mulot (WI6), and farther to the north, Capteur de Rêve (WI5+). The Gaspé Peninsula in Quebec is home to small and quaint riverside villages offering numerous world-class, roadside routes, right above the majestic St. Lawrence River. With short approaches and a smaller climbing community spread out over an infinite number of routes, Quebec is an ice climber's dream.

Upper Peninsula, Michigan

Michigan, although far from the mountains, has a great local ice climbing scene including an annual Michigan Ice Fest in February that normally draws around 1,000 participants. The scenic Pictured Rocks National Lakeshore hosts over 150 ice routes, with most of them being vertical and challenging, rising right out of Lake Superior. Unlike many destinations, climbs here are accessed from the top more than normal, and sometimes you have to rap in, commit, and pull the rope. Grand Island, which is accessed near Munising, is just across the channel and has 45 kilometers (28 miles) of shoreline, much of which is cliffs, but make sure the ice is formed to get across the lake before you make plans to climb here.

Bozeman, Montana

Bozeman is the epicenter of ice climbing in Montana. The route many hope to tick in Hyalite Canyon is Winter Dance (M8 WI6), the namesake for the local guidebook, which rarely forms, but there are 150 other routes in a small area that make Hyalite a top ice climbing destination. Joe Josephson, an extremely well-traveled ice climber, presents a good argument for saying, "Hyalite is the most concentrated, easily accessible, and consistent ice climbing venue in North America." Every year in December, climbers flock to Bozeman for one of the best ice climbing festivals in the United States—definitely one worth checking out.

There is a great variety of climbing in Hyalite, from toprope areas to a higher-than-usual concentration of hard mixed climbs, put up by the late Alex Lowe. If you are looking for adventure,

Montana just might be the destination for you, as parts of Montana are ranked as some of the most remote spots in the Lower 48. The Cabinet Mountains in northwestern Montana will likely quench your thirst to explore.

Cody, Wyoming

If visiting Cody from another location in the lower 48 states, expect the climbing to be more adventurous than you are used to, with longer approaches and a sandbagged style to the grades. The South Fork of the Shoshone is easily accessible from the town of Cody, and there is camping available close to the climbs at Deer Creek Campground. The area is reminiscent of the Ghost in Canada in that it is in the Front Range, which means there's usually less snow to deal with than at other ice climbing destinations. There are many routes to choose from in the South Fork of the Shoshone, and instead of having to worry about needing a 4x4 to access the climbs, you can usually get by with something more civilized like a minivan.

The South Fork offers enough ice to keep you busy for a while, with classics such as Moratorium

Doug Shepherd and Aaron Mulkey admire the view in Cody, Wyoming, USA.

Nikki Smith climbs Sugar Snice and Everything Zice (WI4, 225 m) in Zion National Park, Utah, USA.
AUSTIN SCHMITZ

(WI4), High on Boulder (WI4), Moonrise (WI5), Mean Green (WI5), and Broken Hearts (WI5-6) being just a small selection of the high concentration of quality routes.

Utah (by Nikki Smith, author of Bee Hive Ice)

Utah has plenty to offer in the "standard" mountain ice scene, such as the spring-fed ice pouring out of stepped limestone buttresses in Provo Canyon, the long waterfall ice on the granite gullies of Little Cottonwood, or the frozen cascades hidden in the pines of the Uintas. But it also offers some of the most diverse and interesting ice climbing around. Formed by snowmelt, the carved conglomerate walls of Maple Canyon create unique climbs in a setting unlike anything else in the state, which holds one of the highest concentrations of natural ice climbs in the United States.

A paradox to the uninitiated, beautiful blue cascades of ice pour off cartoonishly featured orange sandstone buttresses right next to sagebrush and cacti in the middle of Utah's southwest deserts. Below the horizon from Moab to Zion, hidden subterranean slot canyons twist and turn in a labyrinth of mostly undocumented potential for ice climbing. Adventure climbing at its finest, you have to rap in, then climb out (if you can). It's a committing experience in one of the most unique and beautiful settings in the world.

Colorado

In the Front Range, Rocky Mountain National Park and Pikes Peak offer quality routes high up on granite peaks. Vail is home to a selection of single-pitch routes like the Fang, and some of the hardest-touted mixed grades in North America. A little farther west along I-70 you can find Hidden Falls (WI3-4), the Drool (WI4-5), and Rifle, but the main area for ice climbing in Colorado is the San Juan Mountains.

Ouray, with its ice climbing park, is one of the most unique towns for climbing ice in North America. Over 200 routes are farmed and manufactured in the park within a quick walk of downtown, and it hosts one of the biggest ice festivals every year with over 3,000 festival participants descending on the town for an exciting extended weekend of fun.

Ouray Ice Park is certainly worth a visit, but the best ice in the area is found outside the park. Camp Bird Road features mixed classics like Bird Brain Boulevard (WI5 M5) and the Talisman (WI6 M6), while Eureka has Stairway to Heaven (WI4), and close by in Telluride you can find Ames Ice Hose (WI5 M6) and Bridal Falls (WI6). Although the ice park is what the area is known for, the local classics make up some of the best climbing in Colorado.

White Mountains, New Hampshire

New Hampshire has some of the best ice climbing in New England. With technical testpieces and an alpine environment on Mount Washington, it is a fantastic place to climb ice during the winter. North Conway is the hub of winter climbing in the state. Within a short drive are the popular routes at Frankenstein Cliff and The Black Dike (WI4-5) at Cannon, and just outside town at Cathedral Ledge are the classic multi-pitch routes Repentance (WI5 M5) and Remission (WI5+ M5). For more of an alpine feel, Mount Washington can't be beat on the East Coast. Head up to the scenic Huntington Ravine and check out the longer gully routes for some mountain training.

Lake Willoughby, Vermont

Vermont is home to the famed Lake Willoughby. It's been referred to as possibly the largest concentration of hard ice routes in the United States. The approach is relatively short, but the collection of quality multi-pitch routes is high. For a single cliff the selection of routes here can't be beat. At the end of the day, you might even get to enjoy the butt slide back to the road. Smuggler's Notch is another location in Vermont that offers a large selection of routes and some great mixed climbing.

New York

Upstate New York has great ice climbing, with many options near Keene Valley for beginner to advanced climbers. The Chapel Pond area offers a great introduction to multi-pitch ice with options like Chouinard's Gully (WI3) and Chapel Pond Slab (WI2+). Located right beside them is the classic Power Play (WI4-5) and Chapel Pond Canyon with a selection of single-pitch climbs. Within a short drive is another classic, Positive-Thinking (WI5) at Poke-O-Moonshine. If you are looking for more of a backcountry experience, try checking out the Avalanche Lake area.

North American Ice Climbing Festivals

Ice climbing festivals are a great place to learn skills, try out new gear, and make new friends. If you are looking to learn more about ice climbing, a festival can be a great place to learn the skills in a supervised environment at a lower cost than normal. Another great thing about ice climbing festivals is that typically the major manufacturers attend the festivals, and you can demo their ice climbing gear. If you are considering buying new tools or crampons, it's a good opportunity to try them out before purchasing.

Here is a selection of ice festivals in North America. There is a tendency for some of the smaller ones to change from season to season or for new ones to be added, so search online before you put them in your calendar.

Adirondack International Mountainfest, Keene Valley, New York

Bozeman Ice Festival, Bozeman, Montana

Catskill Ice Festival, New Paltz, New York

CityROCK Ice Fest, Colorado Springs, Colorado

Cody Ice Climbing Festival, Cody, Wyoming

Duluth Ice and Mixed Fest, Duluth, Minnesota

Festiglace, Pont-Rouge, Quebec

Festival Grimpe En Ville, Riviere-du-Lou, Quebec

Lake City Ice Climbing Festival, Lake City, Colorado

Michigan Ice Fest, Munising, Michigan

Mount Washington Valley Ice Fest, North Conway, New Hampshire

Nipigon Ice Fest, Nipigon, Ontario

Ouray Ice Festival, Ouray, Colorado

Portland Alpine Festival, Portland, Oregon

Smuggs Ice Bash, Smuggler's Notch, Vermont

Southern Ontario Ice Festival, Maynooth, Ontario

Valdez Ice Climbing Festival, Valdez, Alaska

Ryan Vachon finishes the competition route in good style at the 2018 Ouray Ice Climbing Festival, Colorado, USA.
AUSTIN SCHMITZ

Appendix A

Dynamic Shock Load Evaluation of Ice Screws: A Real-World Look

J. Marc Beverly, BS-EMS, M-PAS
Stephen Attaway, PhD
November 2005

ABSTRACT

Background: It is unknown how many climbers take lead falls on ice screws placed in waterfall ice. Generally, what is reported are accidents that occur when ice screws fail or are pulled from the ice. To date, there is very little information regarding ice screw testing.

Methods: Over the period of eight days of drop testing, we conducted a randomized placement of short ice screws in real-world vertical waterfall ice. Different fall factors, including the UIAA standard, were evaluated to determine what a climber might expect from dynamic shock loading of an ice screw in real climbing conditions.

Results: 61 drops were performed on real world ice on ice screws.

Conclusions: We show that while ice is a variable medium, a predictable and surprisingly strong normogram can be produced in the conditions we performed our testing in. However, because the methods of judging ice conditions are based solely on experience, it may be difficult for novices to discriminate these conditions. The perception that ice screws are weak protection when "good" ice is utilized is unfounded.

A definition of terms has been created that may help provide a nomenclature for discerning ice conditions.

INTRODUCTION

The main objective was to gain an understanding of the behavior of ice screws under dynamic shock loading and peak forces needed to hold a falling ice climber in a real-world setting. There is little information regarding real-world testing. Rather, most testing is done in laboratories and the tests performed there only evaluate the tensile strength of the materials and not necessarily the application for which they were intended to be used in the first place. Climbers rely on word of mouth, books, periodicals, and training from others to gain insight on the equipment used. Good data are not only hard to find but are difficult to acquire outside in real-world conditions. This was an attempt to find scientific-based data that might help climbers think more critically about their ice screw placements.

HYPOTHESES

1. Peak forces seen in ice climbing are equivalent to those seen in rock climbing. It is thought that ropes with more stretch decrease shock load and thereby decrease peak forces on an ice screw. Does using a new rope play a role in what peak forces are seen? If so, how?

2. Considering only being able to place the shortest ice screws on the market and using the UIAA test configuration for dynamic mountaineering ropes for lead falls, do peak forces seen in dynamic shock loading of ice screws in the orientation of $\geq +10°$ but $\leq +30°$ hold in fair to good ice?

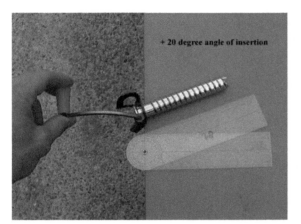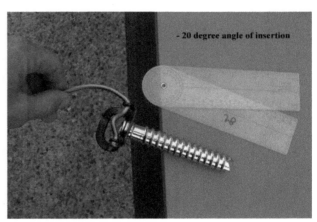

Figure 1: *Defining the angles:* left: *a positive 20°;* right: *a negative 20°. These angles are relative to vertical ice from the horizontal/perpendicular line relative to the ice face.*

3. A large spread of results has been reported on ice screw strengths, and the CE tests ice screws in a non-ice medium for approval. The tests that abound are at different forces and time durations. Can drop testing in a natural forum of actual ice climbing produce more realistic and repeatable results?

BACKGROUND

To date, there is very little information regarding ice screw testing. One of the major factors for this is the lack of consistency of ice quality. This makes the science of testing anything in ice obscure at best. Volumes of research have been performed on oceanic and glacial ice, but there is sparse information of anything regarding waterfall ice especially in application to ice climbing. The general thought has been that "climbers essentially take their lives in their own hands should they take a fall onto an ice screw." Their only protection, aside from luck, has been experience. The rule of thumb has been that the "leader must not fall."

Craig Luebben[1] and Chris Harmston did some drop testing on ice screws and found poor results in aerated ice. Using a solid mass of 185 pounds of iron, Luebben reports having "pulled out entire lengths of ice screws" in some tests resulting in a ground fall from the top of the climb. "The ice had lots of aeration and bubbles in it; the way the ice was made was different back then," in a conversation I had with Luebben. The drops were from 16-28 feet, with corresponding fall factors of 1 to 1.7. A total of twelve drops on screws were performed: the top screw failed in seven tests, ice hooks failed three out of three times, and a pound-in screw with a stitched load-limiting device failed under a fall factor of 1 using a 16-foot fall. The 10.5 mm dynamic rope ran from the iron, down through the protection, and was clipped into an equalized anchor. A single dynamometer was used to record peak forces. However, how many tests were performed in each configuration or what the exact data were from those falls are unavailable and unclear. Perhaps the most confounding variable is that the same rope was used repeatedly.

Luebben went on to perform more tests, this time using a dynamic belay with an ATC and "back weighted the rope with 75 pounds (not a mechanical hand)." The fall factor was reduced to somewhere between 0.9 and 1.2 and no failures were reported. An Abolakov (treaded tunnel) held a 0.8 fall factor and again, three of three ice hooks failed. No configurations were reported to ascertain how the fall factors were obtained and the forces produced from these tests is unknown, but the results were clearly separated into fail or no fail.

Further testing on the strength of varying lengths of ice screws in ice, what angle of ice screw placement is better, and if tying off a foreshortened screw was a good idea or not, was also performed. These tests were done using a come-along. Chris Harmston, then the quality assurance manager at Black Diamond, performed similar tests.

Harmston's methods were as follows[2]:

"The top few inches of really bad ice is chopped off and a new layer of water is added and allowed to freeze. A screw is placed in one half of the cell and pulled to failure at 12 cm per minute. The screw generally fails by cratering the top 5-8 centimeters of ice away from the screw, bending of the screw and finally, either levering the hanger off the head of the screw, breaking the tube of the screw, or pulling the screw out of the ice. A second screw is placed in the other half of the cell near the first screw's hole and similarly pulled to failure (yes, the ice is shattered and broken from the first test). After the tests are completed, any broken-off screws are removed by chopping them out with an ice axe. The cell is placed back into the freezer and water is added to the old test holes and allowed to freeze onto the remaining ice. The cells are used repeatedly in this fashion up to 20 times before the entire cell is allowed to thaw and be 'regenerated.' As can be inferred, this technique of ice preparation is highly variable and unpredictable (not unlike real world ice) yet has yielded conclusive and supportable results."

The trends that Luebben observed followed those of Harmston's regarding strength of ice screw material in slow pull testing where force is applied for a relatively longer period and at sustained high forces. The results are interesting and may be extrapolated to similar real-world uses, but only Luebben has reported actual drop test data.

Luebben's results have prompted some significant changes. Perhaps the most important one is in the way ice screws should be placed. Placing the screw at +10 to +20 degrees has shown a significant increase in strength from –10 to –20 degrees, as the positive angle does not compress and thereby fail the ice under the screw and relies on the friction of the threads for holding strength.

Most recently, testing at three placement angles (–30°, 0°, and +30°) was evaluated[3]. Their conclusions agreed with both Luebben and Harmston reports in that negative placement angles showed reduced failure load. However, their data also suggest that positive angle placement had a dependency on loading rates of 125 N/s and 12,500 N/s and two manufactured ice types. Unfortunately, a third loading rate was not performed to provide for a graphical representation of what the scale of the difference might be: linear, logarithmic, or otherwise. They also report that a faster loading rate reduces failure load, but they did not do actual drop tests to validate what force reached upper threshold limits.

"If a metal screw was placed in a similar metal material, the thread surface area equaling at least 1.5 times the diameter of the screw is significant in strength to hold the screw in the material. However, all bets are off when two materials of differing characteristics are used, such as metal and ice," according to Frank Zanner, a PhD in metallurgy retired from Sandia National Laboratories in Albuquerque, New Mexico. Therefore, an assumption of how an ice screw might behave based solely on its physical characteristics is unreliable. Drop testing must be performed.

In drop testing, the UIAA[4] uses an 80 kg load on a single rope and 55 kg on a half rope as a test mass for dynamic falls. The reasoning behind the lower test mass on the half rope is that a half rope should ideally see only 70% of an 80 kg dynamic fall factor of 1.74. In the UIAA test this is a solid mass, not a human form such as the Rescue Randy, and represents an ideal worst-case scenario for placing loads on the protection seeing the load. The UIAA test insults the rope further in that the anchoring system is a bollard and backed up by a non-slipping mechanical hand.

Dynamic loads on this medium may vary from static loads in the way that moving a body through water slowly such as a swimmer is different than a body hitting the water that is moving at 9.8m/s/s. This is a gross analogy, but one that cannot be dismissed at this time. The point being that behavior of ice on screws may be different with different velocities of force applied.

Joe Josephson showed that Ice Threads (aka, an Abolakov), were shown to be substantially strong[5] and today they are standard practice in use for retreating off an ice climb. Abolakovs are also used as protection points while climbing but were not evaluated by our testing in Ouray.

LOCATION

The Uncompahgre Gorge is the setting of the Ouray Ice Park in Ouray, Colorado. It was selected as the site for the drop tests for several reasons. The gorge is a slot canyon with greater than a one hundred foot vertical to overhanging drop and is the site of over 180 established popular ice climbing routes. The sun does not hit the bottom of the route on any day but does reach the retro-base formation[6] for a brief period between noon and 14:00 hrs. This is like many natural ice climbs in other areas. Ouray is known for having many different types of ice during a season.

Figure 2: *Configuring the data collection node and preparing the test weight on the "Rhythm Method" WI5 in Ouray, Colorado.*

The ice route used was the "Rhythm Method," WI5+, located on the northwest side of the lower bridge and represents undulating vertical and overhanging ice to ensure free fall in the vertical axis. Testing occurred throughout the two months of January and February over a total of seven days.

TESTING METHODS

A. DATA

The testing system used was a wireless Microstrain V-link data logging system that was modified to meet the needs of data acquisition while on the ice climb. The V-link stores the data and then it is downloaded through a wireless transceiver into the laptop for later analysis. We used a Pelican case to house the V-link and made quick disconnects from the case that attach up to four load cells and one manual triggering device. An automatic triggering system that allowed a single user the capability to run tests quickly and efficiently was also engineered.

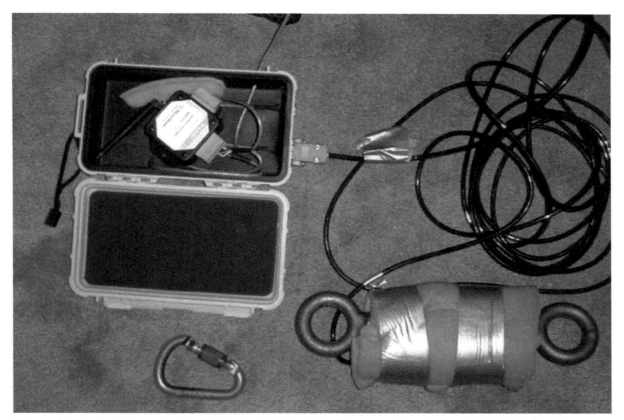

Figure 3: *Typical S-type load cell attached with quick disconnect to wireless V-link data logging system.*

B. ICE TYPE

Although one can consider that ice is an ever-changing medium with varying properties, "it is neither a 'simple elastic' nor an 'elastic/plastic' solid[7]." Furthermore, "ice has at least twelve different crystallographic structures and two amorphous states. The structure formed most commonly in nature is the Ih-type. This is formed by simply freezing water and has a hexagonal structure[8]," and is likely the structural form most often found in the Ice Park as well as abroad. Further analysis should be done in this area to confirm consistency where other waterfall ice forms and is climbed.

Density measurements were taken by chipping a sample from where the top piece ice screws were placed. On site, the sample was weighed, then was melted in a beaker and allowed to reach 47°C and the volume measured. The ice densities measured were $\bar{x} = 0.97$, $n = 8$. The density of the Ouray Ice is equivalent to that of the ice made by Ready Ice in Albuquerque, NM: $d = 0.97$, $n = 4$ for comparison.

Figure 4: *Typical placement and typical ice conditions throughout the Ouray Ice Park.*

Ambient air temperature varied from 20F°/-7°C to 33 F°/1°C, and the ice temperature diurnal variation was -6.6°C at 08:00 hours to -1.9 °C at 13:00 hours but was consistent on a daily evaluation. Temporal variability could not be accounted for due to the slow and tedious process of doing drop testing in real-world conditions.

What will not be described here is the form or quality of the ice. Instead, *Appendix A* provides a descriptive vernacular used to make an attempt to better portray the quality of the ice as seen by a lead climber placing an ice screw.

Figure 5 (left) *weighing the test mass, and* **Figure 6 (right)** *displaying the results of why a stopper knot is necessary—note the over camming of the Grigri that allowed no slip.*

C. CONFIGURATIONS

Several lead climbing orientations were performed using a (172 pound = 78.0178876 kilogram [two pounds of clothes and gear])[9] Rescue Randy for the simulation of a fallen lead climber. The Randy had a seat harness and a chest harness.

For all tests:
Grigris were used at both the test mass side and the anchor side. Stopper knots were placed behind each device to prevent and control for slip. For the appropriate tests, the rope ran freely through the top piece carabiner as in lead climbing orientation. Otherwise, the rope hung freely and without obstruction.

Stopper knots allow for all belays to be equivocal and non-dynamic for consistency of the experiment as it would be nearly impossible to account for a dynamic belay's variability. This method is like the UIAA test where a bollard wrap is used and creates a non-dynamic belay condition. The Grigri retains full strength of the rope[10] by using a bollard. It was important to consider having no knot at the anchor as it absorbs energy.

FALL ORIENTATION

Orientation #1 Fall Factor 1–Anchor (Figure 7)
The test weight is placed at the same level of the ice screw acted upon. The test weight is dropped 2 m on 2 m of rope. This would replicate a slip from the belay stance.

Orientation #2 Fall Factor 1–UIAA Variant (Figure 8)
The testpiece was placed at 2.3 m above the anchor and at a 30° angle. The test weight was raised to 2.3 m above the testpiece (straight up) and released. This test was also a fall factor of 1. However, it is also a likely scenario. *Understand that it places more force on the ice screw testpiece than Orientation #1.*

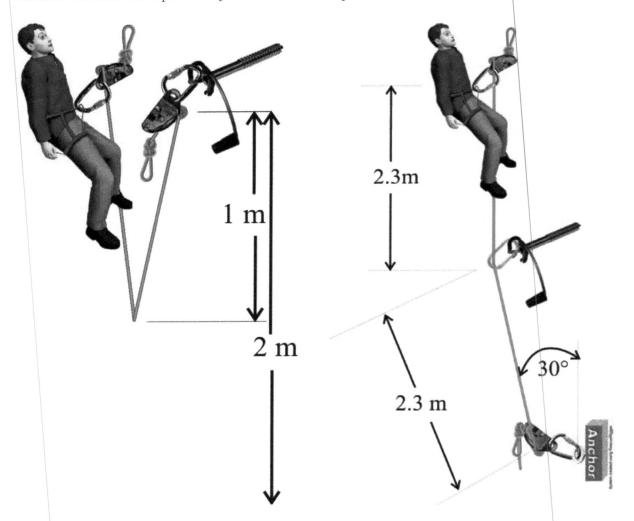

Left to right: Figure 7, *fall factor 1 from an anchor;* **Figure 8,** *fall factor 1 in lead climbing formation UIAA-variant.*

Orientation #3 Fall Factor 2 (Figure 9)
The test weight was placed at 2 m above the ice screw testpiece and released.

Orientation #4 Fall Factor 1.71–UIAA drop test (Figure 10)
From the anchor point to the ice screw test piece was 300 mm (30 cm) and at a 30-degree angle to the anchor. The test weight was lowered to 2.5 m from the testpiece. The weight was raised up to 2.3 m above the testpiece and released.

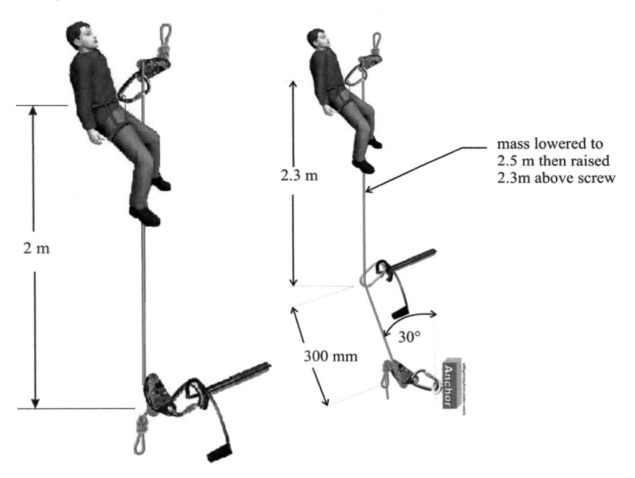

2 m

2.3 m

mass lowered to 2.5 m then raised 2.3m above screw

300 mm

30°

Anchor

Left to right: Figure 9, fall factor 2; Figure 10, fall factor 1.71 (the UIAA test).

LIMITATIONS

Several confounding factors are evident:

Choice of protection placement–Not everyone will be able to perceive ice quality in the same way. There is simply no substitute for experience. Sometimes that is experienced in the face of grave danger while leading and it seems to exhibit operantly conditioned responses from seasoned ice climbers as can be seen from the choice of tool and protection placement.

Ice screw manufacturer–Each manufacturer has its own style of production. Only three styles were tested: the Grivel 360°, Petzl Laser, and Petzl Laser Sonic, all of which were the shortest of their make.

Ice/environment–Certainly, ice is an ever-changing medium. Conditions were generally what one might expect to climb in, but there was no way to control for environmental variation. This might best be done in a facility capable of producing waterfall ice and maintaining stable conditions, day or night.

Test mass–This is an area of continuing debate and cannot possibly be covered in this paper. Further mention of possible research in this area should be investigated.

RESULTS

We looked at the data in several different ways and asked several questions that were pertinent to ice climbers and those interested in ice screw placements. Other questions arise as one was answered. We used statistical analysis to verify our hypothesis.

passing screws			failing screws			total all	
Mean	8.294		Mean	10.1		Mean	8.63
Standard Error	0.348		Standard Error	0.88		Standard Error	0.34
Median	7.93		Median	10.8		Median	8.17
Mode	6.07		Mode	#N/A		Mode	6.07
Standard Deviation	2.464		Standard Deviation	2.91		Standard Deviation	2.62
Sample Variance	6.072		Sample Variance	8.49		Sample Variance	6.88
Kurtosis	1.003		Kurtosis	1.04		Kurtosis	0.05
Skewness	1.178		Skewness	-0.67		Skewness	0.78
Range	9.95		Range	10.6		Range	10.9
Minimum	4.93		Minimum	3.98		Minimum	3.98
Maximum	14.88		Maximum	14.6		Maximum	14.9
Sum	414.7		Sum	112		Sum	526
Count	50		Count	11		Count	61

Table 1: *Descriptive analysis: pass, fail, and all-inclusive.*

First, we looked at pass versus fail. What could someone expect if a mass was exerted on an ice screw protection point while using a single rope and a static belay?

To show breakdown of variance of impact force by fall factor we tabulated Figure 11. Higher fall factors produced a higher impact force, but note that ff 2 did not get above 10kN, nor did any ff 2 fail on a single screw. Figure 12 shows a complete breakdown of peak impact forces by individual test.

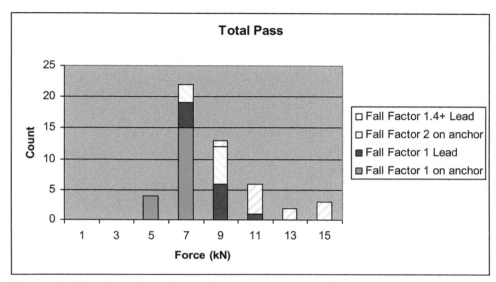

Figure 11: *Total number of pass drops relevant to peak impact force.*

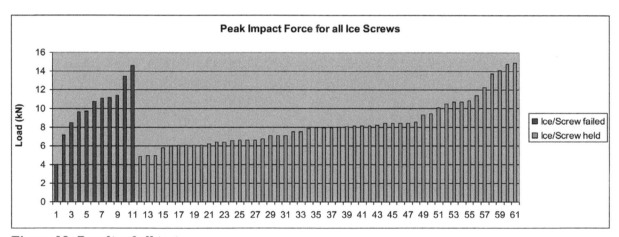

Figure 12: *Results of all tests.*

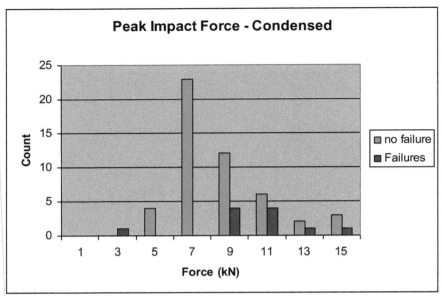

Figure 13: *Condensed count of all tests separated out in no failure (pass) and failures vs. force (kN).*

The results of our tests were surprising. At first glance it appears that there is no significant difference in impact force between passing and failing screws, and that it looks like a 50/50 shot at failing a screw. Both categories of pass/fail fall into the same relative bins.

In evaluation of the statistical analysis, we use the standard formula for the one-sample t confidence interval of 95%,

$$\bar{X} \pm t\frac{s}{\sqrt{n}}$$

Where, $\bar{x}$ = mean, t = how far $\bar{x}$ is from m in standard deviation units, $s/\sqrt{n}$ = standard error (estimation of standard deviation). This is assuming that one puts ice screws into what appears to be "good" waterfall ice as outlined earlier.

For the normal distribution in our experiment:

Pass (held)

$8.63kN \pm 2s = 7.29 < \bar{X} < 9.97$

$8.63kN \pm 3s = 6.62 < \bar{X} < 10.64$

Failed (pulled)

$10.14kN \pm 2s = 6.24 < \bar{X} < 14.04$

$10.14kN \pm 3s = 4.29 < \bar{X} < 15.99$

$$t = \frac{\bar{X} - \mu}{\frac{s}{\sqrt{n}}}$$

A t-test for the normal distribution curve shows:

Where $a = 0.05$, we find the p = 0.0365. This shows that there is a significant difference that out of 100 samples, there is less than a 3.65% chance that the samples we obtained were due to sampling error.

Therefore, we can support the hypothesis that there is a significant difference in impact force between failing and non-failing ice screws in real-world ice. What is attributed to this difference? Likely, it is the ability of the individual placing the screw to discriminate the ice conditions where the screw is placed.

The failure of 3.98 kN is close to the 3 standard error (standard deviation) from the mean. This was indeed an outlier in the fact that I was able to make the statement that it was "psychological pro" and would likely not hold a high impact force when I placed the screw. This explains the lower end of the failures.

Evaluation of High Fall Factors >1.0

Looking at fall factors of 1.4–1.7, there was no significant difference in pass or fail.

t-Test: Two-Sample Assuming Equal and Unequal Variances:
Setting $a = 0.05$ we find that p = 0.017 and 0.037, respectively.

What was observed is that the stubby screws saw high impact forces of nearly 15kN without failure. This fact only supports the reasoning that _ice placement selection ability becomes the important factor._

COMPARISON OF PREVIOUS TESTING AND AVAILABLE DATA

We used the Black Diamond data to look at relevant comparison to our own.

For 13 cm length ice screws in lab ice at Black Diamond:
N = 63
$\bar{x}$ = 4279/19.0
Std. Dev (s) (IbF/kN) 1275/5.7
High (lbF/kN) 8269/36.8
Low (lbF/kN) 2387/10.6

Calculating the Black Diamond's 2 and 3 sigma, we see that it is much greater than our results:
$19kN \pm 2s$ = $16.1 < \bar{X} < 21.9$
$19kN \pm 3s$ = $14.7 < \bar{X} < 23.3$

Calculating our results with those of Black Diamond's with a two-sample t-test:

$$t = \frac{\bar{X}_1 - \bar{X}_2}{\sqrt{\frac{s_1^2}{n_1} + \frac{s_2^2}{n_2}}} = 10.99$$

We find that _t=10.99 > p=0.05,_ and therefore it could be said loosely that, the type of testing that Black Diamond did in the lab cannot be compared to our testing in Ouray on real-world ice, but a larger sample and further testing should be done to confirm these results. Perhaps overdriving our system either using static rope or increasing the mass to force-fail all screws would be indicated.

Addressing Fall Factor 2

A total of nine drops of ff 2 were performed before discovering futility.
$7.8kN \pm 2s = 6.8 < \bar{X} < 8.8$

The maximum impact force reached was only 8.6kN with no failures. This opens the door to a large debate that could be justified in several ways of, "when should I put in my first ice screw when leaving a belay stance on a multi-pitch ice route?"

Certainly, the classic thought process has long been to either clip the master point if the anchor points are potentially weak, and/or place a screw immediately to avoid a ff 2.

Entertain the following scenario: No research has ever been done to establish the "non-elastic deformation," also known as the "double whammy phenomena." This occurs when a climber leads off from the anchor as in a multi-pitch climbing scenario, places a piece right away, and places a fall factor large enough on the system to produce an impact force that will not only stretch the dynamic rope to a high dynamic elongation but also to fail a protection piece. Using our data, the average ice screw might likely pull out somewhere between 3.98-14.6 kN in good ice. The question becomes, once the rope has just been stretched, possibly to near its UIAA limit, what is the behavior of the rope if it does not have time for the elastic properties to recoil and provide for more shock load absorption? If the belay is not "bomber," the possibilities could be grim. This is an area in need of further research.

DISCUSSION

It is always safe to say that climbing in any form is inherently dangerous and nothing substitutes for good training, experience, and expertise, and our investigation supports that notion. We have made an effort to help those who use ice screws to stack the odds in their favor by performing real-world application to an enigmatic topic. This exercise has shown many things of importance in addition to the use of good judgment:

1. Higher impact forces can cause more failures. A narrow margin appears to exist. Simply overdriving a system not designed for heavier masses can be one way to accomplish this. There are other ways at achieving this same result such as using an old rope, clipping two double ropes together when only one should have been, or increasing friction in the system by any modality are several of those ways.

2. Short ("stubbie") screws when placed in good ice provided a significant amount of protection that was quite unexpected and equivalent to that of rock gear. It is of the opinion of the authors that poor ice gear is as good as "rattly" rock gear or just throwing your rack on top of the rock, clipping your rope to it, and jumping off the cliff only to hope that the gear somehow miraculously catches on something and holds your fall. In essence, ice gear is good if placed in zones of compression or areas devoid of large air pockets within 15-30 cm of the screw placement. Anecdotally, small air bubbles within the ice do not seem to matter.

3. There was a significant difference between lab ice and real-world ice in our analysis. Lab tests and lab ice may not reflect real-world ice, but further investigation into this topic should be performed before drawing any conclusions.

4. Temperature varies greatly in waterfall ice. It has been shown that ice becomes brittle below -5°C. We did see more failures in the morning than in the afternoon hours. However, the ice did not get above

-1.9°C. The density of the ice itself does not appear to be a significant factor, but temperature may be. Colder ice (less than -5°C) should be studied.

5. Research should be performed looking specifically at non-elastic deformation of rope when a protection point fails during a fall and the relative forces placed on the subsequent piece(s)/anchor. Indeed, a complex matter.

6. We were able to validate the concept of what angle ice screws should be placed in vertical waterfall ice as previously studied by Luebben and Harmston.

7. During the course of our ice screw testing, we were able to test three ice hooks, all three failed, did not slow the test mass down at all, and became a sharp flying projectile heading toward the test mass (climber). In one instance the "double whammy phenomena" was possibly observed and failed a back-up screw immediately.

Certainly, many other inferences about these results can be made. More discussion about application is in order, and testing in some of the aforementioned areas is appropriate.

Glossary

ICE TYPES

This glossary of terms is by no means extensive or definitive. Terms may also vary according to any given changes on any given day. This is only to help for sake of discussion.

EXCELLENT
Goo, Block of Cheese, blue, solid, vertical hockey rink, sinker, thunker, stonker, hero, bomber, thick, windshield ice;
Cold yesterday, warm (perhaps humid today)

GOOD
Opaque, rivulet surface, good screw placement, small occasional dinner plating (tension release fracture), minimal fracturing on tool and screw placements, psychologically encouraging;
A little colder out or less humid than Fair Ice conditions

FAIR
Large dinner plating, exfoliating surface (radial cracking), beginning to chandelier, small cauliflowers

POOR
Large cauliflowers, deep and extensive chandeliering, sublimated surface, brittle, gray, sun bleached, baked out, back warmed, hollow, low gonging, air pockets upon insertion of screw, baby heads, bobbles

PITIFUL
Verglass, very warm, extremely cold, crap, shit, crumbly, full raking, 8-10 swing ice, slush, porridge, rotten

Ropes used

UIAA drop testing:
Brand new Sterling Evolution Kosmos Dry 10.2 mm rope. Lot # R1-092704DPC/DJC

FF0.3 and 1.0 (free fall from anchor) drop testing:
Brand new Sterling 8.8 half rope Lot #R47-082404
Brand new Sterling 10.4 single rope Lot #04-110504

UIAA variant drop testing FF1.0:
Brand new Sterling 10.4 single rope Lot #04-110504

Credits

Special thanks are in order. If not for the following this study would not have been done: Mountain Rescue Association, American Alpine Club, Albuquerque Mountain Rescue, Sterling Rope, Grivel North America, Petzl, Ouray Ice Park, Ouray Mountain Rescue, Rescue Rigger, Jayne's Corp., Collette and Mark Miller, Nick McKinley, Ryan from the Ice Park, Jerome Stiller, Eric Nilan, Nancy Attaway, Christine Beverly, and all the ice climbers who allowed the research to carry on each day and kept our fall-zone safe.

Notes

1. Luebben, Craig. *How to Ice Climb* (pp143-158). Connecticut: The Globe Pequot Press, 1999.
2. Harmston, Chris. *Climbing* no 172 (Nov 97), pp106-115; or http://www.needlesports.com/advice/placing screws.htm.
3. K. Blair, D. Custer, S. Alziati, W. Bennett. (2004). "The Effect of Load Rate, Placement Angle, and Ice Type on Ice Screw Failure." 5th International Engineering of Sport Conference.
4. UIAA EN-892, dynamic mountaineering ropes, UIAA-101.
5. Joe Josephson. "Ice Anchor Review," The *Canadian Alpine Journal*, 76, 1993, pp66-67.
6. Retro-base–large formation of ice made by the sprinkler system that serves as the source reservoir during the day preserving the ice route.
7. Bennett, Warren. (10/2002). "Simulating and Testing Ice Screw Performance in the Laboratory," Final Design Proposal.
8. Schulson, Erland M., "The Structure and Mechanical Behavior of Ice." The Minerals, Metals and Materials Society, http://www.tms.org/pubs/journals/JOM/9902/Schulson-9902.html. 09/30/02.
9. http://www.onlineconversion.com/weight_common.htm.
10. Beverly, Marc, Attaway, Stephen. "Hang 'Em High: How Good Are Belay Devices?" ITRS 2005.

Appendix B

Ice Climbing Anchor Strength: An In-Depth Analysis

J. Marc Beverly, PhD, IFMGA
Stephen W. Attaway, PhD
November 2008

ABSTRACT

Ice climbing anchors are seemingly simple yet have a mystique that surrounds their use and overall strengths. Not all ice climbing anchors are used in a standard configuration.

Placing an ice screw into an already existing ice screw hole is called re-boring. Re-boring of ice screws is a common practice among ice climbers. Re-boring is typically preferred when placing a screw to avoid creating adjacent holes that could serve as a potential fracture propagation point.

We evaluated re-boring strengths for several ice screw designs to determine the strength as a function of length of screw. Slow pull tests were performed, and the results were compared with prior data from drop testing on ice screws. Static pull testing using lake ice was compared with drop testing on waterfall ice and found to be a good substitute test medium.

In addition, we evaluated Abalakov anchors (aka V-thread anchors) with 7 mm perlon cord as well as 1" tubular webbing in different configurations. Their strengths were then compared with that of the single re-bored ice screws.

The nature of ice is a continually changing medium and hard to predict in the field. However, the actual strengths shown from our testing methods in the real-world environment make a strong case for the strength of re-boring. Recently, re-bored holes in a freezing environment were found to be strong enough in most configurations. Abalakov ice anchors were also found to be strong, provided that enough ice area was enclosed by the anchor. Placing Abalakov anchors vertically appeared to be stronger than placing them horizontally. Precautions and recommendations for use of ice climbing anchors stem from our evaluation of the data.

INTRODUCTION

Ice climbing anchors have traditionally been shunned as not being strong anchors, especially when compared to rock. Perhaps this arises in part from the fact that ice is a poorly understood medium and has a mystique about it due to its perceived unpredictable nature at times.

In technical ice climbing, the technique of re-boring (Figure 1) has been utilized over the years. Several legitimate scenarios exist for re-boring an ice screw. Finding a good placement for an ice screw is often difficult. With the advent of more traffic on ice climbs, the usual "easy" ice screw placements may have already been used. What remains is the conundrum of choosing where to place a screw. One option is to place a screw into an already existing hole that was created by a previous ice climbing party. That hole is an uncontrolled factor as to what type of screw was used initially, when it was drilled, and what environmental conditions have occurred since the hole was left behind.

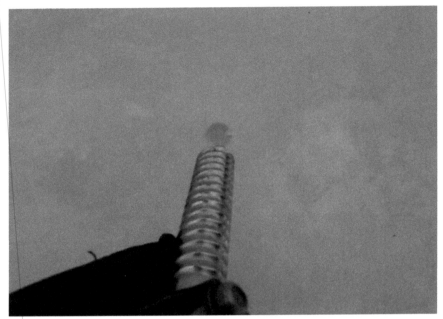

Figure 1: *Placing a screw into an existing hole is called re-boring.*

Another scenario that often occurs is when an ice climber may be leading a pitch of ice at their difficulty threshold, finds an old hole that appears to be usable, and wonders if it is reasonable to use that hole. A dull screw that doesn't "bite" into the ice to start a new hole is always problematic. Time can be of the essence when the climber loses all strength and risks a dangerous fall. Re-boring an ice screw seems to be a quick alternative to creating an entirely new hole and can save the climber strength by decreasing the amount of time spent to place a fresh ice screw.

Other legitimate scenarios exist for re-boring an ice screw. The above are merely examples and are non-exhaustive.

Much conjecture has been created, leading to dogma, about how good these placements are or are not. We now know that "psychological protection" (a piece of protection that the climber may think dubious) produces less of an impact force on the system, even if a piece fails, rather than just climbing quickly for the belay stance. "Running it out" produces larger forces than a fall that pulls out a piece of protection because of the residual fall factor after a failed anchor point[1]. We also know that air pockets (not aerated ice) near ice screw placements are bad and cause fracturing of the ice more readily. Ice is a difficult medium to understand, and its fracture mechanics can be explained to a certain degree[2], but inherently, it is not yet possible to anticipate the nature of fracture, propagation, and collapse in the field.

Other types of ice anchors exist, such as the bollard and Abalakov. The bollard is fairly passé and somewhat dangerous on ice because of decapitation and slipping, but it is used in the alpine environment. The threaded Abalakov, however, is used extensively.

Threaded Ice Anchors: Abalakovs (aka V-threads)

Vitaly Mikhaylovich Abalakov, a Russian, is credited for the innovation of drilling into the ice in two places, such that the two drilled holes would come together as far back as possible to create a continuous hole. A rope or piece of cord could then be threaded through and used as an anchor, as shown in Figure 2. This technique is also commonly known as a "V-thread." With it, a climber can retreat without leaving much, if any, gear behind, thereby being able to abseil many pitches in a row. Commonly, climbers will leave a piece of webbing or cordage behind in the anchor so that climbing ropes do not become stuck in the back of the Abalakov. At other times, the V-thread is used as an anchoring point for climbing competitions, rescue anchors, toprope anchors, or other applications.

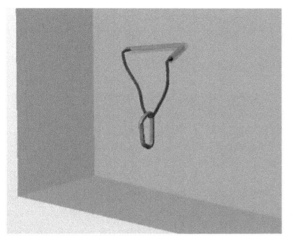

Figure 2 *shows a traditional horizontally made Abalakov ice anchor. Notice that in the example on the right, the cord is tied off with a flat overhand. This is usually acceptable for rappelling only and not advocated for lead configuration.*

Anchor strength studies were first evaluated and published in Canada by Joe Josephson[3]. Since then, many people have accepted the Abalakov anchor as a standard rappel anchor for descent from ice climbs. The pendulum then swung in public opinion that the Abalakov was stronger than an ice screw. This led to the idea that an Abalakov anchor was strong enough to belay from in the multi-pitch climbing environment.

HYPOTHESES

The working hypotheses to be tested are:

1. Re-bored ice screws are strong enough★ to arrest a UIAA[4] fall.
2. The over-driven ice screw in a shorter original hole is strong enough★ to take a leader fall on.
3. Shorter screws placed in longer screw holes are as strong as longer screws placed in longer screw holes.
4. Abalakovs are stronger than ice screws.
5. Abalakov strength is directly related to the area it encompasses rather than the orientation.

★ Strong enough to hold 7–8kN

BACKGROUND

Fortunately, there are very few case reports for failed re-bored ice screws resulting in injury. The lack of published literature available limits our ability to perform a retrospective study.

Climbers gain experience through feedback mechanisms, both positive and negative. Therefore, the thought process is that "if an anchor doesn't fail, then that type of anchor should be good enough to use the next time." In other words, those who never fail a placement will gain a sense of comfort from experience. Fortune smiles on climbers most of the time, but it is impossible to know how strong is "strong enough" without formal testing where failure is observed.

Much has been assumed about re-boring. The comments typically heard include: "the placements aren't strong enough to hold a fall; it's a waste of time to place them; and they're psychological pro."

When considering whether an ice screw is stronger than an Abalakov/V-thread placement, unpublished preliminary testing proposed that Abalakov anchors are weaker than single screw placements in streambed ice[5].

The actual mechanics of ice fracture have been studied, especially in the marine ice realm. Although it is not our focus to evaluate these characteristics, it is important to understand that freshwater ice fails in uniaxial tension via transgranular cleavage[6]. The mechanics of tensile failure are described in both nucleation and propagation. A direct correlation exists between grain size and fracture propagation: the larger the grain size, the greater the propagation of fracture. Brittle compressive failure is more complex and fails via longitudinal splitting in unconfined fresh-water ice[7].

Research by Schulson indicates that ice strength depends on the square root of grain size, rate of loading, and temperature.

For ease of testing, a static pull test was used to load ice screws placed in lake ice. The grain size of ice typically found on ice walls and lake ice will be about the same, so grain size effect for lake ice and wall ice will be similar. Likewise, the temperature of the lake ice and waterfall ice were comparable and not considered to be a source of strength difference between lake ice and waterfall ice.

The ratio of rate of loading between slow pulls and drop test are on the order of 1000x. At really slow rates of loading (i.e., moving as slow as a glacier), ice will be ductile, with the yield strength increasing with load rate. For faster loading rates, the strength of ice decreases with rate of loading. Based on laboratory testing by Schulson, failure stress at 1e-3/sec (slow pull) are about 20% higher than strain rates at 1e-1/sec (drop test). Thus, for our slow pull test, we could expect some increase in the strength of ice under slow pull compared to drop testing. Differences may also exist due to the difference between lake ice and waterfall ice. Lake ice will likely have fewer defects than waterfall ice.

METHODS

We did slow pull tests on ice screw re-boring configurations based on ice screws placed at a positive angle relative to perpendicular of the ice face. This positive angle is considered the proper configuration for lead climbing[8,9].

Slow pull test in accordance with the Cordage Institute standard rate of pull of 0.5"-1.0" per second powered by a hydraulic ram was used for pull testing of the screws. The ram was anchored to the ice. Ice and air temperatures (Figure 3), as well as times and details of each test, were recorded for the slow pull tests at Echo Lake, Colorado (Figure 4), located near the town of Pagosa Springs. Several slow pull tests were done on Abalakovs in Ouray at the new Kid's wall, since the ice was convenient and homogenous.

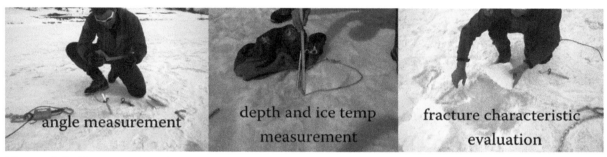

Figure 3 *(left) measuring air and ice temperatures (°C); (middle) measuring depth and angle of holes (cm); (right) simple evaluation of fracture characteristics.*

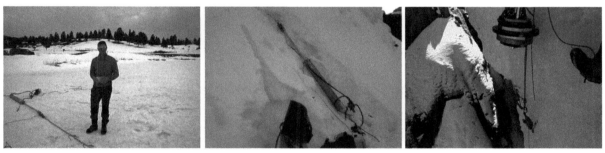

Figure 4 *(left) showing the nature of homogenous lake ice as a control medium; (middle) slow pull tests on waterfall ice in Ouray; (right) the drop testing grounds for waterfall ice in Ouray Ice Park.*

For our testing, we needed to use the same medium for making a direct comparison analysis. We chose lake ice for pull testing, not only because it is a good control but also for ease of access and reproducibility of our testing worldwide.

A control medium with variability as small as possible is hard to find. The UIAA has recently published a safety standard[10] on how ice screws are to be tested to receive a Comité Européen de Normalisation (CEN) rating for sales in countries. YTONG[11] has also been considered for ice screw testing, but this medium is not readily available for our testing purposes.

Our drop testing was performed at the Ouray Ice Park, Colorado. Two routes were used to perform the drop testing on, both located at the Lower Bridge: *Rhythm Method* WI5 (the same route that we used in 2005-06), and the *2008 Competition Route* (on the ice section between the mixed rock climbing and the diving board) that had not been used by any ice climbers prior to our testing. This site provided a good control area. The two routes are on distinctly different aspects in the Uncompahgre Gorge in order to get a better sampling of the ice at the Ouray Ice Park.

Ice Screws

The general specifications of the UIAA are outlined in Figure 5. There is no mention of any testing that has been performed where ice screws had been tested in re-bored holes. Our approach did not follow UIAA specifications. The UIAA specifications call for strength testing for screws loaded in shear and loaded in tension. The UIAA specifications were designed to test the strength of the screw, not the strength of the screw placement in ice. The specifications require that the screw not fail below a critical load. Our testing considered loads in shear only and included the tests where each screw was loaded to ice failure.

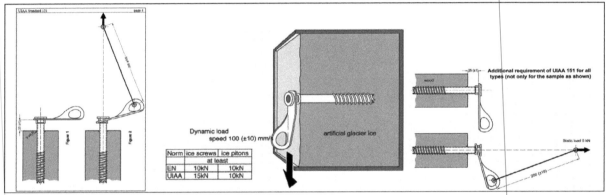

Figure 5: *UIAA specifications for testing ice screws in different mediums.*

We performed two drop tests on re-bored and over drilling in combination using a longer screw in a shorter hole. The results were as strong as if it were a new hole. We then focused our remaining tests on the worst-case scenario, whereby a climber would come upon a long hole and only have a short screw for placement. We alternated holes drilled by the same and different manufactures in conjunction with using a short screw.

We repeated testing on some screws that had either been used in drop testing already or used in a slow pull test. The rationale is that we were not as concerned with the strength of the screw as we were with the strength of the re-bored hole. Interestingly enough, the strengths of the screws did vary somewhat as a function of multiple uses, as some screws would break before the re-bored hole failed. If the screw showed obvious signs of fatigue, then it was not used again. In one case during a slow pull, the screw fractured at the midpoint of the tube; several other times the eye of the screw would fracture. Screw failure was not observed for new screws that had not been used in prior testing.

Orientation

There is still debate, as well as inconclusive results, from screw angle placement[11,12,13]. It has been fairly well documented that on static pull testing, "confirming that the most effective threads are those near the hanger (and that the reverse thread orientation may be stronger than regular thread orientation) . . . the holding strength does not depend significantly on thread type, but rather on the radial and axial dimensions of the screw." The general strength of an ice screw is based on loading rate duration rather than a faster loading rate[13].

It is well understood that placement of an ice screw, whether in dynamic shock loading or slow pull testing, produces the strongest results when NOT placed in a negative angle (i.e., using the screw in a levering configuration). So, from somewhere between 0° and +20° is the ideal angle, and that was our target range for testing re-bored screws.

RESULTS

Re-bored Ice Screw Results

A statistical comparison of drop test results and slow pull testing is presented in Table 1. These results indicate drop tests on waterfall ice and slow pull tests on lake ice produced similar results.

Drop testing statistics	
	kN
Mean	10.6
Standard Error	1.3
Standard Deviation	4.9
Minimum	3.9
Maximum	22.0
Count	15.0
Confidence Level (95.0%)	2.7

Slow pulls in lake ice—all screws	
	kN
Mean	11.1
Standard Error	0.6
Standard Deviation	3.7
Minimum	5.5
Maximum	19.7
Count	38.0
Confidence Level (95.0%)	1.2

Table 1: *Re-bored ice screws; all results by testing type.*

Redline Failures—Re-bored Ice Screws	kN
Beverly/Attaway 2005-06—Drop Tests (non-re-bored)	10.14
Beverly/Attaway 2007-08—Drop Tests	10.58
Beverly/Attaway 2007-08—Slow pulls Lake Ice	11.09

Table 2: *The overall averages of failure forces.*

A very high failure strength (22.5 kN) for a re-bored ice screw was achieved by leaving a re-bored screw overnight with a test mass of 80 kg hanging from it for more than ten hours. The temperatures recorded were less than –30°C in the Ice Park that night. There was no evidence of melt-out from the ice screw, even with a test mass hanging from it. This correlates well to Schulson's evaluation that ice becomes stronger (<25% when cooled from –5°C to –20°C).

Angle

The regression line shown in Figure 6 shows that $14° \pm 5°$ is the optimal angle for re-bored ice screws. Placing a screw at $0°$ or as great as $25°$ shows a marked decrease in overall strength.

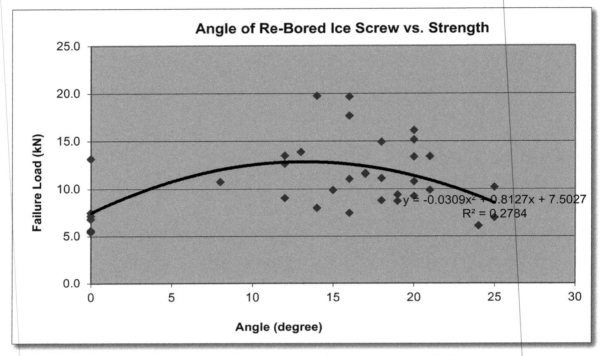

Figure 6: *A regression line indicates the area where the strongest + angle is.*

Length of Re-Bored Ice Screw

For slow pull testing on lake ice, ice screw strength was a strong function of length. In slow pull tests, as shown with the blue line in Figure 7, even having a few extra centimeters can, on average, increase the strength of the ice screw placement.

The dependence of strength on screw length was not as evident for drop testing. There still remains a slight positive correlation, and one might attribute that to chance alone. Only a limited number of drop tests were performed on long screws. Drawing a conclusion on strength–versus–length for ice screws loaded with drop test will require more data.

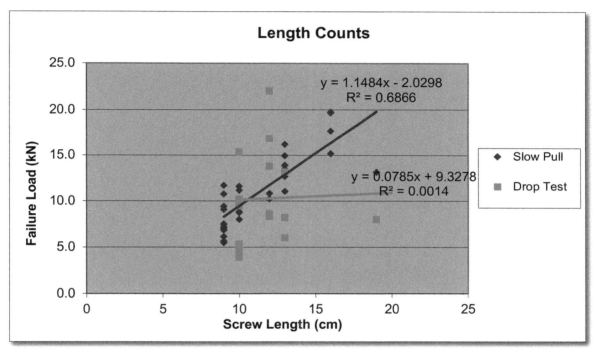

Figure 7: *Length of re-bored screws placed into long holes. A regression analysis shows the strength correlation for slow pulls and drop tests.*

Results: All Threaded Ice Anchors

With regard to our Abalakov ice anchors, we found the following data to be quite insightful and very interesting.

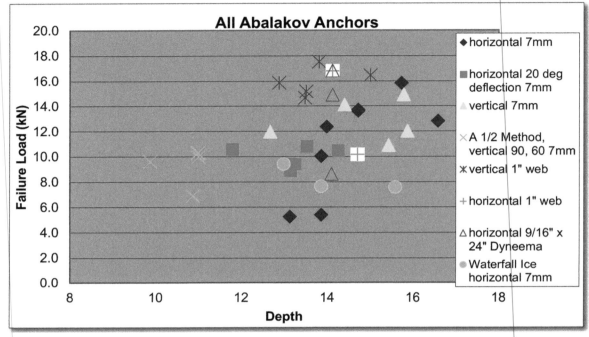

Figure 8: *A scatter plot of threaded ice anchors by type.*

We tested several different configurations of Abalakov anchors. Temporal variations were limited by pre-setting all the anchors and pulling each anchor to failure within a couple of minutes of each other. Figure 8 shows the data for all Abalakovs, while Figure 9 depicts the protocol and techniques used in the slow pull process.

Figure 9 (left) shows multiple Abalakov slow pull testing in action; (middle) logging data and quickly moving the pull testing device from anchor to anchor; (right) showing the strongest Abalakov configuration and material used (1" tubular webbing).

Test results showed that Abalakov anchor strength was a strong function of geometry and orientation.

Ice fails by fracture in zones of tension more easily than in compression. In our testing, the failure mechanisms for Abalakovs and ice screws resulted in large segments of ice above the anchor point failing in tension. The ice located below the Abalakov and located below the screw are both placed in compression and actually have a higher failure load due to the increased strength of ice under compression.

Large amounts of ice were displaced superiorly from the zone of tension when visually compared to the inferior zone (toward the force applied), as shown in Figure 10. Notice that both ice anchors have similar modes, with lots of ice seen coming out above the anchor and almost no ice noticed coming out below the anchor.

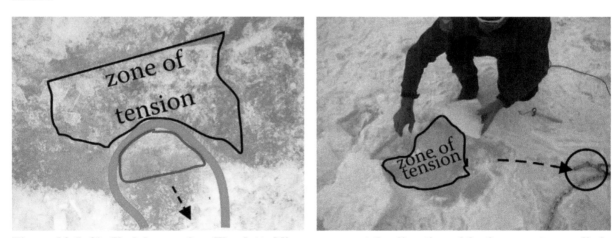

Figure 10 (left): Abalakov anchor. The dotted lines represent the direction of the force vector applied: the blue line shows where the 7 mm Perlon Abalakov cordage was. The red line indicates where the bulb was released. (Right): Ice screw anchor. Notice the large amount of ice superior/above to ice screw from the zone of tension.

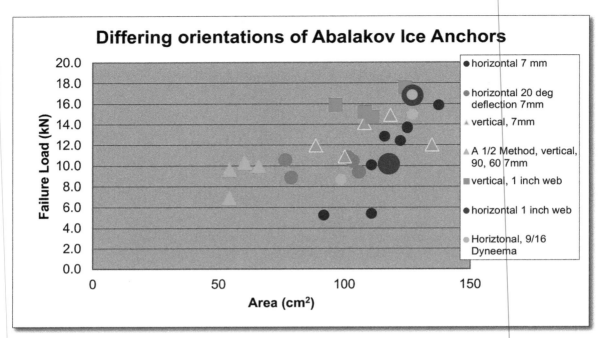

Figure 11. *Differing orientations of Abalakovs vs. total strength with good grouping.*

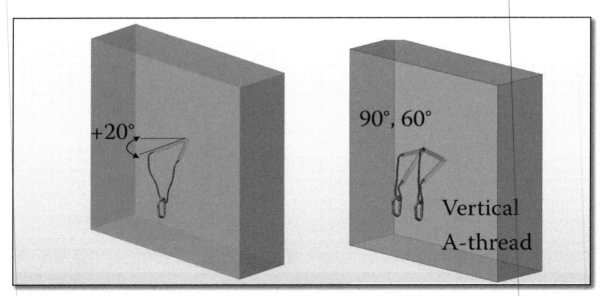

Figure 12. *Digital pictograph of the other orientations tested. (Left) a V-thread with both holes placed at +20 degrees and adjoining in the back; (right) A-threads (Anderson threads) with the top hole 90 degrees perpendicular and the other using the 60x60x60 degree method.*

Figure 11 shows a plot of Abalakov anchor strength as a function of the area enveloped by the anchor. Test results indicate that the more total area enveloped by the Abalakov, the higher the ice anchor's strength.

Enclosed area is not the only mechanism upon which the strength is based. The strength is also a strong function of the anchor orientation. A vertical (A-thread) placement increases the overall anchor strength.

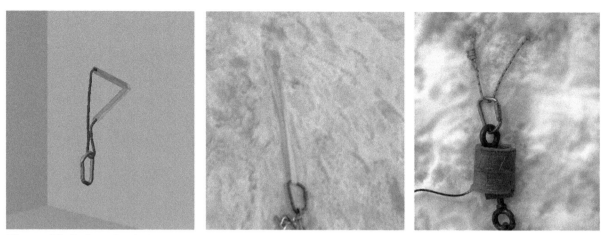

Figure 13 *(left and middle) strongest orientation; (middle) strongest orientation and material-vertical 1" tubular webbing single loop; (right) weakest of the three, but still strong enough*.*

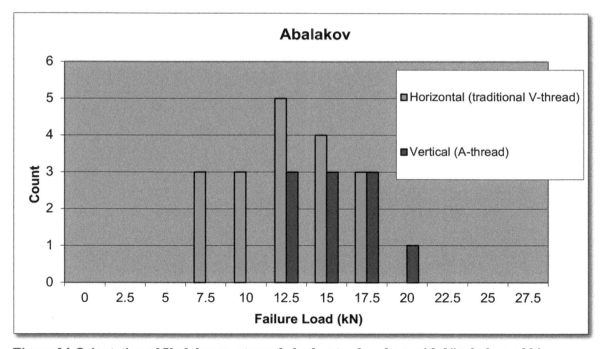

Figure 14 *Orientation of Abalakov vs. strength, both sets of anchors with 1" tubular webbing.*

Figure 13 displays the configuration and type of materials used to make the threaded ice anchors. Figure 14 shows how the strongest orientation was in the vertical configuration. This is also outlined in Table 3.

From our testing data, 1" tubular webbing tied off with a standard water knot/ring bend was measured to be the strongest on a consistent basis.

data for horizontal (V-threads)			data for vertical (A-threads)	
	kN			kN
Mean	11.3		Mean	14.4
Standard Error	0.8		Standard Error	0.7
Median	10.3		Median	14.8
Standard Deviation	3.6		Standard Deviation	2.1
Sample Variance	12.7		Sample Variance	4.6
Range	11.6		Range	6.6
Minimum	5.2		Minimum	10.9
Maximum	16.8		Maximum	17.5
Count	18.0		Count	10.0
Largest (1)	16.8		Largest (1)	17.5
Smallest (1)	5.2		Smallest (1)	10.9
Confidence Level (95.0%)	1.8		Confidence Level (95.0%)	1.5

Table 3: Data comparison of traditionally placed horizontal (V-threads) vs. vertically placed (A-threads).

The good news is that all of the configurations and materials used were strong enough★ to hold abseilers/rappellers with a significant safety margin from a single anchor point. Testing showed that anchors could fail at below expected climber fall (7.5 kN) forces and should be backed up if in any doubt.

Comparison of Types of Ice Anchors

Figure 15 compares the strength of ice screws drilled into virgin ice, with the strength of re-bored ice screws testing in both drop test and slow pull. All three were shown to have comparable normal distribution curves with most failures occurring within the 10-15kN range. Also plotted on this graph is the strength of the Abalakov anchors in both the horizontal and vertical orientation.

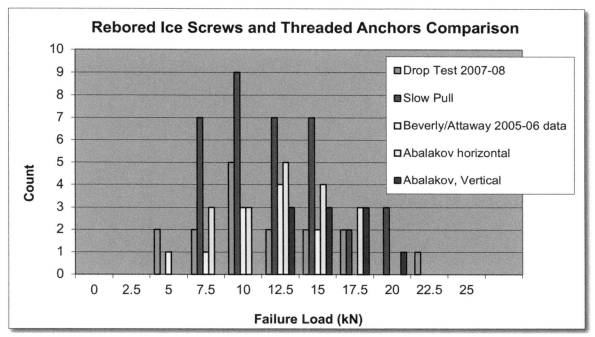

Figure 15: *Re-bored ice screws compared to overall strengths of our drop and slow pull tests to our previous data from 2005-06 as well as to our data from Abalakovs in both horizontal and vertical orientation.*

Figure 16 compares the strength of re-bored ice screws with the horizontal and vertical Abalakovs anchors. While the number of tests may be too limited to draw conclusions, the preliminary testing results show that longer ice screws are stronger than Abalakovs. Vertical Abalakovs are stronger than horizontal Abalakovs. Horizontal Abalakovs are on average about the same as re-bored short screws. The data also show that a considerable spread exists in all anchor strengths, with the potential for failure in loads below the expected (7.5 kN) loads generated by ice climbers.

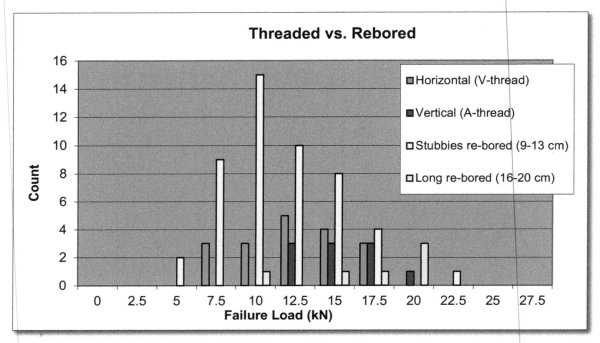

Figure 16. *Shows peak force compared to ice anchor type and configuration.*

Discussion

Using a re-bored ice screw as a first placement off a multi-pitch climb is a sufficient load reduction method that can aid the falling climber from placing the entire impact force on the anchor system that results from a residual fall factor.

The most risk of high impact forces on an anchor/anchor system in climbing is when a climber is starting from a hanging belay. A single ice anchor (screw or Abalakov) is unlikely to arrest a high impact force from a lead climber in this position. In Figure 17, the leader would have been better off not to have clipped the anchor and thereby taking a fall factor of 2, as the rope would place a lesser peak force to the system than in the configuration shown.

Figure 17. Multi-pitch scenario: Leader falling onto a single ice anchor (in this case a single horizontal Abalakov) that the belayer is also attached to in the UIAA fall test scenario, a potentially deadly combination.

Our sample size is still what we consider to be small and non-exhaustive. The spread is large, and ice is a variable medium. Learning good skills at where and when to place ice screws remains an art, although our science is helping us to compose a better picture of ice anchor behavior experienced in real-world conditions.

CONCLUSIONS

These tests were performed in what the authors consider to be "good ice." Lake ice appears to be a good testing medium for comparison analysis to waterfall ice that is homogenous.

1. Based on the variability of anchor strength observed in our test results, we must accept the null hypothesis that re-bored ice screws are too weak to withhold a UIAA fall factor *all* of the time. They are, however, stronger than expected and compare closely with an ice screw placed in virgin ice.

2. Re-bored ice screws are nearly as strong as freshly drilled holes. It is likely that any refreezing process that decreases the diameter of the hole over time is of benefit for a re-bored screw.

3. A re-bored ice screw that is left in frozen temperatures overnight will likely freeze in quite solid, even with a mass of 80 kg suspended from it, and not experience "melt-out," even if placed in a positive angle.

4. The greater the area an Abalakov anchor has, the more likely it is to be a stronger anchor. So, save the longest screw for the belay to make an Abalakov using 60° x 60° x 60° as the best guideline for angle drilling.

5. We accept the null hypothesis that a single ice screw, even a short re-bored screw, is generally about the same in strength as a horizontal Abalakov anchor.

6. The longer the ice screw is, the stronger the ice anchor will be, regardless of whether it is a freshly placed screw or a re-bored screw.

7. There is no significant difference when comparing the three manufacturers' brand ice screws when placed into an old hole of the same or different manufacturer.

8. Reverse threads did not appear to make a difference in any regard.

9. The optimum angle placement is >8° and <16° from our regression analysis.

10. The vertical Abalakov is superior in strength to the tradition horizontal or other configurations tested. We call this the "A-thread" since discussions with Vince Anderson inspired investigation into other configurations.

11. Drop test data on waterfall ice were weaker than slow pull test data on lake ice. Rescue anchors for slow pulls will likely act as stronger placements than when climbers fall onto ice screws.

12. NEVER use a single anchor (A-thread, V-thread, or ice screw) as the only anchor when high forces are expected, as seen with multi-pitch climbing.

FUTURE RESEARCH

1. Numerical simulations to evaluate zones of tension and compression for a better understanding into the mechanics of ice anchor fracture for both Abalakov-style ice anchors and ice screws.

2. Evaluate other types of screws that have diameters and threads of different sizes.

3. It is likely that a re-bored screw may be stronger when compared to the alternative of placing a new hole next to an old hole. Nearby holes can result in stress concentrations and act as a fracture nucleation site. We did not evaluate the possible reduction in anchor strength due to nearby drill holes.

4. A slight strength difference was observed between 7 mm cord and 1" tubular webbing. More testing may be needed to see if this strength difference is significant.

Note: Overdriving (red-lining) ice screws in the drop testing environment is dangerous. Flying ice debris, ice screw missiles, snapping ropes, and the general objective hazard of being in the vertical ice environment, plus having to record data and also be aware of everything else going on, is taxing as well as expensive. Many thanks go out to Angie Lucht for her help in drop testing and to Nic McKinley for his efficient help on the slow pull tests performed on lake ice.

We humbly and gratefully thank our sponsors PMI Rope, Grivel North America, Petzl, Black Diamond Equipment, Ltd, and the Mountain Rescue Association. Without their help, this research would not have been possible. Also, we thank the Ouray Ice Park for the use of their facilities.

Notes

1. Beverly, M., Attaway, S. *Measurement of Dynamic Rope System Stiffness in a Sequential Failure for Lead Climbing Falls*. ITRS, 2006.
2. Schulson E.M. *Brittle Failure of Ice*. Eng Fracture Mechanics 68 (2001) 1839–87.
3. Joe Josephson. "Ice Anchor Review," The *Canadian Alpine Journal*, 76, 1993, pp66–67.
4. http://www.theuiaa.org/upload_area/cert_files/UIAA101_DynamicRopes.pdf.
5. http://video.google.fr/videoplay?docid=1863958284744514965.
6. Schulson, E.M., Baker I., Robertson C.D., Bolon, R.B., Hanimon, R.J. *Fractography of Ice*. J. Mater Sci Lett 1989;8:1193–4.
7. Smith, T.R., Schulson, E.M. *The Brittle Compressive Failure of Fresh-Water Columnar Ice Under Biaxial Loading*. Acta metall mater 1993;41(1):153–63.
8. Beverly, M., Attaway, S. *Dynamic Shock Load Evaluation of Ice Screws: A Real-World Look*. ITRS, 2005.
9. Harmston, Chris. *Climbing*, no 172 (Nov 97), pp106–115.
10. http://www.theuiaa.org/upload_area/cert_files/UIAA151_IceAnchors01-2004.pdf.
11. Cracco, S., Meneghetti, G. *Holding Strength of Ice Screws in YTONG Concrete*. Session of the UIAA Safety Commission. Sept. 2006.
12. Heshka. *Holding Strength of Climbing Ice Screws vs. Placement Angle*. Annual Report Scholarly Activity Committee, 2005.
13. Blair, K., Custer, D., Alziati, S., Bennett, W. *The Effect of Load Rate, Placement Angle, and Ice Type on Ice Screw Failure*. 5th International Engineering of Sport Conference, 2004.

References

Beverly, J. M., PhD, and S. W. Attaway, PhD. "Dynamic Shock Load Evaluation of Ice Screws: A Real-World Look." International Technical Rescue Symposium (November 2005). http://itrsonline.org/dynamic-shock-load-evaluation-of-ice-screws-a-real-world-look/.

Beverly, J. M., PhD, and S. W. Attaway, PhD. "Ice Climbing Anchor Strength: An In-Depth Analysis." International Technical Rescue Symposium (November 2008). http://itrsonline.org/ice-climbing-anchor-strength-an-in-depth-analysis/.

Burns, B., and M. Burns. *Wilderness Navigation*. Seattle, WA: Mountaineers, 1999.

Descamps, P., and S. Lozac'hmeur, ed. *Alpine Skills: Summer*. Bern: International Mountaineering and Climbing Federation (UIAA), 2013.

Haegeli, P. *Avaluator: Avalanche Accident Prevention Card*, 2nd ed. Revelstoke, BC: Avalanche Canada, 2010.

Hinch, S. W. *Outdoor Navigation with GPS*, 3rd ed. Birmingham, AL: Wilderness Press, 2011.

Klassen, K., ed. *Technical Handbook for Professional Guides*. Canmore, AB: Association of Canadian Mountain Guides, 1999.

LaForge, C. "To Screamer or Not to Screamer," QC Lab. Black Diamond website (2011). https://www.blackdiamondequipment.com/en_CA/qc-lab-to-screamer-or-not-to-screamer.html.

Letham, L. *GPS Made Easy*. Surrey, BC: Rocky Mountain Books, 2003.

Marshall, P. *Avalanche Skills Training 1: Instructor Manual*. Revelstoke, BC: Avalanche Canada, 2015.

McCammon, I. "Heuristic Traps in Recreational Avalanche Accidents: Evidence and Implications, Part 1." *The Avalanche Review*, vol. 22, no. 2 (2003): 16. Whitefish, MT: American Avalanche Association.

McCammon, I. "Heuristic Traps in Recreational Avalanche Accidents: Evidence and Implications, Part 2." *The Avalanche Review*, vol. 22, no. 3 (2004): 11. Whitefish, MT: American Avalanche Association.

Pasteris, J. "When to Retire Climbing Gear." *Co-op Journal*. REI website (July 3, 2018). <https://www.rei.com/blog/climb/when-to-retire-climbing-gear>

Piche, M., ed. "Belay Device Categories." *ACMG Tech Files* vol. 1, no. 1 (2012): 10. Canmore, AB: Association of Canadian Mountain Guides. https://www.acmg.ca/05pdf/TechFiles/TechFiles_Vol1_No1.pdf.

Piche, M., ed. "Fixed-Point Belay." *ACMG Tech Files* vol. 1, no. 1 (2012): 4–6. Canmore, AB: Association of Canadian Mountain Guides. https://www.acmg.ca/05pdf/TechFiles/TechFiles_Vol1_No1.pdf.

Piche, M., ed. "Use of Auto-Braking Belay Devices." *ACMG Tech Files* vol. 1, no. 1 (2012): 7–9. Canmore, AB: Association of Canadian Mountain Guides. https://www.acmg.ca/05pdf/ TechFiles/TechFiles_Vol1_No1.pdf.

Powick, K. "Sling Strength in 3 Anchor Configurations." QC Lab. Black Diamond website (2009). https://www.blackdiamondequipment .com/en_US /qc-lab-sling-strength-in-3 -differentanchorconfigurations.html.

Richards, D. "Knot Break Strength vs Rope Break Strength." Cordage Institute. http://caves.org/ section/vertical/nh/50/knotrope-hold.html.

Statham, G. (2008). "Avalanche Hazard, Danger and Risk: A Practical Explanation." Whistler, BC: International Snow Science Workshop. http://arc.lib.montana.edu/snow-science/ objects/P__8153.pdf.

Touche, F. *Wilderness Navigation Handbook*, illustrated edition. CA: Touche Publishing, 2004.

Wilding, D., ed. *Top Rope Climbing Instructor Tech-Manual*. Canmore, AB: Association of Canadian Mountain Guides, 2018.

Further Reading

The Art of Ice Climbing by Jerome Blanc-Gras and Manu Ibarra (Blue Ice Press, 2012).

Autonomy, Mastery and Purpose in the Avalanche Patch by Bruce Kay (self-published, 2015).

Avalanche Essentials: A Step-by-Step System for Safety and Survival, 1st ed., by Bruce Tremper (Mountaineers Books, 2013).

The Avalanche Handbook, 3rd ed., by David McClung and Peter Schärer (Mountaineers Books, 2006).

Backcountry Avalanche Awareness, 8th ed., by Bruce Jamieson (Canadian Avalanche Association, 2011).

Blink: The Power of Thinking Without Thinking by Malcolm Gladwell (Little, Brown and Company, 2005).

Climbing: From Rock to Ice by Ron Funderburke (FalconGuides, 2019).

Climbing Ice by Yvon Chouinard (Sierra Club Books, 1978).

Climbing Self-Rescue: Improvising Solutions for Serious Situations by Andy Tyson and Molly Loomis (Mountaineers Books, 2006).

How to Climb: Self Rescue, 2nd ed., by David Fasulo (FalconGuides, 2011).

Ice and Mixed Climbing, 2nd ed., by Will Gadd (Mountaineers Books, 2020).

Ice World: Techniques and Experiences of Modern Ice Climbing by Jeff Lowe (Mountaineers Books, 1996).

Life in the Cold: An Introduction to Winter Ecology, 4th ed., by Peter J. Marchand (University Press of New England, 2014).

Mixed Climbing by Sean Isaac (FalconGuides, 2005).

The Mountain Guide Manual: The Comprehensive Reference from Belaying to Rope Systems to Self-Rescue by Marc Chauvin and Rob Coppolillo (FalconGuides, 2017).

Mountain Weather: Backcountry Forecasting and Weather Safety for Hikers, Campers, Climbers, Skiers, and Snowboarders by Jeff Renner (Mountaineers Books, 2005).

Staying Alive in Avalanche Terrain, 3rd ed., by Bruce Tremper (Mountaineers Books, 2018).

Index

About the Authors

Sean Isaac is a fully certified Alpine Guide with the Association of Canadian Mountain Guides. He has been ice climbing for thirty years and instructing ice and mixed climbing for the past twenty years. During that time, he has taught more than a thousand people the art of moving over frozen waterfalls. Based in Canmore, Alberta, in the Canadian Rockies, Sean was a key member of the modern mixed climbing movement in the late 1990s and early 2000s, establishing classics like Cryophobia, The Asylum, Mixed Monster, Uniform Queen, and The Real Big Drip, to name a few, and repeating testpieces like Musashi (M12). He has competed in the Ice World Cup, Ouray Ice Festival Competition, Bozeman Ice Festival, and Festiglace, with a handful of podium placements. He has traveled all over the world in search of new routes—to the remote ranges of Alaska, Patagonia, Peru, Pakistan, and Kyrgyzstan. Sean is also the author of several ice and mixed books including *Mixed Climbing in the Canadian Rockies* by Rocky Mountain Books, *Mixed Climbing* by FalconGuides, and *Ice Climbing Leader Field Handbook* by the Alpine Club of Canada. In addition, he has been the editor of the *Canadian Alpine Journal* for the past fourteen years. For more information, visit Sean at www.seanisaac.com, IG: @seanisaacguiding, and FB: @seanisaacguiding.

Tim Banfield has been ice climbing for sixteen years and has worked in the climbing photography industry for the past decade, gaining experience in his niche—ice climbing—while at the same time writing feature climbing articles that focus on destinations. Tim has journeyed to Alaska, Nepal, South America, the Alps, and all over Canada pursuing icy and snowy objectives. As a seasoned climbing photographer, he is passionate about capturing authentic ice and mixed climbing images taken in the moment. In addition to writing and photography, he is also involved in real estate. Outside of the "office," Tim enjoys climbing, skiing, and taking photos of his dog Trango. For more information, visit Tim at www.timbanfield.com, IG: @timbanfield, and FB: @timbanfieldphotography.